LINCOLN LESSONS

LINCOLN LESSONS

REFLECTIONS ON
AMERICA'S GREATEST LEADER

EDITED BY
FRANK J. WILLIAMS AND
WILLIAM D. PEDERSON

Southern Illinois University Press
Carbondale

12 11 10 09   4 3 2 1

Library of Congress Cataloging-in-Publication Data
Lincoln lessons : reflections on America's greatest
leader / edited by Frank J. Williams and William D.
Pederson.
     p. cm.
 Includes bibliographical references and index.
 ISBN-13: 978-0-8093-2891-8 (alk. paper)
 ISBN-10: 0-8093-2891-7 (alk. paper)
 1. Lincoln, Abraham, 1809–1865—Influence.
2. Lincoln, Abraham, 1809–1865—Political and
social views. 3. Political leadership—United
States. 4. Democracy—United States. 5. United
States—Politics and government—Philosophy.
6. Presidents—United States—Biography.
I. Williams, Frank J. II. Pederson, William D., date.
 E457.2.L833 2009
 973.7092—dc22   2008018043

Printed on recycled paper. ♻
The paper used in this publication meets the mini-
mum requirements of American National Standard
for Information Sciences—Permanence of Paper for
Printed Library Materials, ANSI Z39.48-1992. ∞

CONTENTS

Acknowledgments vii

Introduction
    FRANK J. WILLIAMS AND WILLIAM D. PEDERSON   1

1. Getting Right with Mary Lincoln; or, How a
First Lady Taught Me to Be a Feminist
    JEAN H. BAKER   4

2. Lincoln on Democracy
    MARIO M. CUOMO   18

3. A View from the Lincoln Museum
    JOAN FLINSPACH   23

4. The Evolution of a Lincoln Editor
    SARA VAUGHN GABBARD   28

5. Transforming Foes to Allies: The Political
Alchemy of Lincoln
    DORIS KEARNS GOODWIN   32

6. The Lincoln Visual Image: A Personal
Journey of Discovery
    HAROLD HOLZER   41

7. A Political Philosopher's Defense of Lincoln
    HARRY V. JAFFA   55

8. Lincoln through the Eyes of a Civil War and
Civil Rights Historian
    JOHN F. MARSZALEK   65

9. Lincoln's Legacy for Our Time
    JAMES M. MCPHERSON   75

10. Lincoln and African American Memory
    EDNA GREENE MEDFORD   91

Contents

11. Suspension of Habeas Corpus
SANDRA DAY O'CONNOR   101

12. Lincoln and the Meaning of Equality: How I
Became a "Lost Cause" Apostate
MACKUBIN THOMAS OWENS   110

13. Crossing Borders to an International Lincoln
WILLIAM D. PEDERSON   122

14. Tell Me What You Want to Believe, and I'll
Tell You What You Will Believe
EDWARD STEERS JR.   130

15. Sixteen Feet Tall: Abraham Lincoln and
History
CRAIG L. SYMONDS   140

16. Historian, Editor, and the Assassination
Legacy
THOMAS REED TURNER   151

17. The Compleat Lincolnator: Enthusiast,
Collector, and Scholar
FRANK J. WILLIAMS   160

Selected Bibliography of Works by Contributors   169
Contributors   173
Photo credits   175
Index   177

ACKNOWLEDGMENTS

It is difficult to get scholars to write about the personal side of their professional work, so we remain grateful to the contributors not only for their work but also for going beyond the third person norm of the scholarly profession. A third of the contributors performed double duty as speakers at the Frank and Virginia Williams Abraham Lincoln Lecture at Louisiana State University in Shreveport—the only annual Lincoln lecture series in the state. We appreciate their willingness to travel to the Deep South and to endure the occasional "Wanted Dead or Alive" flyers and other protests directed not at them personally but at the subject of their presentations.

We are also grateful to the Louisiana Endowment for the Humanities—especially its president, Dr. Michael Sartisky—and to Glenda and Neil Erwin for supporting the annual lectures and the triennial presidential conference series at LSU in Shreveport as well as the nation's first Summer Teachers Institute on Abraham Lincoln for secondary teachers held in 1993. The concluding follow-up event to that institute led to the creation of the annual Lincoln lectures and the formation of the Louisiana Lincoln Group, which launched *The Lincolnator,* the first newsletter on America's sixteenth president in the Deep South.

The editors are also appreciative of the work and continual support of Southern Illinois University Press executive editor Sylvia Frank Rodrigue for this volume, which observes the bicentennial of Abraham Lincoln's birth. Her assistance in its production was crucial, as was the support of our assistants Donna Byrd and Donna Petorella. We also extend a special thanks to Lincoln artist Wendy Allen for permission to use her beautiful oil painting of Abraham Lincoln for the jacket of *Lincoln Lessons.*

This book is dedicated to students of Abraham Lincoln, both at home and abroad, who continue to learn from him.

Frank J. Williams and William D. Pederson

Abraham Lincoln attracted others to him during his lifetime. He liked people, and they liked the original Great American Commoner. It is an appeal that continues today. Even in death, professionals and amateurs, scholars and the public, remain keenly interested in him, visiting the Lincoln Memorial in the nation's capital, reading books about him, and seeing films that address his legacy. There are far more films devoted to him than any other president and more books written on him than any other democratic political leader in world history.[1]

This book brings together a number of contemporary professionals who have been drawn into Lincoln's orbit. The following essays are primarily personal rather than third person narratives. The contributors make an effort to explain how they became interested in Lincoln and what lessons they have derived from him.

Because Abraham Lincoln is America's highest ranked president, it is not surprising that all the contributors first encountered him during their elementary school years. But their first serious work with Lincoln typically came during their undergraduate and more often their graduate years. Some became biographers (Jean H. Baker and Doris Kearns Goodwin) or editors of Lincoln periodicals (Sara Vaughn Gabbard and Thomas Reed Turner). In a sense, Joan Flinspach, as president and CEO of the Lincoln Museum in Fort Wayne, Indiana, was drawn into Lincoln's world as a museum director. A significant portion of Harold Holzer's work on mid-nineteenth-century American iconography grows out of his association with art collections and his expertise on Lincoln images.

Civil war historians (John F. Marszalek, James M. McPherson, Mackubin "Mac" Thomas Owens, and Craig L. Symonds) inevitably encountered Lincoln during their graduate training in history. Owens's story is somewhat reminiscent of Woodrow Wilson's. As sons of the South, they grew up as men without a country. They had first identified with Confederate heroes and only much later became Lincoln men after encounters with political science. In the case of Owens, it was due to the influence of another contributor to this volume, Harry V. Jaffa, a political scientist interested in political philosophy. For Woodrow Wilson, it was after he had given up the practice of law for the study of political science.[2]

As one of the top ranked lawyers in American history, Lincoln heavily influenced other contributors to this volume (Mario M. Cuomo, Sandra Day O'Connor, and Frank J. Williams).[3] The Great Commoner has served as a role model for many Americans who desired to rise in society. In Cuomo's case, he became a lawyer-politician like Lincoln. Both became involved in democratic politics at home and abroad.

Coining the standard definition of democracy in the world, Lincoln has left a greater international legacy than any other American president. The International Lincoln Center (see William D. Pederson's chapter) attempts to document this often overlooked dimension of the Lincoln legacy. There are more schools, stamps, streets, and statues in honor of him around the world than any other American political leader. In addition to the American adaptation of federalism, Lincoln's style of leadership is the other great gift that the United States has made to world democracy.[4] Not only Republicans and Democrats but liberals and conservatives around the world continue to admire Lincoln.

Of course, his role as the Great Emancipator continues to inspire people everywhere (see Edna Greene Medford's chapter). Moreover, his classical magnanimity left a mark on Nelson Mandela in South Africa and Mahatma Gandhi in India.[5] As the first assassinated president, Lincoln's legacy has been transformed into a civil religion (see Edward Steers Jr.'s and Thomas Reed Turner's chapters).

A common theme among the contributors is Abraham Lincoln's prescient understanding of what was morally right in the civil contest. Many were inspired by his profound sense of morality. He was always careful not to blame the South. Rather than engaging in "ethnic cleansing," his philosophy was "with malice toward none." Prudent morality and the pursuit of justice rather than mere power politics became a touchstone of his style of leadership. His administration is credited with establishing the first humanitarian standards for the conduct of warfare, thus setting the precedent for the eventual Geneva conventions of the twentieth century.

This volume, then, reveals how a group of contemporary Americans has encountered the Lincoln legacy and the personal lessons they derived from it.

NOTES

1. Peter W. Dickson, "Experts' Pick," *Book World*, September 12, 1999, 7; "Picture-Perfect Chiefs," *U.S. News and World Report*, July 10, 1989, 62.

2. Mary Stockwell, *Woodrow Wilson: The Last Romantic* (New York: Nova, 2007).

3. Bernard Schwartz, *A Book of Legal Lists* (New York: Oxford University Press, 1997), 210–36.

4. James C. Davies, *Human Nature in Politics* (New York: John Wiley and Sons, 1963), 320.

5. William D. Pederson, "The Impact of Abraham Lincoln's Constitutional Legacy: A Global Outlook," *Lincoln Lore*, no. 1885 (Summer 2006): 18–22.

Getting Right with Mary Lincoln; or, How a
First Lady Taught Me to Be a Feminist

W hen I first met Mary Todd Lincoln, she was dressed in a gorgeous white gown from that emporium of nineteenth-century high fashion in New York, A. T. Stewart's Department Store. Her satin dress was decorated with flounces and cattails, her hair interlaced with fresh flowers, her gloved hands graciously extended to her guests in the crowded East Room of the White House. She was presiding at one of her famous receptions in the lithograph published in *Frank Leslie's Illustrated Newspaper.* At the time, I was a harried wife of a surgeon and mother of four children, trying to combine motherhood with a doctorate from the Johns Hopkins University. For a paper in the premier Lincoln scholar David Herbert Donald's seminar, I had chosen the 1864 presidential election as my topic. I was years away from any interest in First Ladies.

Nor did I have any appreciation of how a First Lady's use of White House entertainment and what is awkwardly dubbed "public space" could provide not only the symbol for a husband's administration but also an opportunity for officials to discuss important matters of state privately—in less formal settings. Catherine Allgor has called this "parlor politics," and she means by this term an arena in which women "appear as political actors in their own right, using social events and the private sphere" to participate in politics.[1] As a novice historian, I was far removed from anything beyond the motto emblazoned in our seminar room: "History is past politics and politics present History."

My seminar paper focused on Lincoln's famous humble and incorrect prediction that he would not win the election of 1864, but as president he went on to assure the passage of power during the interregnum to his successor. I focused as well on his principled statement about the importance of holding elections during wartime. And, of course, many of us were using statistics in those days of quantitative history. I ran regression analyses of who voted for Lincoln in this campaign against his erstwhile general, the Democrat George McClellan. Did disproportionate numbers of farmers from Illinois support the incumbent over those from Vermont, or was it Congregationalists in New England but not Presbyterians in Maryland, or merchants in seaports but not inland cities who provided the core of his votes? As is usually the case in this kind of research, the results were uncertain and ambiguous. I can't remember my conclusion, although I would never have survived the seminar without one. At the time, I was hardly cognizant of the extent to which the study of nineteenth-century politics, including (perhaps especially) the Lincoln story, was a gendered enterprise—of male voters and politicians, by male historians, and for late-twentieth-century male graduate students.

Even as I continued to study past politics, that image of Mary Lincoln continued to haunt me. In part, this was because the only thing I thought I knew about Lincoln's wife was her insanity. To be sure, she did not look unbalanced in the lithograph. Nor was she demure and retiring in any of the Mathew Brady photographs, as other nineteenth-century First Ladies, except the indomitable yellow-turbaned Dolley Madison, seemed to be in their portraits. As I worked on a very traditional dissertation about Maryland politics during the Civil War, I also filed away—not on note cards but in some part of my brain—those polarized statements about Mary Lincoln I had picked up in my research.

Some said that she was a vixen, others that Lincoln had not wanted to marry her and, in fact, according to his law partner William Herndon, had gone so far as to stand her up at the altar. For revenge, she made his life miserable in the White House. Treasonously, she supported the Confederacy and consorted with Southern spies. She spent outrageous sums of public money on the White House, and when Lincoln was assassinated, their son Robert finally had to put her away in an insane asylum.

On the other hand, there were more sympathetic accounts, especially by those who knew her best. These included her husband, who had placed a ring on her finger at their wedding engraved with the sentiment "Love is Eternal." In her own memory, he was "Always-lover-husband-father and *all all* to me—Truly my all."[2] Family members noted what a good mother she was, involved and engaged with her children and, perhaps for that reason, overly sensitive to their deaths, more so than other nineteenth-century mothers who often accepted the loss of a child with resignation. Many visitors praised her tasteful redecorating and refurbishing of the White House that transformed what had looked like a third-rate hotel into a mansion symbolically conveying the power of the Union during a destructive Civil War in which the Confederate States of America nearly became a reality. Others admired her spirit and intelligence, especially in the informal salon she established in the Blue Room. From many sources, it was apparent that she made the White House into a national focus for all Americans—from soldiers to foreign ministers—in a way it had never before been. Certainly, novelists like Irving Stone and historians like Ruth Painter Randall did not think she was a termagant, playing Xanthippe to Lincoln's Socrates.

Among other reasons, these clashing views encouraged me to write her biography. I was increasingly tired of doing the kind of political history that required feeding statistical information about groups of voters into a computer to identify their characteristics in an era before exit polls. Where were the people in such exercises? Besides, political history in the nineteenth century had nothing to do with women, and I was coming to understand this neglect at a time in which American women were increasingly organized and active. It was the historical moment of the struggle for the passage of the Equal Rights Amendment, and during the 1970s, women were on the march. I was among them, and in the adage that surprises only the naive and disingenuous, all history is contemporary history.

But before I embarked on such an offbeat project—and for an academic historian, a biography of a First Lady was that—I inquired of colleagues, friends, and other historians whether they approved. Overwhelmingly, they did not. If you want to write the story of a nineteenth-century woman, went the argument, choose someone like the suffragists Susan B. Anthony or Elizabeth Cady Stanton. Tell the life story of someone who did something on her own, not that of a woman who achieved notoriety only because of her marriage. And indeed, Mary Lincoln did not fit any model of "contributory history." Hers was what biographers have dubbed "a minor life." Mary Lincoln did not lead armies or write novels or become president or join reform movements. Mary Lincoln did not author Lincoln's speeches or instruct him about military tactics. Still, she encapsulated aspects of the human condition, and I was drawn to her by a need in my own thinking to study a woman whose public achievements did not eclipse her private existence.

Time passed. I wrote other books. My children grew up. I had more time; I had tenure. Then in the 1980s, I returned to Mary Lincoln, in part because of the historical dilemma posed by the polarized reviews about her, in part because while she was by no means "everywoman" during the course of her life, she confronted the challenges common to millions of nineteenth-century women, including domesticity, an absentee husband, the death of children, and widowhood with its attendant struggle to survive emotionally and financially. Were her detractors or her admirers correct? Or was she, like most of us, something in between—a multidimensional human being with some good traits, some bad ones? In time, it seemed that both Mary Lincoln's strengths and weaknesses were exaggerated. But when I began my research, I did not recognize what telling this story would do to enhance my own understanding of women's issues.

Fortuitously, a volume of her correspondence edited by Justin Turner and Linda Levitt Turner had appeared in 1972, and a quick perusal of the six hundred surviving letters revealed a highly intelligent woman—a helpmate who indeed encouraged her husband, as William Herndon once said, "up to action." Boldly, Mary Lincoln went beyond traditional support to offer herself to her husband as a companion and a partner in what she liked to call "our Lincoln Party." This, it seemed to me, was the public motive of her existence.

Like all biographers, who necessarily gather energy and commitment from the notion that they will get it right as others have not, I felt that Mary Lincoln's story had never been properly told. Other biographies glossed over her early life. At a time when I was struggling against the reflexive societal definitions that automatically named me Mrs. Robinson Baker—that is, Dr. Baker's wife—Mary Lincoln offered a prism through which I observed the status of nineteenth-century women and its legacy for those of us who were in the twentieth century. Unsurprisingly, the best biography of Mary Lincoln dealt with her as Lincoln's wife. Her relative Katherine Helm even gave her sympathetic portrait the asymmetrical title *Mary, Wife of Lincoln,* while Ruth Painter Randall dubbed hers *Mary Lincoln: Biography of a Marriage.* In Ishbel Ross's historical fiction, she was *The President's Wife: Mary Todd Lincoln, A Biography.*

The more I researched, the more certain I became that Mary Lincoln was a historical archetype of what some historians of women have called a disorderly woman—a woman, as Carroll Smith-Rosenberg has written, who challenges convention and deviates from the expected norms of female behavior.[3] She did not accept the traditional submissive roles assigned her at the same time that she was a conventional mother and wife. She suffered in the judgments of some of her contemporaries and in the opinions of the male historical fraternity who admired Lincoln and found his wife so impossible.

Mary Lincoln's story began in Lexington, Kentucky, home of the proud, aristocratic Todds who had founded a community they intended to make the Athens of the West. What struck me immediately about the twenty years that Mary Lincoln spent in Lexington, from her birth in 1818 until her departure in the late 1830s, was how painful her early life was. Her mother died when she was six, a critical age for any child. Her father, Robert, quickly remarried a bossy woman loathed by his first set of children. Soon Robert and his new wife had their own children, who displaced the first Todds. In a unanimous migration, all four of Robert Todd's first set of daughters fled the city of their birth, where they enjoyed a privileged status, for Springfield, Illinois, as soon as they could get away from the second Mrs. Robert Todd. In family remembrances, Mary was the one who most bitterly contested the authority of her stepmother.

Among other areas in her early life, Mary Todd taught me about women's education, a topic I had never much considered, though I had lived it in the series of single-sex schools and college that I attended and, of course, their corollary, the overwhelmingly male seminar room at Johns Hopkins. More-over, the dismissive stereotypes I held about unschooled Southern women who knew only how to flutter a fan, embroider, and manage a house with, of course, the forced labor of their slaves, who did most of the work, dissolved when considering young Mary Todd's schooling. Granted, she was an exception, for she stayed in school for twelve years, a length of time that placed her among a tiny proportion of American women and, indeed, men. She resisted that period of flat, empty time endured by late-adolescent upper-class women between the end of their schooling and their marriage. In a town like Lexington, they did little but attend parties and observe the social rituals of calling.

Instead, young Mary Todd continued for four more years in one of the most rigorous boarding schools in the United States, the French-born Madame Victorie Mentelle's seminary in the outskirts of Lexington. A year later, she was back at John Ward's school taking advanced courses. This was a far longer period of education than that of her sisters. It was obvious that she was a talented scholar, once running to school so fast that a local observer thought she must be eloping. At Mentelle's, Mary Lincoln learned how to act in school theatricals, how to parse Latin verbs, how to speak French, how to appreciate English literature and write forceful English prose, and, of course, in the requirement necessary for all young ladies of society, how to dance. She was not the traditional Southern belle on the pedestal but rather served as an example of what the English writer Mary Wollstonecraft in her path-breaking *A Vindication of the Rights of Women* described as the necessity of schooling women so that they might become interesting companions for their husbands. I came to see her intellectual cultivation as one of the reasons that Lincoln loved her. But I also envisioned her lifelong interest in politics, reading, and the theater as part of an intellectual autonomy she had created against all odds in the Todd household.

Of course, Mary Todd did not go to college. She was prohibited, on the grounds of her sex, from attending all but two institutions of higher learning in the United States. In the 1830s, only Oberlin in Ohio and, after 1839, the Georgia Female College in Macon, later known as the Wesleyan College, accepted women. Unlike the North, where Catharine Beecher was pressing for teaching as a natural, suitable female occupation, young Southern women like Mary Todd were discouraged from becoming teachers. Hence there was no reason for any further academic training.

I discovered that Mary Lincoln, in addition to her education, was independent in other ways. After her years at Mentelle's and Ward's, she defied the conventions of her time and place by not marrying. Nearly all her friends in Lexington had wed by the time they were twenty; several were already mothers. Mary Lincoln delayed until she was almost twenty-five, nearly a spinster in the calculations of this period but to our generation the sign of a woman who would not march to custom's drums. "I will not give my hand where my heart is not," she once said. "I would rather marry a good man—a man of mind with a hope and bright prospects ahead for position."[4] In the independence that remained one of her most signal characteristics, she moved to Springfield, first in 1837 and then permanently in 1839. There she lived in her married sister Elizabeth Todd Edwards's home until her own marriage in 1842. And there on the uncomfortable horsehair sofa in the parlor of a dwelling that was a social center for many aspiring Illinois politicians, she met her future husband, Abraham Lincoln. In Elizabeth's memory, "Lincoln would listen and gaze on her as if drawn to some Superior power."[5]

Of course, their courtship is a much-disputed topic, though invariably it is Lincoln who is thought to have temporarily broken off the engagement. But to an awakening feminist armed with a growing body of research by women historians about courtship, this was a classically male-oriented interpretation. By every account of the power dimensions among young men and women on the eve of marriage, women held the trumps during the period of courtship. True, they could not proactively pursue their mates, but they did have veto authority over the process, especially in the United States, where mate choice had passed from parents to the future bride and groom. And one-third of these courtships in antebellum America, I discovered, endured some disruption. Viewed from her perspective, Mary Todd had plenty of reasons to end her courtship with Lincoln. Her sisters and brother-in-law, Ninian Edwards, objected on the basis of the couple's different backgrounds, by which Elizabeth Todd Edwards meant that a young man raised on a hard-scrabble farm with only two years' formal education was an inappropriate spouse for an aristocratic Todd.

In other ways, too, Lincoln was not such a catch for the belle of Springfield, who had other suitors, including Stephen Douglas, while Lincoln, whose name at the time was linked in Springfield only to Mary's, had no other prospects. Could he support her in the style to which she was accustomed? And, according to Mary's sister Frances, he was the ugliest man in town, who sometimes infuriated his hot-tempered girlfriend when he arrived late for parties.

There is no definitive evidence about who broke off the engagement, but those in the Lincoln fraternity are reluctant to grant Mary Todd any leverage in this relationship. They persist in what seems to me a one-dimensional view of what is necessarily a relationship that requires mutuality. Believing in the uniqueness of Lincoln, they fail to place his domestic arrangements in the context of their time. Some even explain the couple's eventual marriage in 1842 as an example of Lincoln's high ethical code. Having once promised himself to Mary, he married her only because it was the honorable thing to do. (This view has encouraged legions of practical-minded Americans to wonder if Mary was pregnant "at the altar," a question I am often asked.)

With no conclusive evidence, some historians provide other women whom Lincoln would have preferred to marry, such as Ann Rutledge (whose fictional but enduring claim on Lincoln's affections has recently been demolished by Lewis Gannett) or an Edwards cousin or perhaps Sarah Rickard, who was fifteen years his junior. As I developed the stages of Mary's life, which fell into three segments of approximately two decades each, the judgments of history seemed unfair. The intense dislike of Mary Lincoln, nurtured in a vague misogyny about noncompliant women and promoted by knowledge of her supposed insanity, led most observers to read history backward. In the ultimate androcentric view of the courtship, C. A. Tripp in *The Intimate World of Abraham Lincoln* has argued that Lincoln's melancholic crisis in 1841—"the fatal first of January"—had nothing to do with Mary Todd but rather was the result of a lover's agony over the departure from Springfield of his homosexual partner, Joshua Speed.[6]

After her marriage, Mary Lincoln lived for eighteen years as a wife and mother in Springfield. She ran her home, with Lincoln often on the circuit and increasingly engaged in politicking. While beating rugs, fighting with servants, raising young sons, and cooking chicken is not the stuff of historical drama, I certainly identified with it. Similar domestic routines define the existence of most nineteenth-, twentieth-, and twenty-first-century women. As such, they deserve study, whether through research on the often-barbed relationships of domestic servants with their mistresses, on the adoption of new household technology, such as the Lincolns' new Thompson stove, or even on changing standards of cleanliness. In Mary Lincoln's case, such transformations involved iron stoves, more finished consumer goods in the shops of Springfield and, therefore, less sewing, and more household bric-a-brac to dust. Faced with my own domesticity, I admired Mary Lincoln's efficient management of the house at Eighth and Jackson, especially since, to the manor born, she had grown up in a wealthy household with eighteen slaves where she had few assigned domestic tasks and little training in such mundane chores.

In these eighteen years in Springfield, Mary Lincoln also immersed herself in her husband's expanding political career. At first I thought her interest an aberration and part of her uniqueness. For what did disfranchised women care about the male endeavors of politics? But now we understand that even in the years before women could vote or hold office, they vicariously shared men's interest in politics as they slipped over the divide between the public and private spheres, just as less-remote fathers like Lincoln sought companionship with their wives and children in the privacy of their homes. Mary Lincoln, raised by a father prominent in Kentucky Whig politics, already knew the difference between a Democrat and a Republican. Politics was in the air everywhere, and she wanted some part of it.

Ultimately, she served her husband well as confidante and cheerleader. In her anticipation, as Lincoln several times told his friends, she expected him to be president. Of course, he thought such a prediction ludicrous, but it was surely a stimulant to his ambitions that his wife shared the ultimate goal of any American politician. Mary Lincoln gave political parties; she wrote patronage letters; she informed friends of his stands. Later, believing in the intuitive understanding of women about human behavior, she insinuated herself into even his cabinet choices. And, in what I considered to be a testament to what Lincoln perceived as her contributions to his political career, when he heard in 1860 that he had carried Pennsylvania, he hurried home, calling out as he neared his house, "Mary, Mary, We are elected."[7]

Mary Lincoln's most controversial years occurred in the final two decades of her life—from 1861 when she became First Lady until her death in 1882. Writing about her in the 1980s, when Nancy Reagan was adorning our contemporary White House and being criticized for her borrowed gowns and haughty presence, I sympathized with Mrs. President Lincoln's understanding of her role, which, like so much that she did, was ahead of her time. To her credit, she immediately grasped the importance of her home to the nation. Just as the still-domeless United States Capitol conveyed the sense of an unfinished, second-rate republic, so a shabby President's House revealed the powerlessness of the chief executive. Foreign ministers such as Britain's Lord Lyon and France's Henri Mercier would report to governments already disposed to support the Confederacy how feeble the Union was if they were to observe flaking wallpaper and soiled rugs in the home of its chief executive. Few First Ladies comprehended the profound significance of the White House to public affairs at the level Mary Lincoln did during the Civil War.

With characteristic energy and good taste, she transformed the dismal interiors of the president's home into stately ceremonial rooms, available for the entertainments that introduced Abraham Lincoln to thousands of Americans. He called these "Handshake Days"—and dreaded them. When his wife overspent the budget for the White House, the president angrily complained that her improvements would "stink" in the land and that she must take personal responsibility for her "flub-a-dubs."[8] Of course, her husband's criticism has echoed through the historical evaluations of Mary Lincoln in the White House, and she has been demonized as a cheating mistress who took bribes and even, with no evidence to support the claim, sold state documents to adventurers.

I came to see her role differently. First, I wondered why she should take the blame when in fact the commissioner of public buildings, who signed the payment vouchers sent to the U.S. Treasury, controlled the federal budget for the White House. Wasn't it the commissioner's responsibility to stop any extravagance? Wasn't a public official to blame rather than a First Lady who had no official standing and certainly no staff or office? Was Mary Lincoln, to whom all criticisms stick like barnacles, so persuasive and powerful that she could suggest purchases beyond the budget and get the commissioner to sign for them? I wondered because, if so, it suggested another side of Mary Lincoln—her authoritative ability to transcend the limitations of female influence. Still, the failure to consider the commissioner's culpability reminded me symbolically of the double standard applied to men and women.

From another perspective, it seemed to me that Mary Lincoln was following what students of women's history define as "domestic feminism," and she was doing a good job at it. By 1860, many middle-class American women whose husbands worked away from home were taking greater authority over household matters. The First Lady was simply practicing what was going on elsewhere, though her home was a special one—the People's House, as the press sometimes called it.

While historians remember Mary Lincoln's public fits of temper and her interference with patronage matters, few credit her success. The fact that the White House emerged as an effective physical statement of the power of the Union government as well as of the authority of its chief executive whose election had led to the secession of the South testified to her achievement. The Lincolns used all the renovated public rooms of the first floor of the White House to entertain Washington society (many of whom thought both Lincolns vulgar), the press corps (who constantly criticized the First Lady and the president), the Congress, the judges, the foreign diplomatic corps, and, most poignantly, the nation's soldiers. William Crooks, who served nine presidents, from Abraham Lincoln to Theodore Roosevelt, as a doorman and guard, believed that the White House "was never so entirely given over to the public as during Mr. Lincoln's administration."[9]

Nor in the myths about Mary is there room to acknowledge her bold insistence to stay by her husband's side during the fearsome early days of the war in the spring of 1861, when most wives left Washington because of the possibility of a Confederate attack across the Potomac. Nor is there attention given to her frequent visits to hospitals crowded with wounded soldiers. "I am sitting by the side of your soldier boy," she wrote to Mrs. James Agen from Campbell Hospital in 1864. "He tells me to say to you that he is all right."[10]

In the end, the White House brought tragedy to a woman whose life had often been marred by the abandonment through death of those she loved. The family circle represented her spiritual center, and it was vanishing. As a young mother in Springfield, she had lost her second son, three-year-old Eddie, to tuberculosis. In the White House, eleven-year-old Willie, perhaps the favored son of both parents, died an agonizing death from typhoid fever. And then on that dreadful night in April 1865, John Wilkes Booth murdered her husband. The Civil War had claimed over 600,000 lives, and in a merging of her private life with the nation's, it had exacted casualties from the Lincoln family. But Mary Lincoln's melancholy did not preclude enough energy to wage an eventually successful battle with the fathers of Springfield about where her husband would be buried.

Now Mary Lincoln became a wanderer, uncertain of her financial circumstances and unsure as she departed from one of the grandest houses in America about whether she could afford to maintain a home in Chicago for her youngest son, Tad, and herself. She represented the sad plight of many widows who, for reasons having to do with the dual standards of a society that made women outsiders to financial matters, found themselves ill-equipped to deal with the emotional burdens of their family losses coupled with the economic ignorance about their future lives without a provider. Abraham Lincoln left no will, an extraordinary oversight for a lawyer, and her male protectors, executor Judge David Davis and her son Robert, delayed the process of probation, which would assure her of $34,000, a third of her husband's estate.

Restless and miserable but determined to raise young Tad as best she could, Mary Lincoln even organized a sale of her old clothes, which led to more humiliation when the New York newspapers featured stories about her stained gowns. I came to see this episode of the "Old Clothes Sale" as a gallant, if mistaken, effort by a widow to try to help support herself. In any case, an embarrassed son hastily dispersed the monies from Lincoln's estate. Mary Lincoln, ever portrayed as greedy, offered to give her portion of twelve-year-old Tad's estate coming to her as his guardian to Robert, and she eventually gave her eldest son over $10,000.

Long attuned as a Christian to the possibilities of an afterlife, Mary Lincoln now found comfort, along with many Americans, in the heresy of spiritualism. She had begun her efforts to recall dead members of her family in the White House to the amusement of the press and her husband's secretaries and to the horror of her half-sister Emilie Helm. Increasingly, she traveled to the centers for spiritualists who claimed they could return her lost loved ones. In 1868, she began a long pilgrimage to Europe with Tad. Three years later after living in Frankfurt, where Tad went to school, she returned to Chicago. There, in the penultimate tragedy of Mary Lincoln's star-crossed life, she watched her youngest son, eighteen-year-old Tad, die of pleurisy in a Chicago hotel room in 1871.

Four years later, Robert initiated another devastating blow. In May 1875, Mary Lincoln was taken to the Cook County Courthouse in Chicago, charged as a lunatic, convicted, and sent off to an asylum. It did not take a feminist to appreciate the inequity of a kangaroo court, but in researching this episode, I was inspired by unprofessional anger at Robert Lincoln's filial disloyalty and at the judicial system that denied Mary Lincoln any possibility of defending herself. Why, if Robert was so worried about his mother's spending, didn't he have a conservator appointed to control her money, an easy enough procedure and one used by the Adlai Stevenson family for their mother, Ellen Borden Stevenson, in 1965? Why didn't Robert provide some kind of emotional solace for his bereaved mother? Why didn't he hire a housekeeper or companion for her?

Mary Lincoln had no warning before she was hauled off to court. Her son never advised her of his intentions. Instead, Leonard Swett, a friend of her husband's, arrived at her Chicago hotel room armed with a writ of arrest and persuaded a resistant Mary Lincoln that she must go to the courthouse for a trial that very afternoon. She was never called to testify and explain the examples of aberrant behavior presented by her son and his witnesses, nor did the lawyer chosen by Robert and his advisers defend her. In fact, Isaac Arnold said nothing. Instead, Robert's lawyers summarized the prosecution's case with stories of Mary Lincoln's uncontrollable grief after Lincoln's assassination, her old clothes sale, her mania for buying things she could not use, and her peculiar delusions. The last witness against her was her son, who testified that he had no doubt that his mother was insane. "She has long been a source of anxiety to me. She has no home and no reason to make these purchases."[11]

Then the jury—not of her peers, but of twelve men—heard testimony that confused migraine headaches with hallucinations and excessive shopping with psychosis. Her judges included a friend of Robert's, who informed the jury as they deliberated about what he considered Mary Lincoln's overwrought reaction to Tad's death. And within the hour, Mary Lincoln was adjudged *non compos mentis* and given an indeterminate sentence of confinement to take place in Dr. Robert Patterson's asylum, Bellevue.

Recent students of this trial have pointed to the improvements in the Illinois law, and that of three other states, which now guarantee a trial by jury, thereby making it more difficult to confine married women and minors, as had been the case in the past, simply at the behest of a male family member and the agreement of a supervisor of an asylum who had an unused bed. Mary Lincoln was again teaching me a lesson—this time about the imbalance and lack of judicial fairness in a system that still did not allow women to serve on juries or testify. This time, the instruction concerned the utter lack of protection for women, especially disorderly, eccentric ones who did not conform and behave. These women could be institutionalized on the sole grounds that their male relatives thought they should be. I was disappointed that historians interpreted the trial as just, especially since it did not take long for even Mary Lincoln's contemporaries to complain publicly about such a proceeding.[12]

I interviewed three psychiatrists about Mary Lincoln's insanity trial. One thought that I thought that I was Mary Lincoln, exaggerating even the supposed cliché of identification and transference that biographers supposedly have with their subjects. (It was true that I did occasionally have conversations with Mary Lincoln, but only when I was swimming.) The other two psychiatrists saw her behavior as annoying and improper but not dangerous to herself or to society. Nor did she fall into the nineteenth-century medical categories of insanity—mania, melancholia, and dementia. Instead, according to my experts, she suffered from the personality disorder of narcissism, a common neurosis of today but not a psychosis and one that hardly requires hospitalization. In a more practical vein, a pharmacologist explained that the overuse of chloral hydrate, which Mary Lincoln used for insomnia, might have caused some of the symptoms described by her doctors.

Mary Lincoln stayed only three months and three weeks in the Bellevue asylum, and she spent most of it fighting for her release. Given that Robert was her official guardian and had control of her money and that the superintendent of the asylum read and censored all her mail, freedom was not easily obtained. Several women had been in Bellevue for years, and I admired her persistent and cunning efforts to gain her freedom. Mary Lincoln began smuggling letters to influential public figures on her carriage rides. Sometimes she used two envelopes, addressing the outside one to an innocuous correspondent. A few recipients responded, including a newspaper reporter and, more critically, Myra Bradwell, America's first woman lawyer.

Bradwell was no stranger to public controversy. Her first public battle involved her efforts to practice law, for although she had passed the Illinois bar exam and edited the influential *Chicago Legal News,* she suffered from what the courts called the "Marital Disability." In a word, she was a married woman, Mrs. James Bradwell, and was not an independent agent. In 1873, the U.S. Supreme Court had decided in *Bradwell v. Illinois* that "the natural and proper timidity and delicacy which belongs to the female sex evidently unfits it for many of the occupations of civil life. The paramount destiny and mission of woman are to fulfill the noble and benign offices of wife and mother."[13] Two years later, Bradwell took up Mary Lincoln's pleas for freedom. Soon, Bradwell threatened a writ of habeas corpus (which only her husband could introduce); she wrote letters to the newspapers proclaiming that Mary Lincoln was being held as a prisoner and that the former First Lady was "no more insane than I am."[14] By September, an embarrassed Robert grudgingly agreed to release his mother, and Mary Lincoln left for her sister's home in Springfield to reclaim the liberty she might never have obtained without the intercession of a female advocate. And later, in behavior that testified to her sanity, Mary Lincoln lived independently for four years in Pau in southern France, where she moved because she still feared the patriarchal reach of her son.

Mary Lincoln's story is a woman's tale, but it is not just that. As I lived through transformations in my own life relating to the roles of women in the late twentieth century, I came to see her paradoxically as an exceptional yet representative woman—not so much because she married Abraham Lincoln and became a First Lady but rather because I viewed her story as that of the universal human condition. Granted that she played the role of an agent provocateur in some of her humiliations, still the range of her experience, the hammering persistence of her tragedies, the degree to which she was willing to be different, her struggle to gain her release from Bellevue, her survival those four years she lived alone in Pau—all seemed to reveal something more than a wife's tale. She came to represent the human experience, with its vagaries of fortune so often beyond our control. Observing her through the historical prism of her life, I felt a profound sense of compassion and sadness when I wrote about her death in Springfield at her sister Elizabeth's home in 1882. For me, what had begun as the study of politics in my professional career had been transformed into feminism. Through Mary Lincoln, in the slogan of the woman's movement, the personal had become the political.

NOTES

1. Catherine Allgor, *Parlor Politics: In Which the Ladies of Washington Help Build a City and a Government* (Charlottesville: University of Virginia Press, 2000), 1, 63.

2. Justin Turner and Linda Levitt Turner, *Mary Todd Lincoln: Her Life and Letters* (New York: A. A. Knopf, 1972), 534.

3. Carroll Smith-Rosenberg, *Disorderly Conduct: Visions of Gender in Victorian America* (New York: A. A. Knopf, 1985), 17, 23, 197–244.

4. Douglas Wilson and Rodney O. Davis, *Herndon's Informants* (Urbana: University of Illinois Press, 1998), 444.

5. Ibid., 443.

6. C. A. Tripp, *The Intimate World of Abraham Lincoln* (New York: Basic Books, 2003), 134–38.

7. Jean H. Baker, *Mary Todd Lincoln: A Biography* (New York: W. W. Norton, 1987), 162.

8. David Herbert Donald, *Lincoln* (New York: Simon and Schuster, 1995), 313.

9. Colonel William Crook, *Through Five Administrations: Reminiscences of Colonel William H. Crook*, ed. Margarita Gerry (New York: Harper and Brothers, 1910), 17. Crook, in fact, served nine administrations.

10. Turner and Turner, *Mary Todd Lincoln*, 179.

11. Baker, *Mary Todd Lincoln*, 321.

12. I also discovered the power of the Lincoln fraternity when I was refused access to a new source about the trial—the so-called insanity file that had been discovered in Robert Lincoln's home, Hildene, in Manchester, Vermont, after his grandson Robert Beckwith's death in 1985. Although this box of papers was public property owned by the state of Illinois, it had been "lent" to two historians who were writing a book on the insanity file. They refused to let me see it until I threatened to hire a lawyer, and even then I had to wait until their book came out. Inadvertently, Mary Lincoln had taught me another kind of lesson.

13. *Bradwell v. Illinois*, 83 U.S. (16 Wall), 130; Robert Spector, "Women against the Law: Myra Bradwell's Struggle for Admission to the Illinois Bar," *Journal of the Illinois State Historical Society* 68 (June 1975): 228–42.

14. *Bradwell v. Illinois*, 130, 141.

Lincoln on Democracy

Editors' note: Governor Cuomo first encountered Lincoln in the sixth grade at Public School No. 50 in South Jamaica, Queens, New York. America's sixteenth president was offered as evidence to the students of this poor neighborhood that they could survive and thrive. He would encounter Lincoln again in the courses he would take. After the *Collected Works of Abraham Lincoln* was published in 1953, it was given to him as a gift from his sister and took him down the path as a student of Lincoln. Throughout his career as a lawyer and public official, he has written numerous articles, coedited with Harold Holzer *Lincoln on Democracy*, and authored *Why Lincoln Matters: Today More Than Ever.*

In July 1989—months before democracy blossomed in the capitals of Eastern Europe—the seed for a book on democracy was planted halfway around the world, in the capital of New York State.

As governor, I had the privilege of welcoming to Albany a delegation of leading educators from Poland, a nation with a long history of yearning and fighting for liberty but, at the time, only the briefest experience in enjoying liberty itself. They were members of the Teacher's Section of Poland's Solidarity Union, the heroic coalition of working people who had been advocating democratization in the face of rigid, historic repression. They had come to the United States on a tour sponsored by the "Democracy Project," a global exchange program organized by American teachers to foster understanding and opportunity among teaching professionals here and overseas. The American hosts had invited me to greet their Polish colleagues, and I was delighted to accept, hardly realizing that their visit would inspire a new work on Lincoln.

When they arrived in July, I proudly guided those in the delegation through our recently restored and refurbished "official" governor's office. This is an ornate chamber in the capitol building known as the "Red Room," where many of my predecessors, including Theodore Roosevelt, Franklin D. Roosevelt, and Thomas E. Dewey, all enjoyed working but which I used only for ceremonial purposes, preferring to work in smaller quarters next door. The Red Room, with its gleaming wood paneling, stately chandeliers, formal drapery, and gilt molding, is an architectural marvel. And it is more. It is a reminder of all that was accomplished by those who came before us and of our obligation to preserve what they left us and to build upon it for the benefit of those who will come after us.

What better room to display to our Polish visitors, I thought, than a chamber where so much of our own history had taken place, where democratically elected chief executives had administered one of the largest states in the Union? The Poles seemed to share my enthusiasm for these surroundings. But our visitors had something more on their minds than the highlights of our capitol. There is no shortage of graceful public architecture or lavish interior design in Warsaw. What *had* long been missing there was the guarantee of freedom, not its trappings; the privilege of self-determination, not monuments in its honor. What had been lacking there, in those dark days before Poland and its neighbors in Czechoslovakia, Hungary, and East Germany so dramatically threw off the stifling yoke of longtime oppression, was the personal experience of democracy and with it a meaningful, inspiring credo of freedom and self-determination that could be relied on to illuminate democratization in the future.

Speaking through translators, the Polish teachers asked whether I might help them begin building an archive of great thoughts and writings on democracy by telling them which American writings on the subject had meant the most to me in my life and career and might provide similar guidance for them. I did not need to reflect on the question. My choice of a source was immediate and unequivocal: Abraham Lincoln.

I enjoyed joking with people in those days that I had always admired Lincoln because he was reassuring to politicians like me. He was himself a big, homely-looking politician from a poor family who started off by losing a few elections, yet in the end succeeded brilliantly. Of course, my fascination with Lincoln went far deeper. Lincoln was the president who argued that government has a responsibility to "do for people what they cannot do, or do so well for themselves."[1] I have quoted those lines many times to support my own belief that government today is no less obligated.

For me, Lincoln's writing—his unique ability to craft arguments of raw power and breathtaking beauty, arguing the seamless logic of a great lawyer and the large heart of a great humanitarian—is among the best produced by any American, ever. I have read Lincoln's words over and over from the volumes of the *Collected Works*. I am always taken by the humor, the pathos, the determination, and the compassion that resonates in those words. And by the great ideas.

Above all, the theme that courses through so many letters, speeches, and fragments, the great addresses and the simple greetings alike, is the unyielding commitment to the principles of our Declaration of Independence, what Lincoln called the "sheet anchor" of our democracy. Lincoln talked about the Declaration as a stump campaigner, during the debates with Stephen Douglas, and again as president at Gettysburg. All people shared the right to advance as far as their talents could take them. America, Lincoln believed, was a great society because it promised to "clear a path for all," to provide opportunity for anyone with skill and ambition.[2] When the institution of slavery blocked that road, it was Lincoln who cleared the path. Some have since argued that he did it too slowly, or too halfheartedly, or too imprecisely. But the fact remains that it was he who did it. He saved our democracy. He improved our democracy. And he characterized our democracy in timeless words of inspiration for the benefit of all the generations of Americans who have followed.

Lincoln has been an inspiration to me and to others for as long as his words have been heard or read. He was a man of principle and purpose who not only forged in war America's new birth of freedom but hallowed it in words as well—unforgettable words that his mind sharpened into steel and his heart softened into an embrace, words he spoke in Illinois and Washington and Gettysburg, calling for the highest sacrifices Americans could make to preserve their unique experiment in government, a system Lincoln believed was "the last best hope of earth." Lincoln brought the American people to their feet, cheering, crying, and laughing, an unforgettable reminder of the indomitability of the human spirit.

Lincoln was a model of active presidential leadership in crisis. He fought to maintain our system of majority rule, then broke the chains that bound four million Americans to slavery, and finally showed us the way to expanding democratic rights. His presidency was a crucial turning point in the evolution of democracy here and remains an example to people everywhere who aspire to exercise the full measure of their own freedom.

And so I thought, when my Polish guests asked for my advice on which expressions on democracy were worth reading, that surely Lincoln could now provide such guidance for countries too long denied the basic rights and freedoms Lincoln fought here to preserve. Surely the brilliance of his prose could withstand translation into a foreign tongue. Surely the logic of his argument would transcend the decades and the distance, as well.

"Do Polish students study Lincoln's words today?" I asked the Polish teachers. "No," they told me, because Lincoln's words were simply not available in Poland—not since World War II, when freedom went into retreat there. When the Russians marched in, Lincoln went out; not surprising, since his passion for liberty was not suited for coexistence with tyranny. The teachers said that not a single volume of Lincoln's words in Polish existed in their country. That seemed a tragedy that startled and saddened me but also a challenge that could be overcome.

Without anything more than a quick, powerful impulse, I promised on the spot to use whatever influences I had or could produce to see that Lincoln's words on democracy were promptly translated into Polish and delivered to Poland for the fullest possible use of the Polish people. The teachers instantly greeted the idea with tremendous enthusiasm. "Why not bring the volumes over yourself?" they asked. I said I would be pleased to consider doing so. And the visit ended.

My promise was, indeed, the product of the moment. But even as the idea flashed into my mind and spilled out in unrehearsed conversation, there was good reason to believe that the promise could be kept. For one thing, New York State had an International Partnership Program, which we created specifically to establish cultural and economic links to foreign nations. With an already proven record of outreach to Italy, Israel, Africa, and Spain, we found Lincoln a perfect way to launch a relationship with the reemerging nations of Eastern Europe.

For another thing, I was fortunate in that the professionals in the world of Lincoln scholarship were not strangers to me, and I knew I would be able at least to ask for their help. Harold Holzer, for example, who later became the coeditor of the volume, had worked with me since 1984, and I had known him since 1977.

The promise proved easier to make than to keep. Frankly, I had thought that all we needed to do was select the best existing treasury of Lincoln's expressions on democracy and have it translated. Then I learned something that surprised me even more than the revelation that no such volume existed in Poland. No such volume existed here, either! Lincoln's unique prose on the subjects of freedom, self-government, and equality had never before been assembled together in English.

As it turned out, what might have dampened our enthusiasm for the Polish project instead heightened our enthusiasm for an English-language edition to be published in the United States. Lincoln's *Collected Works* boasts a 378-page index, but not once does it mention the term "democracy."

And that is how and why *Lincoln on Democracy* was born. It is an American book inspired by the Polish people, just as it will be a Polish book devoted to an American—an American who belongs to another time and place but whose devotion to democracy offers a sublime and universal diplomacy in transcendent prose.

On November 17, 1989, I had the further pleasure of formally announcing the *Lincoln on Democracy* project at an event honoring the chairman of the Solidarity Union, Lech Walesa, during his first visit to the United States. I told this extraordinary freedom fighter, "As you shake off four decades of doctrinaire rigidity, working to open the windows of liberty in every library and schoolroom in Poland—letting the sun shine in on minds too long denied the birthright of free expression—we want to help." *Lincoln on Democracy*, I suggested, constituted "a tangible way to link your struggle for freedom with our historic respect for liberty and democracy." The Polish edition might be only the first of many. Future translations might include Hungarian, Czech, German—even Russian and Chinese—books for every nation where there is a yearning for democracy, a need for the guidance of historical truth, and the absence until now of available materials.

"This makes me feel even more warm," Mr. Walesa said in his reply. "But I don't know if you will be able to keep pace with the other languages, because the line is forming already."

Lincoln belongs at the head of that line.

Lincoln brought forth a "new birth of freedom" for America, as he put it at Gettysburg. But it was not just for Americans that he struggled. It was to save democracy for the world. He knew that by preserving *our* Union, he would guarantee "the civil and religious liberties of mankind in many countries and through many ages."[3]

Early in his administration, President Lincoln reminded a foreign visitor that Americans "cherish especial sentiments" for "those who, like themselves, have founded their institutions on the principle of the equal rights of men."[4] We cherish the same sentiments for everyone, everywhere, and therefore we continue to do what we can to make Lincoln available, reminding people how relevant his idea of democracy continues to be in this "work in progress" of a world.

NOTES

1. *The Collected Works of Abraham Lincoln*, ed. Roy P. Basler, 9 vols. (New Brunswick, N.J.: Rutgers University Press, 1953–55), 2:221.

2. Mario M. Cuomo and Harold Holzer, eds., *Lincoln on Democracy*, rev. ed. (New York: Fordham University Press, 2004), xxix.

3. *Collected Works*, 5:212.

4. Ibid., 5:143.

JOAN FLINSPACH

A View from the Lincoln Museum

O ne December holiday season, when I was ten, I traveled with my family down the Great River Road from my hometown of Fairfield, Iowa, through Missouri, Arkansas, and Louisiana and returned "up north" through Mississippi, Tennessee, Kentucky, and Illinois. My parents meticulously planned all of our family trips, complete with maps and tourism material from the cities and towns that responded to my mother's requests for visitor information. After we had purchased our pickup camper, we took major trips that coincided with both the school and farming schedules that dominated our lives. Usually they were planned for the summer months, during late July and early August, when the planting, fertilizing, and herbicide applications were done and before the harvesting season began, but this year we had a rare holiday break, with Christmas and New Year's Day both falling on a Wednesday, which made our break a little longer.

My mother, a schoolteacher, suggested, "What a great time to go south! It will be cold up here, and we have two full weeks. The kids will drive us crazy with no school, especially if the weather is bad and they are cooped up inside. Let's go." My father agreed, provided the harvest was completed.

The first stop was St. Genevieve, Missouri, a town on the Mississippi River settled by French fur traders. This unique place had stone buildings constructed by hand in the late 1700s. I remember thinking how amazing it was to find something that old. We toured the city, learning about the French settlement. In Arkansas and Louisiana, we visited historic plantations.

New Orleans was the next destination—the French quarter, the Café du Monde, lunch at the Court of Two Sisters, and a Greyhound tour featuring the history of the city. But after seeing Natchez and Vicksburg, Mississippi, my brother refused to leave the camper, saying if he had to look at one more historic site he would die. I, however, was in total rapture.

This family trip awakened my love of history. Like Lincoln, as a child I was an avid reader, frequently winning the local public library's summer reading competition for children. I had discovered before taking this memorable family trip that our library carried a series of biographies for children. During this holiday vacation, I was able to see history in the third dimension, and I knew, by the end of the trip, that I had to find a career that would incorporate the study of American history, preferably the nineteenth century. At college, I was an extremely rare class of student—a history major without an education degree. Teaching history would never satisfy my desire to be *surrounded* by history.

Under the guidance of my wonderful University of Iowa undergraduate advisor, Dr. Lawrence Gelfund, I learned that one could be a part of the museum world through graduate study. After three years, I completed my master's degree in historic preservation and began the great American job search. I found my first permanent position at the Historic General Dodge House in Council Bluffs, Iowa. Working there was a terrific experience, but after two years, knowing that I wanted to make a career of the museum world, I sought opportunities that would further my knowledge in settings beyond that of the historic house museum. During a great job at Father Flanagan's Boys' Home, or Boys Town, as it was known then, I got to build the archive area of a museum and see to the structure and organization of both an archival and an artifact collection. I was the manager of the Hall of History.

It was, however, the opportunity of a lifetime to take a position as director at the Lincoln Museum in Fort Wayne, Indiana. Here, I have overseen the multimillion-dollar construction of a new museum, hired the staff, and watched it (and them) grow. I was back in the era I loved, nineteenth-century American history, and I have gotten to know a man I honor—Abraham Lincoln.

I have come face-to-face with Abraham Lincoln through my involvement with the Lincoln Museum. The museum's growth includes the establishment of temporary exhibits, a membership program, a volunteer program, lectures, an authors' series, a museum theater program, a Web site, an online store, teacher institutes, a partnership in the Lincoln Colloquium, and a new in-school program. We have established the Friends of the Lincoln Museum, which, together with our operating partner, Lincoln Financial Group Foundation, underwrites much of this programming. We are on the cusp of launching distance learning via video conferencing.

The museum's collection has evolved over the years. The executives of Lincoln National Life Insurance donated more than 1,600 items, forming the basis of the museum collection in 1928. Louis A. Warren, the museum's first director, expanded it when he brought three more collections with him to Fort Wayne. Through his research, he had obtained the Helm-Haycraft and the Hanks-Hitchcock collections. The former, assembled by John Helm, surveyor, and Samuel Haycraft, historian, consists of documents and manuscripts from the communities where Lincoln's parents lived. The Hanks-Hitchcock collection includes over 1,200 lists of Hanks families and hundreds of family records and letters. Amassed by Warren, the third collection is called the Warren collection. It encompasses thousands of Virginia, Kentucky, Indiana, and Illinois records referencing the Lincolns and neighboring families.

As his first major acquisition after his arrival at the museum, Warren purchased the Richard Thompson collection from his estate in 1928. Thompson had gathered over 2,000 manuscripts, which included such items as Lincoln letters and the correspondence of his contemporaries. Thompson had been a friend of Lincoln's and a leading Indiana Whig. Warren also bought the library of Judge Daniel Fish of Minneapolis, one of the five largest collections of Lincoln books and documents in the nation. Judge Fish died in 1906, so to augment his collection, Warren bought the Albert H. Griffith collection, which complemented the Fish acquisitions because it added twentieth-century Lincoln material.

The museum's second director was R. Gerald McMurtry, who acquired the life mask of Lincoln's face and hands made in 1860 by Leonard Wells Volk. And like his predecessors, third director Mark E. Neely Jr. made important additions, including the Lincoln family collection of photographs, purchased in 1986.

With 300 Lincoln-signed documents, 18,000 books, 7,000 nineteenth-century prints and engravings, rare nineteenth-century newspapers, 5,000 original photographs, 350 sheet music titles, scores of period artifacts, a vertical file of 200,000 newspapers and magazine clippings capturing the scope of interpretation of Lincoln throughout the twentieth century, Lincoln family belongings, and manuscript collections, only major pieces were missing from the collection. In 1998, a Leland-Boker edition of the Emancipation Proclamation signed by Lincoln was added, and in 2005, the museum purchased one of the thirteen Lincoln-signed copies of the Thirteenth Amendment to the Constitution.

One could not encounter the world's second-largest Lincoln collection daily and ignore this amazing man. I had studied him before coming to the museum, but I did not come to know him personally until I had the opportunity to lead this remarkable institution. The mission of the Lincoln Museum is to interpret and preserve the life and legacy of Abraham Lincoln through research, preservation, exhibits, and education. We use both traditional and innovative means to bring Lincoln to life for our visitors. The permanent exhibit offers hands-on and interactive opportunities to learn about Lincoln. It also presents him in the traditional written word. A detailed time line tells the story of the Civil War, which appeals to history buffs and reenactors, but in the same gallery, we illustrate just the highlights of the war for those who have less of an interest in it. With tools such as these, we reach multiple audiences. Our temporary exhibits feature topics from Lincoln's era or his legacy that appeal broadly and attract our museum "regulars" or draw in new visitors who will also enjoy the permanent exhibit. The museum store completes the cycle by making available many forms of take-home remembrances.

The first Lincoln lesson I learned is the importance of lifelong learning. Even as president, Lincoln was not afraid to check books out of the Library of Congress and teach himself military strategy. The more I learn of this man, the more I need to learn. I am not afraid to ask questions, research a topic, or solicit an opinion. This fearless approach comes from Lincoln.

I use Lincoln's example of assembling his adversaries within his cabinet so that he could hear all sides of an issue to guide my decisions about having controversial or anti-Lincoln speakers and authors at the museum. His "public opinion baths" with the general public were used by him to keep in touch with what others were thinking. We do open our doors to those who do not revere this man so that we can present all sides of him. Lerone Bennett Jr., author of *Forced into Glory*, has spoken at the museum; we have through a temporary exhibit examined Lincoln's conflicts with the Constitution; and we show how Lincoln has been used over the years as both a symbol and an advertising icon.

Lincoln hated war and violence of any kind. In our telling of the Civil War, we recite an account of Lincoln's search for a general and note the battle losses of each of the fired generals, teaching that the price of war is costly and war should not be glorified. His second inaugural address, with its emphasis on "with malice toward none," was delivered as the war was clearly winding down. It was more meditative than celebratory.

We exhibit a sale bill and use figures to illustrate the sale of a mother and her three-year-old daughter as they stand on the auction block, where they will be sold separately. This scenario depicts one of slavery's greatest tragedies, the separation of family members. It ties into Lincoln's personal hatred for the institution but his awareness that, politically and constitutionally, the issue was very difficult.

Lincoln loved the theater. He frequently read, recited from, and attended plays. We have a museum theater program that captivates audiences. I think that Lincoln would enjoy knowing that we use existing and original theater to teach audiences about him and his era. *Lincoln Lore*, our quarterly publication, is the longest continuously published periodical (since 1929) devoted exclusively to Abraham Lincoln and his era.

Lincoln loved innovation and still is the only president with a patent. He was fascinated by the latest inventions. We have replicated his interest in innovation by using technology to present him. Our video conferencing program will bring him to the world at large, creating a museum without walls for the twenty-first century.

In his first inaugural address, Lincoln connected the Declaration of Independence and its principles to his 1861 audience. At the Lincoln Museum, we have the privilege of connecting Abraham Lincoln and his principles to future generations through "the mystic chords of memory."

I have learned from this man. As I enter my second decade working with the public to educate them about him, it is second nature to me to resolve tough issues by asking myself, "What would Lincoln do?" When a project or event that was funded through grants comes in under budget, we offer to return the unused funds to the funder. We learned this lesson from Lincoln, who walked for miles to return a small amount of change to a customer. His honesty, practicality, patience, and adherence to the ultimate goal have guided me many times. It has been a privilege to get to know him and to share him with the world.

Editors' note: The Lincoln Museum closed on June 30, 2008, at the direction of the Lincoln Financial Foundation, the charitable arm of the Lincoln Financial Group.

4

SARA VAUGHN GABBARD

The Evolution of a Lincoln Editor

While not as eloquent as the other contributors, I will surely win the "serendipity award" by virtue of the fact that my first encounter with Abraham Lincoln was on May 14, 1936, the day that I was born (and subsequently raised) in Lincoln, Illinois. My hometown, located twenty miles north of Springfield, was the first named for and by Abraham Lincoln before he became famous. The people of this modest settlement, just another stop for the circuit-riding prairie lawyer, wagered on his future claim to greatness and decided in 1853 that their town should carry his name. Lincoln, in one of the odder bits of Lincolniana, obliged by christening the courthouse steps with juice from a watermelon. To my great embarrassment, my parents were involved in raising money for one of the town's centennial projects, a statue of a watermelon to be placed at the train depot.

My guess is that I am also the only contributor who has met a child of Governor Richard J. Oglesby, early Lincoln political supporter and three-time governor of Illinois in the second half of the nineteenth century. Just a few miles south of Lincoln, there is a glacial moraine standing in the midst of flat farmland. Governor Oglesby built a mansion, Oglehurst, on top of this moraine, and memories of my childhood are filled with images of playing at Oglehurst, raking leaves there (with subsequent bonfires and wiener roasts), and sledding during the winter. I was, however, somewhat frightened by the thought of approaching his tomb on the property. I met his daughter Louise Felicite several times during my elementary school years, and I remember being thrilled when she told me that I could address her as Aunt Felicite instead of her proper title of countess, a title merited by her marriage to Italian count Alessandro Cenci-Bolognetti. Twins Carolyn and Jacqueline Oglesby, direct descendants of the governor, also born in 1936, were two of my closest friends. They lived just a few doors away from me. We went through elementary school, high school, and even Sunday school together.

I did not have a "eureka moment" to awaken my interest in Abraham Lincoln. He was always present in my life. Trips every summer to New Salem, Illinois, included surviving swarms of mosquitoes when we stayed to watch an outdoor play in the evening, and I have early memories of the Lincoln home and tomb. (I don't know if this is true or simply a transposed memory, but I seem to recall that on my first visit to the tomb, the "Battle Hymn of the Republic" was playing softly in the background. Whether it was or not, my mother often recounted the fact that she had to lead her sobbing daughter from the tomb after that first visit.) Our high school sports teams were, of course, the Railsplitters, as was our school paper. Our pep song ended with the stanza, "If dear old Abe would return, I know what he would do. / He'd say, Lincoln, I'm proud of you."

Obviously, central Illinois is no longer the same as early pioneers found it. However, it is still possible to gaze upon the vast expanse of land and the rich, dark soil and understand what early settlers, including the Lincolns, must have felt when they first saw it. I have vivid memories of the small courthouses in surrounding communities, and we were aware of the fact that Lincoln practiced law in these buildings. There is no question that Abraham Lincoln was a part of my life.

Some might argue that this early connection with our sixteenth president came not from an intellectual appreciation but from an accident of birth. Would my dedication to the study of Abraham Lincoln and his era be greater if I had "discovered" him as a teenager, a college student, or an adult? I don't see how it could be greater. Surely, given my background, the opportunity to work at the Lincoln Museum in Fort Wayne, Indiana, is either a felicitous coincidence or some sort of subconscious journey on my part. Either way, having a small role in preserving and presenting the legacy of Abraham Lincoln has brought me to the sense of a circle completed.

My experience was no doubt similar to that of many "history buffs" in that my passion was formed at an early age. Perhaps the fact that my father was away for three years "winning World War II" (as he so modestly put it) planted the seed in my mind that things worth fighting for are worth learning about. In fifth grade, I had my first class in U.S. history. There were, of course, textbooks, but there were also exciting trips to the town library, one of so many constructed through the generosity of Andrew Carnegie. At that point in my life, it is difficult to separate the evolution of my feelings about Lincoln from those about history in general. I devoured books during the summer months, especially in the periods during which all children were kept at home because of the "polio scare." I don't think that I developed any sort of "great man" theory of history, but I believe that Abraham Lincoln was absolutely necessary to the preservation of the United States of America.

I was, of course, taught lessons about "right and wrong" as a child, but this was in the context of individual behavior. Serious encounters with Lincoln began at the University of Illinois when, as a history major, I began to think about issues of right and wrong that went far beyond my personal behavior. Slavery was perhaps my first engagement with this larger issue, and I became aware of the contradiction between my somewhat idealistic view of statements in the Declaration of Independence and the reality of that "peculiar institution." Also, it was difficult to accept the fact that, for all practical purposes, the Founders had failed to address the problem in the Constitution. I believe it was at this point in time that my admiration for Abraham Lincoln began to expand. First of all, I was cognizant of the fact that he had not been blessed with the opportunity for education that I had, and I determined that I must make the most of my opportunity. Secondly, I began to understand what it meant to stand up for a cause in which one believed.

I have learned from the life of Abraham Lincoln that it isn't always easy—or popular—to adhere to firmly held principles. I have learned that we cannot always make assumptions about character and that we should not rely on stereotypical behavior to define, for instance, who is "religious" and who is not. I have learned that the term "continuing education" need not apply only to attendance at a formal course; rather, each of us should take the risk of learning on our own by tackling subjects that appear initially to be beyond our understanding.

Reminding myself of Lincoln's magnificent thought in his second inaugural address that "both read the same Bible, and pray to the same God" helps me deal with the inevitable conflicts we all face. I remind myself that we all are trying to contribute to a common goal.

While I consider editing articles written by scholars as my main contribution to *Lincoln Lore*, the bulletin published by the Lincoln Museum, I have on occasion written articles myself. Joan Flinspach, the Lincoln Museum's president and CEO, has been very supportive in allowing me to pursue research that interests me. Some of my articles, including "Assassination Aftermath: Eulogies and Poetry," "For the Bible Tells Me So: The Use of Scripture to Justify Slavery," "His Truth Is Marching On: God and the Union," and "At the Cannon's Mouth: The Founders and Slavery," examine topics that fascinate me because they help to explain and justify events and beliefs.

I am also cognizant of the fact that writing for a public program is much different from writing an article. I give frequent public presentations; these have included "The Insanity File," "Mystic Chords of Memory: The Opening of the West in American Memory," and "Abraham Lincoln: Master of Language."

In 2006, I completed work on a book that Harold Holzer and I coedited, *Lincoln and Freedom: Slavery, Emancipation, and the Thirteenth Amendment.* It is a study of the issue that threatened the very existence of our Union and of the manner in which Abraham Lincoln responded as a politician, president, writer, orator, and commander in chief to address this contentious subject and how he, thereby, changed American society. Working with Harold and other contributors has been an absolutely tremendous experience. In my second coedited book (with Joseph Fornieri), *Lincoln's America: 1809–1865,* leading scholars contributed chapters that put Abraham Lincoln in the context of his times.

Given the amount of material written about Lincoln and his era, one can easily be overwhelmed. There are, for instance, 18,000 volumes in the Lincoln Museum's vault, just a few steps from my desk. I have found some peace and comfort in admitting that I cannot possibly read them all. When I first came to work here in 1996, I read mostly complete biographies, the ones that always begin on February 12, 1809, and end on April 15, 1865. After finishing several of these, I could then allow myself the luxury of delving into more specific areas of Lincoln's life: his faith, his oratorical skills, his political development, and, especially, the evolution of his character. Having grown up in Illinois, I am naturally attracted to the study of his time in New Salem and Springfield. Being fascinated by the general topic of political theory, I enjoy studying his views on our Founding Fathers, the Declaration of Independence, and the Constitution.

I believe that it is "poor history" to take any historical figure out of the context of his or her era, so I try to maintain a study of the nineteenth century. The social movements, the story of the evolution of political parties of the time, and the growing national debate over slavery are particularly fascinating. As far as political parties are concerned, I plan at some point to either write an article or present a program entitled "Mugwumps, Know Nothings, and Loco Focos: Who Were They? Should We Care?"

At the Lincoln Museum, we have an opportunity each day to watch as visitors, both children and adults, experience the reality of Lincoln's place in history. I have learned that, as public schools increasingly deemphasize such subjects as history, it is imperative that those of us who care about such things must somehow pick up the torch. Just as Lincoln's "mystic chords of memory" echoed back to the Founders, so our own memories must be expanded to include New Salem, Gettysburg, and Ford's Theatre. I feel so very privileged to be in a position to share those memories.

5

DORIS KEARNS GOODWIN

Transforming Foes to Allies:
The Political Alchemy of Lincoln

I have often been asked what brought me to focus on Lincoln's relationship with his colleagues in the cabinet—that fascinating, unruly cast of characters who, together with Lincoln, made up the official circle that won the war, saved the Union, and ended the curse of slavery.[1]

The answer is contained in the slow evolution of my research and writing over a ten-year period. I had originally thought I would concentrate on Abraham and Mary Lincoln's relationship during the White House years, much as I had focused on Franklin and Eleanor Roosevelt on the home front in World War II. I suspect I was searching for a familiar handle on which to lean as I entered what was for me an unknown world. I have always found it difficult to shift focus from one president to the next. Attachments develop over the many years it takes me to complete my biographies. Indeed, my study of Franklin and Eleanor Roosevelt and the home front in World War II took longer to write than the war took to be fought! The lengthy time spent in research, however, produces a growing confidence that I have come to know my subjects and their times. This confidence is shattered as each new figure requires starting over. The shift to Lincoln was the most difficult of all, for it meant moving back to the nineteenth century, leaving behind the knowledge I had acquired of the twentieth century through my studies of FDR, JFK, and LBJ. So the thought of focusing on Mary and Abe brought a degree of discomfort in the early stages of the research.

I soon came to realize, however, that Mary could not carry the weight of the public story as Eleanor could. Having played a pivotal role in so many aspects of the home front, Eleanor was present at the events I wanted to cover in a way Mary was not. Moreover, I came to understand that Lincoln was more intimately "married" to several key members of his cabinet than to Mary in terms of the time he spent with them during the day, the long, anxious hours in the evenings waiting for the telegraph to report news from the battlefront, the moments of relaxation shared, the stories told, and the range of emotions expressed.

By focusing on Lincoln's relationship with his colleagues in his cabinet—by bringing individual members on and off center stage as their areas of responsibility came into and out of the spotlight—I hoped to provide a fresh angle for the narrative tale of Lincoln's presidency, to tell the familiar story in a different way. Thus, Secretary of State William Henry Seward would share center stage with Lincoln during the tumultuous transition period between the election and the inauguration, during the diplomatic negotiations with Britain and France over recognition of the Confederacy, and during the Trent crisis. Treasury Secretary Salmon Chase would assume the limelight when questions arose over the financing of the war, the issuance of government bonds, and the circulation of greenbacks. Edward Bates would make his appearances when legal issues were raised over the suspension of habeas corpus and the Emancipation Proclamation. And of course, once Edwin Stanton became secretary of war, he would deal with Lincoln on a wide range of issues relating to the conduct of the war, appointment of generals, issuance of pardons, and exchange of prisoners.

Moreover, by widening the lens to include Lincoln's colleagues, I trusted the story would benefit from a treasure trove of primary sources that have not generally been used in Lincoln biographies. The correspondence of the Seward family contains nearly five thousand letters, including an eight-hundred-page diary that Seward's daughter, Fanny, kept from her fifteenth year until two weeks before her death at the age of twenty-one. In addition to the voluminous journals in which Salmon Chase recorded the events of four decades, he wrote thousands of personal letters. A revealing section of his daughter Kate's diary also survives, along with dozens of letters from her husband, William Sprague. The unpublished section of the diary that Bates began in 1846 provides a more intimate glimpse of the man than the published diary that starts in 1859. Letters to his wife, Julia, during his years in Congress expose the warmth beneath his stolid exterior. Stanton's emotional letters to his family and his sister's unpublished memoir reveal the devotion and idealism that connected the passionate, hard-driving war secretary to his president. The correspondence of Montgomery Blair's sister, Elizabeth Blair Lee, and her husband, Captain Samuel Phillips Lee, portrays a memorable picture of daily life in wartime Washington. The diary of Gideon Welles, of course, has long been recognized for its penetrating insights into the workings of the Lincoln administration.

As the research accumulated, however, I began to see that focusing on the cabinet might produce additional benefits beyond its function either as a narrative device or as a means of expanding the primary materials. By looking closely at the evolution in attitudes toward their chief on the part of each of these individuals who moved, by and large, from initial skepticism to profound respect and warm affection, the elements of Lincoln's remarkable leadership style could be brought into clearer focus. His emotional strengths proved unmatched by his colleagues. His ability to form friendships with men who had previously opposed him; to repair injured feelings that, left untended, might have escalated into permanent hostility; to assume responsibility for the failures of his subordinates; to share credit with ease; and to learn from his mistakes, plus his remarkable calm, good-natured demeanor and life-saving sense of humor, stood in sharp relief to his advisers. While the men in Lincoln's circle were impressive figures in their own right, Lincoln proved the master of them all, intervening with them at critical moments, reinforcing their strengths, countering their weaknesses, sparking them to perform to the best of their abilities, so much so as that when they looked back on the war years, they could honestly say, to paraphrase Winston Churchill, that this was their finest hour.

I had initially thought I would start the book at the Republican convention in May 1860, where Lincoln challenged frontrunners Seward, Chase, and Bates for the nomination. Early in the writing I completed the opening chapter, providing a sequential picture of the four rivals waiting in their hometowns for news of the balloting in Chicago. While those scenes would remain as the opening through the finished manuscript, I soon realized that, much as I might have hoped, I could not confine the narrative to the six years from 1860 to 1865. If I truly wanted to understand the contrasting springs of character, the temperaments and the convictions that each of these men brought with them to the 1860s, I had to go further back, to their childhoods, their young adulthoods, and their early years in politics. Delving into the primary sources for each of these men added at least three or four extra years onto the project, but I'd like to believe the comparative knowledge gained produced a more dimensional picture of the president himself. Lincoln's barren childhood, his lack of schooling, his relationship with male friends, his complicated marriage, the nature of his ambition, and his ruminations about death can be analyzed more clearly when he is measured against these three contemporaries.

Lincoln's early love of learning and his determination to scour the countryside for books, despite being able to attend school only a few weeks here, a few weeks there—which, taken together, amounted to less than one full year—seem even more remarkable when placed against the experiences of his rivals. Seward had only to pick a book from well-stocked shelves, while both local academies he attended and Union College maintained substantial collections of books on history, logic, rhetoric, philosophy, chemistry, grammar, and geography. Chase, likewise, had access to libraries at his uncle's boys' school in Worthington, Ohio, and at Dartmouth College. And while books were not plentiful where Bates grew up, he had the luxury of his scholarly relative's home, where he could peruse at will an extensive collection.

The comparative analysis also shed light on the question as to whether Lincoln was gay. To be sure, Lincoln shared a double bed for four years with his great friend the handsome, blue-eyed Joshua Speed, and he wrote affectionate letters to Speed over the years. "You know my desire to befriend you is everlasting," Lincoln assured Speed, "that I will never cease, while I know how to do any thing."[2] Yet their intimacy, when placed side by side with the friendships between Seward and a colleague of his in the New York state senate or between Stanton and Chase, seems more an index to an era when close male friendships, accompanied by open expressions of affection and passion, were familiar and socially acceptable.

The letters Seward and Albert Tracy exchanged were far more affectionate than those between Lincoln and Speed. "It shames my manhood that I am so attached to you," Tracy confessed to Seward after several days' absence from Albany. "It is a foolish fondness from which no good can come."[3] By return mail, Seward professed "a rapturous joy" in discovering that his friend shared the "feelings which I had become half ashamed for their effeminacy to confess I possessed."[4] Yet no one suggested that either Seward or Tracy were gay; indeed, at a later point, Tracy tried to seduce Seward's wife, Frances.

Even more compelling are the letters between Stanton and Chase when they first became friends after both had lost their young wives. "Since our pleasant intercourse together last summer," Stanton wrote Chase, "no living person has been oftener in my mind;—waking or sleeping,—for, more than once, I have dreamed of being with you."[5] Then, after receiving a particularly affectionate letter from Chase, Stanton fervently replied that it "filled my heart with joy; to be loved by you, and be told that you value my love is a gratification beyond my power to express."[6] Again, no one has suggested that either of these men was gay.

Nor can sharing a bed be considered evidence of an erotic involvement. It was common practice in an era when private quarters were a rare luxury, when males regularly slept in the same bed as children and continued to do so in academies, boarding houses, and overcrowded hotels. The room above Speed's store functioned as a sort of dormitory, with two other men living there part of the time in addition to Lincoln and Speed. The attorneys of the Eighth Judicial Circuit in Illinois, where Lincoln would travel, regularly shared beds—with the exception of Judge David Davis, whose immense girth left no room for a companion.

Analysis of the style of oratory of the various men yields an interesting contrast between the inflammatory, judgmental rhetoric employed by Seward and Chase to denounce slavery in the 1850s and Lincoln's attempt, so evident in his celebrated Peoria speech, to put himself in the shoes of the slaveholders, suggesting that "they are just what we would be in their situation. If slavery did not now exist amongst them they would not introduce it. . . . When it is said that the institution exists; and that it is very difficult to get rid of it, in any satisfactory way, I can understand and appreciate the saying. I surely will not blame them for not doing what I should not know how to do myself."[7] What is more, unlike his rivals, Lincoln regularly employed homey analogies and metaphors drawn from everyday life that people could readily understand.

When he sought to illustrate the Republican pledge to keep slavery from expanding into the western territories, he told a story. "If I saw a venomous snake crawling in the road," Lincoln began, "any man would say I might seize the nearest stick and kill it; but if I found that snake in bed with my children, that would be another question. I might hurt the children more than the snake, and it might bite them. . . . But if there were a bed newly made up, to which the children were to be taken, and it was proposed to take a new batch of young snakes and put them there with them, I take it no man would say there was any question how I ought to decide! . . . The new Territories are the newly made bed to which our children are to go, and it lies with the nation to say whether they shall have snakes mixed up with them or not."[8] The snake metaphor acknowledged the constitutional protection of slavery where it legally existed while harnessing the protective instincts of parents to safeguard future generations from the venomous expansion of slavery.

By contrast, when Seward reached for a metaphor to dramatize the same danger, he warned that if slavery were allowed into Kansas, his countrymen would have "introduced the Trojan horse" into the new territory.[9] Even if most of his classically trained fellow senators immediately grasped his intent, the Trojan horse image carried neither the instant accessibility of Lincoln's snake-in-the-bed story nor its memorable originality.

For generations, people have weighed and debated the factors that led to Lincoln's surprising victory at the Republican National Convention. Many have agreed with the verdict of Murat Halstead, who wrote that "the fact of the Convention was the defeat of Seward rather than the nomination of Lincoln."[10] There is truth to this argument, but it tells only part of the story, for the question remains: Why was Lincoln rather than Chase or Bates the beneficiary of Seward's downfall?

Some have pointed to luck: Lincoln happened to live in a battleground state that the Republicans needed to win, and the convention was held in Chicago, where the strength of local support added weight to his candidacy. "Had the Convention been held at any other place," Illinois politician Gustave Koerner admitted, "Lincoln would not have been nominated."[11]

Others have argued that he was positioned perfectly in the center of the party. He was less radical than Seward or Chase but less conservative than Bates. He was less offensive than Seward to the Know Nothings but more acceptable than Bates to the German Americans.

Still others have argued that Lincoln's team in Chicago played the game better than anyone else, conceiving the best strategy and cleverly using the leverage of promises to the best advantage. Without doubt, the Lincoln men, under the skillful leadership of David Davis, performed brilliantly.

Chance, positioning, and managerial strategy all played a role in Lincoln's victory. Still, if we consider the comparative resources each contender brought to the race—their range of political skills; their emotional, intellectual, and moral qualities; their rhetorical abilities; and their determination and willingness to work hard—it is clear that when opportunity beckoned, Lincoln was the best prepared to answer the call. His nomination, finally, was the result of his character and his life experiences—these separated him from his rivals and provided him with advantages unrecognized at the time.

Having risen to power with fewer privileges, Lincoln was more accustomed to relying upon himself to shape events. From beginning to end, he took the greatest control of the process leading up to the nomination. While Seward, at his manager Thurlow Weed's suggestion, spent eight months wandering Europe to escape dissension at home, Lincoln earned the goodwill and respect of tens of thousands with a strenuous speaking tour that left a positive imprint on Republicans in five crucial midwestern states. After Chase unwisely declined an invitation to speak at the New York lecture series that brought Lincoln to Cooper Union, Lincoln accepted the invitation with alacrity, recognizing the critical importance of making a good impression in Seward's home territory. In addition, Chase refused invitations to travel to New England and shore up his support. Ironically, despite repeated pledges in his diary to do anything necessary to achieve honor and fame, Chase showed a lack of resolve in the final weeks before the convention.

When ardent Republicans heard Lincoln speak, they knew that if their beloved Seward could not win, they had in the eloquent man from Illinois a person of considerable capacity whom they could trust, one who would hold fast on the central issue that had forged the party—the fight against extending slavery into the territories. Though Lincoln had entered the antislavery struggle later than Seward or Chase, his speeches possessed unmatched power, conviction, clarity, and moral strength.

At the same time, his native caution and precision with language—he rarely said more than he was sure about, rarely pandered to his various audiences—gave him great advantages over his rivals, each of whom tried to reposition himself in the months before the convention. Seward disappointed liberal Republicans when he tried to soften his fiery rhetoric to placate moderates. Bates infuriated conservatives with his newly found liberal positions, and Chase fooled no one in attempting to shift his position on the tariff at the last moment. Lincoln remained consistent throughout.

Nor, as the *Chicago Press and Tribune* pointed out, was "his avoidance of extremes" simply "the result of ambition which measures words or regulates acts." It was, more accurately, "the natural consequence of an equable nature and a mental constitution that is never off its balance."[12]

In his years of travel on the circuit through central Illinois, engaging people in taverns, on street corners, and in shops, Lincoln had developed an acute perception of what people felt, thought, needed, and wanted. Seward, too, had an instinctive feeling for people, but too many years in Washington had dulled those instincts. Like Lincoln, Chase had spent many months traveling throughout his home state, but his haughty demeanor prevented him from truly connecting with the farmers, clerks, and bartenders he met along the way. Bates, meanwhile, had isolated himself for so long from the hurly-burly of the political world that his once natural political savvy was diminished.

It was Lincoln's political intuition, not blind luck, that secured the convention site in Chicago. To be sure, the fact that Lincoln was far less well known aided Norman Judd, chairman of the Illinois Republican State Committee, in landing the venue in Illinois. However, it was part of Lincoln's strategy to hold his name back as long as possible and to "give no offence to others—leave them in a mood to come to us, if they shall be compelled to give up their first love."[13] It was Lincoln who first suggested to Judd that it might be important to secure Chicago. And it was Lincoln who first pointed out to his managers that Indiana might be won. Indeed, his guidance and determination were evident at every step along the way to the nomination.

Lincoln, like Seward, had developed a cadre of lifelong friends who were willing to do anything in their power to secure his nomination. But unlike Seward, he had not made permanent political enemies nor aroused envy along the way. It is hard to imagine Lincoln letting publisher Horace Greeley's resentment smolder for years as Seward did. On the contrary, Lincoln took pains to reestablish rapport with Judd and Lyman Trumbull after they had defeated him in his first run for the Senate. His ability to rise above defeat and create friendships with previous opponents was never shared by Chase, who was unable to forgive those who crossed him. And though Bates had a warm circle of friends in St. Louis, most of them were not politicians. His campaign at the convention was managed by a group of men who barely knew him. Without burning personal loyalty, they had simply picked him as a potential winner, dropping him with equal ease when the path to his nomination proved bumpy.

Finally, Lincoln's profound and elevated sense of ambition—"an ambition," historian Don Fehrenbacher observes, "notably free of pettiness, malice, and overindulgence," shared little common ground with Chase's blatant obsession with office, Seward's tendency toward opportunism, or the ambivalent ambition that led Bates to withdraw from public office.[14] Though Lincoln desired success as fiercely as any of his rivals, he did not allow his quest for office to supplant the kindness and openheartedness with which he treated supporters and rivals alike, nor to alter his steady commitment to the antislavery cause.

In the end, though the men who nominated Abraham Lincoln in Chicago may not have recognized all these qualities, they had chosen the best man for the supreme challenge looming over the nation.

I must confess even now, as I prepare for my next project—a study of Theodore Roosevelt, William Howard Taft, and the Progressive Era—I miss waking up with Abraham Lincoln day by day and going to bed with thoughts of him in my head. I miss the conversations with the remarkable group of scholars who have made Lincoln their life work, who have plowed the field so creatively for so many years. When I began this project, they took me in as rookie, sharing information, sources, and insights, and in the process, they, like Lincoln's cabinet, became not my rivals but my friends.

NOTES

1. See Doris Kearns Goodwin, *Team of Rivals: The Political Genius of Abraham Lincoln* (New York: Simon and Schuster, 2005). This chapter grows from remarks made to the Lincoln Forum in 2006 in Gettysburg, Pennsylvania.

2. Lincoln to Speed, February 13, 1842, in *The Collected Works of Abraham Lincoln*, ed. Roy P. Basler, 9 vols. (New Brunswick, N.J.: Rutgers University Press, 1953–55), 1:269. Hereafter *CWL*.

3. Tracy to Seward, February 7, 1831, reel 118, Seward Papers, *The Papers of William H. Seward* (Woodbridge, Conn.: Research Publications, 1983).

4. Seward to Tracy, February 11, 1831, Albert Tracy Papers, New York State Library, Albany.

5. Stanton to Chase, November 30, 1846, reel 6, Chase Papers, *The Salmon P. Chase Papers*, microfilm ed., ed. John Nivin (Frederick, Md.: University Publications of America, 1987).

6. Ibid., December 2, 1847.

7. "Speech at Peoria, Illinois," October 6, 1854, in *CWL*, 2: 248–75.

8. Speech, March 6, 1860, in *CWL*, 4:18.

9. William Henry Seward, "Admission of Kansas," April 9, 1856, appendix to *Congressional Globe*, 34th Cong., 1st sess., 405.

10. Murat Halstead, *Three against Lincoln* (Baton Rouge: Louisiana State University Press, 1960), 176.

11. Gustave Koerner, *Memoirs of Gustave Koerner* (Cedar Rapids, Iowa: Torch Press, 1909), 2:80.

12. *Chicago Press and Tribune*, May 16, 1860.

13. Lincoln to Samuel Galloway, March 24, 1860, in *CWL*, 4:34.

14. Don Fehrenbacher, *Prelude to Greatness* (Stanford: Stanford University Press, 1962), 161.

6

HAROLD HOLZER

The Lincoln Visual Image:
A Personal Journey of Discovery

There were no shortages of Lincoln images swirling about the public eye—or my own—when I was a boy growing up in the late 1950s and early 1960s in Little Neck, Queens, one of the most remote and countrified outposts in New York City. Isolated though we seemed, in those days the *New York Daily News* could be depended upon to publish a painting of Lincoln each and every February on the cover of its Sunday *Coloroto* magazine. *Life* magazine would routinely produce lavishly illustrated Lincoln articles; so, occasionally, would the *New York Times Magazine* and *Look*.

We seemed so far away from the living Lincoln in terms of time and geography. But television, meanwhile, reliably (if unevenly) gave us Lincoln in perpetual motion, gave him form and voice—whether Henry Fonda's, Raymond Massey's, Richard Boone's, or Walter Huston's—in an array of dramatic specials and movie reruns. Were these the real Lincoln? Were they as close as I would ever get?

Amid this barrage of images, some real, some fanciful, Lincoln emerged for me as a puzzling but irresistible combination of qualities: as imposing as the photos of the statue at the Lincoln Memorial, as ubiquitous as the profile on the copper penny. He seemed accessible yet magisterial: an image one could gaze at in wonderment from afar or hold in the palm of one's own hand, to touch and feel. And he seemed to symbolize, in that face of suffering, the bloody fight to save the country and end slavery.

But these were observations made frustratingly from a distance. Then, in 1961, my father took me on my first trip to Washington, D.C., where Lincoln came alive for me in ways that dazzled and moved me, deeply and permanently. For years, whenever my family would pause to recall that weekend car trip, my father would stubbornly insist that I had been far more interested in the indoor swimming pool at the old Hotel Ambassador than in the city's monuments and museums. Respectfully, I chuckled along with him whenever he dragged out this old canard. The truth was—and I hope that, deep in his heart, he knew it—that it was the most important trip of my life. And not for the swimming.

In Washington, I got my first exposure to real Lincoln documents on display at the Library of Congress, to genuine artifacts on view at the old Ford's Theatre Museum, and to the Daniel Chester French statue at the Lincoln Memorial, of course. All along the way, in addition, I encountered curious-looking sepia-toned little photographic cards—some sharply focused, others fading from too much exposure to the light—all showing the great man as he aged painfully in office, growing, as his secretary John Hay later put it, from "a young to an old man" in four short White House years.[1] Here, at last, I came face to face with the Lincoln image.

From the age of twelve to thirteen, I read everything I could about Lincoln's face: first, Carl Sandburg's edition of Frederick Hill Meserve's pioneering photographic compilation, and then, at an unforgettable session at my junior high school library, Stefan Lorant's glorious oversized book, *Lincoln: A Picture Story of His Life*, each page boasting a large-sized reproduction of photographic portraits by Alexander Hesler, Mathew Brady, and Alexander Gardner, pictures that were already beginning to seem to me iconic.[2] I was reluctant to return it. I parted with it unwillingly, fearful that when I called for it the next day it would be gone, not realizing that I was all alone in my obsession.

I remember how hard I worked that fall to convince my younger sisters to buy a copy of that book for me for my thirteenth birthday. It was not an easy sell. For one thing, it was expensive: all of $7.95. For another, there were no Amazon.coms in those days, no Barnes & Noble chain stores proliferating in the City or making titles instantly available on the World Wide Web. Rather, it took a phone call to a neighborhood bookstore to place the order, followed by endless, imploring calls, week after frustrating week, until the book finally arrived after what seemed like an eternity—during which I could think about little else. I'm sure that the bookseller quickly went into another profession shortly after getting rid of her most persistent young customer. But before she could, my mother piled us into the family Ford and drove my sisters and me to the nearby village of Bayside to pick up the book. I still have the photographs I posed for on the morning of my bar mitzvah: sitting in my room, surrounded by my sisters, just a few moments from heading off to the synagogue, holding in one hand the all-important prayer shawl my grandmother had sent me and in the other my brand-new copy of Stefan Lorant's *Lincoln*.

I suppose that readers will not be surprised to learn that my teenage years were spent conducting similar balancing acts, between the life a young man is supposed to lead (school, sports, girls) and the life in which I found myself, frankly, far more interested (Lincoln, Lincoln, and Lincoln). But like the bar mitzvah boy in the picture, I managed to hold one life in one hand and one in the other and, with plenty of stumbles along the way (up to and including a disappointing and disastrous "exposure" to Lincoln and the Civil War in college), managed to graduate, get a job, and get married, with Lincoln still playing a major role in my life.

Credit for my ability to begin seriously exploring the subject for myself belongs to two people: my wife, who first tolerated it and then came to embrace it, and an extraordinary professional photographer from New York named Leo Stashin, who aroused my Lincoln interest even further. In 1968, the *New York Times* had published a story about this tireless researcher, illustrating it with a daguerreotype he had discovered, which, he insisted, against a tide of criticism, was an early, unknown portrait of Abraham Lincoln. I studied the picture closely: the man seemed too old, too wide around the middle. His nose was too pointy, his brow too narrow, the lips too thin. But Stashin had subjected the imposing full-plate to a barrage of scientific tests and computer scans—such as they were nearly forty years ago—and had identified countless points of similarity, including scars, earlobes, and facial moles.

Stashin was insistent. "The portrait is the only photograph of Lincoln taken from a high camera angle," he explained to the *Times*. "This would tend to elongate the nose, foreshorten the brow and change the perspective in which we have been accustomed to seeing his face. The angle makes the nose seem longer."[3]

So what else could a nineteen-year-old do but write a bold letter to this Leo Stashin? To my delight, he not only replied but also invited me to his Greenwich Village home. There, he showed me the actual daguerreotype, discussed it with passion and precision, and introduced me to the other wonderful early photographic images he had collected on antiquing forays into New Jersey, Pennsylvania, Connecticut, and Massachusetts. No sooner did I have a driver's license of my own—Stashin did not, which fortuitously yoked his expertise to my enthusiasm for the next five years until his 1973 death—than we were traveling together, with our wives. My friend Leo went in search of daguerreotypes and I on a quest for Lincoln prints and photographs, then not only remarkably easy to find but easy to afford.

On one such trip, I unexpectedly walked in on a country auction in Ephrata, Pennsylvania, where the town's citizens, in their questionable wisdom, were unloading the contents of their local historical society in order to raise money to fix the roof (my lucky day). One of the items resting against a table on the grass took my breath away: a huge, gaudy 1860 Lincoln election poster called the *National Republican Chart*. It boasted crude, hand-colored woodcut images of Lincoln and his running mate, Hannibal Hamlin, surrounded by decorative log rails and the full text of that year's Republican Party platform. It was puckering here and there, the result of being affixed to a wooden plank decades before. But the pink, yellow, and blue coloring was still bright, and Lincoln's emblematic beardless portrait was strong and clear.

When the bidding commenced, I found myself nervously engaged in a pitched battle with a local antique dealer, throwing caution to the wind and "recklessly" bidding up, one dollar at a time, as my wife tugged nervously at my sleeve, wordlessly urging caution. Seventy dollars. Seventy-five. Seventy-six. Seventy-seven. And then, at last, at seventy-nine dollars, the competition bowed out, and the prize was mine. I felt all the guilty pleasure that major collectors must experience when they win a trophy but fear in their heart of hearts that they have overpaid.

When I returned home, I rushed off a letter, with a full description of my print, to Lincoln scholar R. Gerald McMurtry. McMurtry, then the veteran director of the Lincoln National Life Foundation (and soon to become another important mentor), quickly informed me that the print was an authentic, important, and exceedingly rare campaign poster. It was, he said (to my relief), worth at least five hundred dollars at the time and, what was more, was considered the centerpiece of one of the most wonderful little stories in the Lincoln literature. For it was a copy of this very poster that a young Grace Bedell, a Westfield, New York, Lincoln admirer, had spied at her local county fair, inspiring her to write her famous letter to the presidential candidate beseeching him to change his appearance by growing a beard.[4] I was finally able to congratulate myself that I had actually found a museum-worthy treasure for next to nothing. It was well worth keeping and, as I would soon find, well worth writing about as well.

As if this was not enough to transform me into a full-fledged, fully confident Lincoln collector, I stumbled within weeks across yet another seminal image—this one portraying the private Lincoln (the family man) rather than the candidate (the public man). Again I bid for it and won it at auction. Now I also owned a beautifully framed, tinted Anton Hohenstein lithograph of Lincoln, his wife, and their sons sitting outside the White House.

I mention these purchases not just because they invigorated my collecting impulse—for life, as it turned out—but because they helped further to focus my interest in understanding the Lincoln image. They beckoned me now to direct my energies toward engravings and lithographs of the sixteenth president, if only to learn thereby the geneses of the pictures that I now seemed to be buying every week, until they filled every inch of wall space in our apartment and overflowed into bulging stacks along the walls.

Happily, another unexpectedly inspiring incident occurred around the time of the Watergate controversy that encouraged me to share what I had learned as a researcher and collector. It happened when *Life* magazine published a 1974 photograph of President Nixon sitting on an easy chair in his

White House study. Framed above him was a period print of the Lincoln family—very much like the Hohenstein I had purchased in New York, yet vexingly not quite an exact duplicate. The face of Lincoln in each appeared to be based on separate photographic sources. How, I asked myself, could prints of Lincoln be so different—yet so very much the same?

Investigating this issue, at the encouragement of Gerald McMurtry in his new role as editor of the *Lincoln Herald*, I finally settled at last on the specific focus—the long-elusive research specialty—that I had been so long seeking. The answer was in iconography, the study of the commercial and political impetus for and emotional power of the period Lincoln images that modern scholars had too often relegated to the realm of mere illustration. I would contend—and suppose I have been arguing in print and books and lectures ever since—that while the products themselves were typically inspired by profit, not politics or public service, they came to testify convincingly to their owners' political and patriotic impulses, occupying honored places in the family home where religious icons of old had once held unchallenged dominance. Moreover, it appeared to me, these images—though often clumsy, flawed, retouched, or disguised to hide their origins (or their original copyright)—helped not only to illustrate Lincoln's emergence from prairie politician to presidential candidate, chief executive, emancipator, and martyr but to influence this image metamorphosis as well.

I learned, too, that Lincoln himself, so famously modest and diffident about his personal appearance, so quick to poke fun at his own homeliness, had proven surprisingly cooperative with photographers, painters, sculptors, and even the engravers and lithographers whose works were based on original models from life. Rarely had Lincoln refused to pose for such artists. Seldom had he refused a request for an autograph that could be reproduced on steel or stone. In short, I argued, Lincoln, although a self-proclaimed "indifferent judge" of his own images, was a very willing subject for those who agreed to immortalize it. He seemed miraculously aware of the importance of such pictures in introducing him to the public, winning him elections, enhancing his reputation, and illustrating his accomplishments.[5]

By the mid-1970s, I had introduced these arguments in my first scholarly articles: a general survey of Lincoln prints for the *Magazine Antiques* and a series of explorations of the Hohenstein Lincoln Family print for the *Lincoln Herald*. Within ten years, I was collaborating with Mark E. Neely Jr. and Gabor Boritt on a series of illustrated books that explored not only the theme of the Lincoln image but those of the Confederate and Union images as well. Probing Civil War iconography only served to help us better understand Lincoln's place in the firmament of mid-nineteenth-century American history.[6]

If there was a recurring theme to my own personal passage from enthusiast to collector to student—from generalist to specialist on Lincoln iconography and Civil War–era popular culture—it was the kindness of strangers who evolved into mentors, colleagues, and, in many cases, friends. As a youngster, I corresponded not only with Leo Stashin and Gerald McMurtry but also with McMurtry's venerable predecessor at the Lincoln National Life Foundation, Louis A. Warren. I exchanged notes, too, with Mary Lincoln biographer Ruth Painter Randall. And I visited the legendary curator Josephine Cobb at the National Archives, where I saw the glass plate of the unremarkable-looking crowd scene she had somehow divined might portray the audience at Gettysburg on November 19, 1863—and would, enlarged and reenlarged, reveal the face of Lincoln on the grandstand. Miss Cobb (who signed her letters "your friend, J. C.") taught me valuable lessons about perseverance. But I soon learned that she had an eccentric side, too. Exposure to it prepared me well for the roster of Lincoln aficionados with whom I would be required to interact in the decades to come.

Once, Miss Cobb pressed her forefinger to her lips as if to hush our conversation, then slowly opened a drawer in her old wooden desk, whispering: "I am going to show you a rare daguerreotype. If you can tell me who it portrays, I will consider that you have graduated into a real student of Civil War photography." And then, almost conspiratorially, she handed me a small plate, covered completely in wax paper and secured by an orange rubber band. "But I can't see it," I protested. "It's wrapped in wax paper. May I remove it?"

"Of course not," she snapped, snatching it back and replacing it in her drawer. "That would make it too easy." So much for graduating. I must say that the experience made it easier for me to ignore her most persistent advice to me when I told her I was going to specialize in the popular prints of Lincoln. "Try to engrave something yourself according to the old methods of hand work," she urged in 1974. "I'd *like* to see you do it," she added, as if such a coda might make her idea irresistible.[7] But resist I did. Boasting no artistic ability whatever, I was sure that any attempt by me to carve on a steel plate would be a disaster and, moreover, a ridiculous waste of time better spent doing research. I never regretted, Miss Cobb notwithstanding, my decision to look at pictures rather than make them for myself.

Of course, once I read Stefan Lorant's book, I began corresponding with him as well. One summer he invited my wife and me to his home in Lenox, Massachusetts. It was cluttered with Lincoln files and books, including his specially bound volumes of that essential research tool *Lincoln Lore* (which years later I purchased for myself at his estate sale).

I still remember Lorant, then nearing eighty (he lived well into his nineties), clad in Bermuda shorts and a large polo shirt, leading me down a grassy hill to show me the office he had built in a nearby cabin. As tiny toads scampered to get out of his way, he tramped rapidly down his hill—I could barely keep up—and proudly opened the door to a modern study in a rustic house that boasted such expansive mountainside views I could not imagine how he could ever concentrate on his work here. But I admitted that if I ever had a Lincoln office of my own, I would love it to look exactly like this one.

Later, Lorant took us to Chesterwood, the nearby summer home of the sculptor of the Lincoln Memorial, Daniel Chester French. With special glee, Lorant showed us a roped-off storeroom overflowing with French's plaster models—among which, he laughed, was the unmistakable face of Stefan Lorant. No, Lorant was not old enough to have posed for French himself. Rather, he had sat for the sculptor's daughter, a gifted amateur. Curators had long ago mistaken the handsome bust as one of her father's original studies, and Lorant, delighted to have his countenance resting among statuettes of Lincoln, never told them otherwise. Last time I visited Chesterwood, Lorant, long gone himself, was still there, smiling from the storeroom.

Lorant was an unabashed critic of the man who in 1963 overtook him as the leading authority on Lincoln photographs, Lloyd Ostendorf of Dayton, Ohio. Ostendorf, too, was kind to me but filled with undisguised loathing for Lorant. No two people—though they followed the same pursuit—could have been more different. Lorant was a flamboyant European with an inspiring personal history. As a young editor in Munich, he had been imprisoned by Hitler for criticizing the Nazis and encountered Lincoln by accident when a jailer threw him a copy of Lincoln's speeches translated into German. Liberated before the war ended, he went on to a successful career as a magazine editor in London (where he virtually invented the pictorial magazine style later copied by *Life*) and in America published several books on Lincoln, along with pictorial biographies of Theodore Roosevelt, FDR, and other American presidents. By the time I knew him, he was more interested in reissuing his picture book on Pittsburgh than in focusing on Lincoln. He was a renaissance man who had moved on.

Ostendorf, in turn, was a quintessentially American self-made man, as taciturn as Lorant was expansive, a professional cartoonist who became a passionate collector. He amassed such an astonishing trove of Lincoln photographs and publicized his finds so effectively that before long, everyone who owned a putative new Lincoln invariably gave him first crack at authenticating, and buying, their pictures. Ostendorf eventually sold his entire collection to what later became the Lincoln Museum in Fort Wayne, Indiana, and used the proceeds to begin building a new collection from scratch. Though he spent his last years insisting—unconvincingly, to most scholars—that he had found a long-lost page from the reading copy of Lincoln's Gettysburg

Address, along with a dubious photo of Lincoln in death, shortly before his autopsy, he was all but tireless in promoting his discoveries, genuine and imagined alike. From everything I learned about and from him in more than twenty-five years of acquaintance, I never knew him to be interested in any other subject than the photographs of Lincoln and his contemporaries.

Over the years, I coauthored several magazine articles with Lloyd Ostendorf on Lincoln images—including a piece on hitherto-unknown drawings and paintings from life[8]—after which my contact with Stefan Lorant unavoidably suffered. They simply could not abide each other—especially after both men published, and simultaneously took credit for, discovering a previously unknown 1863 Gardner photo of Lincoln. Whatever their antipathy for each other, however, they were almost always kind and encouraging to me (trading images with Ostendorf, however, was not a good idea; he always got the better of the deal, as I learned painfully in the 1980s).

What was more important, each elevated the study of Lincoln images. Before Lorant and Ostendorf, even Lincoln photographs, now so rarefied and valuable, were relegated to the class of illustrations. Their research and scholarship helped elevate the Lincoln image into a serious study. My own work built on the models and the evidence they amassed. It could not possibly have been accomplished, or even attempted, had they not set the foundation so firmly in place.

In the early 1980s, I decided at last that after more than a hundred articles on Lincoln iconography published in popular magazines and scholarly journals, it was time to collect what I knew for a book. No one had ever written a book on Lincoln prints, save for an ancient compilation by one Winfred Porter Truesdell, so rare it was by then far more expensive than most of the prints it depicted and so incomplete that all that had ever been issued was, curiously and inexplicably, volume 2.[9]

But would anybody publish a new book? More than a year of trying convinced me that the answer was no. Such a project was too specialized, came a typical reply—disappointingly, from Stefan Lorant's old editor. It would be too expensive to produce. I could not imagine anyone resisting a manuscript bearing what I convinced myself was the brilliant title, *Of the People, By the People, For the People: The Engravings and Lithographs of Abraham Lincoln.*

Fortunately, it was then that Gabor Boritt and Mark Neely entered the equation as coauthors, co-curators, partners, and friends. I had encountered the brilliant historian Boritt, like Lorant Hungarian-born, at a lecture I gave on Lincoln sculpture before the Lincoln Group of Boston in East Bridgewater, Massachusetts. Then on leave from Memphis State University, he was kind enough to come forward after the talk and bombard me with questions—without ever introducing himself. I had no idea who he was.

Fortunately, I later asked the club president, Frank J. Williams. Boritt and I have been friends ever since.

The equally dazzling Mark Neely had been a faithful correspondent since he first assumed the directorship of the Lincoln National Life Foundation in the early 1970s. I have never forgotten our first meeting. Together with my wife, our three-year-old daughter, and an elderly photographer named Joseph C. Farber (with whom I would collaborate regularly as well over the next decade), we flew west from New York on assignment from the *Magazine Antiques* to photograph the foundation's Lincoln sculpture for a forthcoming article on the statues and busts of the Great Emancipator.

Unfortunately, we flew into the biggest snowstorm Fort Wayne had experienced in years. Our taxi had to be pushed out of a snowdrift before we reached our hotel, and next morning, when we somehow commandeered a driver to take us to our appointment at the foundation, we found it firmly locked. What else could we do but call Mark Neely at home—luckily he was listed in the phone book—and implore him to open up for us? It was rather presumptuous, in retrospect, but I reasoned that if eighty-year-old Joe Farber could make it all the way from New York, ten boxes of lights and cameras in tow, then the rest of us could try as well. Dressed in snow boots nearly as tall as he was, Neely eventually appeared over a snowbank and turned on the lights. He has been an important part of my life from that day forward.

By 1983, Neely, Boritt, and I determined to gather forces and write the book as a team: a Lincoln and Civil War scholar, a museum director, and a Lincoln iconography expert in full collaboration.[10] To make the project more attractive, we decided to try organizing an exhibition, which would show at both Gettysburg College (Boritt's new headquarters) and the newly renamed Louis A. Warren Lincoln Library and Museum in Fort Wayne. Astonishingly, Boritt's friend the great writer Jacques Barzun took an interest and urged the project on Charles Scribners's Sons. In February 1984, Scribner's published the cannily renamed *The Lincoln Image*, and our show of original engravings and lithographs began a two-year tour of a number of venues around the country

In the years since, our trio published several sequels and another book and traveling show about Confederate prints.[11] We lectured on the subject—separately or in pairs—all over the country and, once, in a suburb of London. And when Professor Boritt turned his attention to his own writing, teaching, and administration of the Civil War Institute and the Lincoln Prize, Neely and I went on to coauthor books on the Lincoln family's personal photograph collection, the prints of the Civil War North, and the paintings of the Union and Confederate experiences at home and on the front.[12] Most of these books are now collectors' items themselves—a somewhat self-deluding way of describing volumes that are sadly out of print, though some have been reissued with new introductions in recent years and appear to be garnering new audiences.[13]

Three things seem clearer than ever after decades of work on the iconography theme: first, audiences seem increasingly interested in the Lincoln image; second, new scholars are producing important new works of their own, moving beyond the books we began publishing in the 1980s; and finally, and perhaps most important, collaboration with peers is just as vital as encouragement from mentors. I have never doubted that the sum of the Holzer-Boritt-Neely partnership is greater than the individual parts might ever have produced on the subject of Lincoln iconography. Our field depends so heavily on the chance observation of what might be the sole surviving copy of a picture that it cries out for collaboration rather than competition. The more people who share the enthusiasm for Lincoln, then, the better—to nourish scholarship (not to mention scholars), to share and advance knowledge, and to perpetuate the understanding of the greatest president America has ever produced.

I am particularly proud that I have played a part—between books (and despite professional responsibilities for full-time employers as demanding as Bella Abzug, Mario Cuomo, and the Metropolitan Museum of Art)—in helping to create and support groups that gather Lincoln enthusiasts to share their knowledge and passion. Together with my local friends Richard Sloan, Larry West, Hal Gross, and the late William Kaland, for example, I helped to found the Lincoln Group of New York, now twenty-six years old and thriving under the leadership of Joseph Garrera (www.lincolngroupny.org).

Later, after serving briefly as a board member of the Abraham Lincoln Association under the leadership of my best friend in the Lincoln field, Frank J. Williams, I worked with Frank and tireless Lincoln aficionado Charles D. Platt to create a new assembly of devotees, the Lincoln Forum. At this writing, the Forum has evolved into a phenomenon of useful scholarship and collegiality. Currently planning its fourteenth annual symposium, it attracts leading historians to lecture before hundreds of enrollees, gives out a prestigious achievement award, publishes a biannual bulletin, has issued two books of papers and proceedings, and has become a vital force in the Lincoln community (www.thelincolnforum.org).

In 2000, President Clinton named me as one of his two appointees to the U. S. Lincoln Bicentennial Commission, and at our first meeting, my colleagues elected me co-chairman to serve alongside U.S. senator Richard Durbin and Congressman Ray LaHood, both of Illinois. The commission is now weighing the creation of a permanent pictorial tribute to Lincoln among its many plans and mandates (one of which may well bring changes to one long-untouchable icon of Lincolniana, the Lincoln penny). As the commission moves toward Lincoln's 200th birthday year in 2009, it is heartening to know that the Lincoln image is now considered such a crucial aspect of the Lincoln legacy that no celebration or appreciation can possibly call itself complete without treating the subject adequately.

Though they led the way, Stefan Lorant, Josephine Cobb, Lloyd Ostendorf, Winfred Porter Truesdell, and the other pioneers might well be surprised. And even this "young" veteran of the field is sometimes astonished at the vigor with which the Lincoln visual theme remains appealing and inspiring to increasing numbers of readers, collectors, and historians.

The palpable, permanent evidence is all around us. In many of the Illinois towns where Lincoln lived or made history, statues are rising with increasing frequency to commemorate his impact. The Lincoln-Douglas debate town of Freeport began a parade with Lily Tolpo's life-size Lincoln and Douglas in 1992. And in 2001, Rebecca Childers Caleel's debaters were unveiled in Ottawa. John McClarey has produced a new heroic sculpture of Lincoln the surveyor at New Salem and created yet another monument for the new Lincoln Presidential Library and Museum in Springfield.

Painters have been busy, too. A new generation of artists, including Richard Wengenroth, Wendy Allen, and Sam Fink, have devoted themselves almost exclusively to Lincoln in a variety of evocative and appealing styles. Not long ago, a world-renowned artist in another medium entirely—the celebrated singer Tony Bennett, whose watercolors have been published and exhibited widely—produced a vivid painting of Daniel Chester French's Lincoln Memorial.[14] Lincoln's appeal to the visual artists remains strong. Perhaps Pablo Picasso expressed it best when he exclaimed of the face of Lincoln: "There is the real American elegance."[15]

So, when Gabor Boritt invited me in 2000 to coauthor an essay on "Lincoln in Modern Art" for his new collection, *The Lincoln Enigma*, I accepted at once, though I was not sure at the time whether the collaboration signified a final reunion for a couple of aging historians or the first iconography study of the new millennium.[16]

In retrospect, I prefer to think it was the latter. Professor Boritt wisely subtitled his volume "The Changing Faces of an American Icon." And those seven words, perhaps better than anything I could have written, seemed neatly to summarize both a lifetime of research and a still-compelling opportunity for new study. Lincoln's image is iconic—set as firmly and unassailably in the public consciousness as the religious icons of the Middle Ages—yet also changeable, reflecting and subtly influencing the still-evolving public response to the man who preserved American democracy and ended American slavery, but at great cost.

On April 5, 2003, I relearned this valuable lesson firsthand in the onetime capital of the Confederacy, Richmond, Virginia. That day, the city unveiled sculptor David Frech's statue of Lincoln and his son Tad as they looked on their visit to the fallen city 138 years earlier—on April 5, 1865. The artist, and the U.S. Historical Society, which commissioned it, might instead have produced a sculpture showing Lincoln striding into the city that day, being greeted by the newly liberated slaves who crowded around him and hailed him as their savior. They chose instead to show the visitors merely resting—sharing a bench that offers modern visitors space to sit and join them while contemplating the brave but modest tour that might, in hands other than Lincoln's, might have turned into a divisive march of conquest.

Nonetheless, as speakers that dedication day gathered on a rostrum behind Richmond's old Tredegar foundry—where, ironically, much of the Confederacy's munitions were manufactured—protesters shouted from behind a distant gate, made their disapproval known from the audience, and even soared overhead to remind participants that Lincoln's legacy was by no means universally embraced, even today.

From afar, angry demonstrators shouted the rebel yell. Portly anti-Lincoln men on the grounds peeled off their jackets to reveal potbellies barely covered by straining T-shirts bearing the likeness of John Wilkes Booth. And in pellucid blue skies above, a small plane towed a banner bearing the toxic declaration "Sic Semper Tyrannus"—thus ever to tyrants—the words Booth had shouted from the stage of Ford's Theatre after shooting Abraham Lincoln. In a way, it is rather exciting to realize that Lincoln icons can still provoke such controversy, just as his image stirred both adoration and revulsion while he lived.

Halfway around the world, at almost precisely the same time, demonstrators in Baghdad pulled down a statue of a leader once revered throughout Iraq—though certainly not by universal choice. It was not lost on the vast majority of the crowd that day at Richmond, or on this student of Lincoln iconography, that Lincoln's image was rising just as Saddam Hussein's was being removed.

Despite the protests of a tiny handful of born-again secessionists that day, despite the obvious power of public art, even Lincoln art, to stir a passionate response, most of Richmond welcomed Abraham Lincoln back. And the statue's unveiling served, too, as a poignant reminder that when wars end, it is possible to feel malice toward none and to express charity for all. And it is possible for an artist to vivify those attitudes in the simple gesture of a father teaching his child how divided people can come together to bind up a nation's wounds.

The enduring power of the Lincoln image to unleash such emotions suggests not only that the study has been well worth pursuing but that there are unimaginable variations on the theme yet unexplored—and more than worthy of attention.

When the Lincoln image was born in 1860, pictures were rare and precious commodities to most Americans. Art museums did not yet exist, newspapers did not yet publish photographs, and mass-produced pictures were purchased to express emotion, patriotism, and political loyalties—not merely to decorate. Motion pictures, of course, had yet to be invented. Television, computers, and the World Wide Web were unimaginable. Amid today's relentless cacophony of pictures, that the Lincoln image can continue to inspire artists, invite commissions, and both thrill and infuriate audiences demonstrates the unique and indelible power it continues to exert.

Why is this so? After so much study, so much renewal of interest in both period and modern Lincoln iconography, the question remains unanswered. Whether it remains unanswerable depends on the next generation of historians.

NOTES

1. John Hay, "Life in the White House in the Time of Lincoln," *Century Illustrated Monthly Magazine*, November 1890, 37.

2. The book was published in 1952 and 1956 editions by Harper and Row. The expanded, definitive edition is Stefan Lorant, *Lincoln: A Picture Story of His Life* (New York: W. W. Norton, 1969). For the Meserve collection, see Frederick Hill Meserve and Carl Sandburg, *The Photographs of Abraham Lincoln* (New York: Harcourt, Brace, 1944).

3. Jacob Deschin, "Lincoln Portrait in Controversy," *New York Times*, January 21, 1968.

4. The poster and Grace Bedell's letter were discussed in Harold Holzer, Gabor S. Boritt, and Mark E. Neely Jr., *The Lincoln Image: Abraham Lincoln and the Popular Print* (New York: Scribner's, 1984), 71–73. For the letter, and Lincoln's reply, see *The Collected Works of Abraham Lincoln*, ed. Roy P. Basler, 9 vols. (New Brunswick, N.J.: Rutgers University Press, 1953–55), 4:129–30.

5. Lincoln to Doney, July 30, 1860, in *Collected Works*, 4:89.

6. See Harold Holzer, "Prints of Abraham Lincoln," *Magazine Antiques* 105 (February 1974): 329–35; "White House Lincolniana: The First Family's Print of the Lincolns," *Lincoln Herald* 76 (Fall 1974): 119–31; and "Hohenstein: Lincoln's Print Doctor," *Lincoln Herald* 76 (Winter 1974): 181–86.

7. Cobb to Holzer, February 11, 1974. Miss Cobb wrote inspiringly that day from her summer home in Cape Elizabeth, Maine: "What next? Now that you have learned of the fascination of engravings and lithographs will you pursue this field and go further with specific images or keep on to cover pictures of Lincoln as they appeared

in foreign countries, or sheet-music covers, patriotic envelopes, and in advertising? I hope you will do them all, and luckily, you are young enough and have now a true interest in the man."

8. See, for example, "A New Discovery: Lincoln Portrait," pts. 1 and 2, *Civil War Times Illustrated*, February and April 1980.

9. Winfred Porter Truesdell, *Engraved and Lithographed Portraits of Abraham Lincoln*, vol. 2 (Champlain, N.Y.: Troutsdale Press, 1933).

10. The most frequently asked questions at our subsequent lectures were, invariably: "How did you divide up the work? Who did what? How could writers in Fort Wayne, New York, and Gettysburg write a book together?" We decided at the outset to keep the details to ourselves, and we've never discussed the process since. Although this chapter marks the first time I have ever written reminiscences about my Lincoln career, I am honoring the promise to keep the Holzer-Boritt-Neely process our little secret.

11. See, for example, *Changing the Lincoln Image* (Fort Wayne, Ind.: Louis A. Warren Lincoln Library and Museum, 1985); and "Francis B. Carpenter (1830–1900): Painter of Abraham Lincoln and His Circle," *American Art Journal* 16 (Spring 1984): 66–89.

12. The books referred to are *The Lincoln Family Album* (New York: Doubleday, 1990); *The Union Image: Popular Prints of the Civil War North* (Chapel Hill: University of North Carolina Press, 2000); and *Mine Eyes Have Seen the Glory: The Civil War in Art* (New York: Orion Books, 1993).

13. *The Lincoln Image*, for example, was reissued by the University of Illinois Press in 2001.

14. Harold Holzer, "Lincoln by Bennett," *American History Magazine* (April 2002): 6

15. Calvin Tomkins, *Living Well is the Best Revenge* (1963; New York: Modern Library, 1998), 33–34.

16. Gabor Boritt, ed., *The Lincoln Enigma* (New York: Oxford University Press, 2001). Our long epilogue was entitled "Lincoln in 'Modern' Art."

7

HARRY V. JAFFA

A Political Philosopher's Defense of Lincoln

Author's note: I have been asked to write something personal about how I became a Lincoln scholar. The seed may have been planted—unbeknownst to myself—in my boyhood, when my mother put a sampler in my room with the words described therein, "Stand with anybody that stands RIGHT. Stand with him while he is right, and PART with him when he goes wrong."[1] I don't remember paying any attention to it whatever and don't remember whether Lincoln's name was on it. Of course, years later I recognized it in the Peoria speech of October 1854, which is the foundation of Lincoln's career from that moment forward.

I discovered the Lincoln-Douglas debates in a secondhand bookstore on New York's Fourth Avenue in 1946. If this was chance or providential (or the fulfillment of my mother's intention), I cannot say. (I suspect it was Providence and my mother working in tandem). I fell in love with the debates and eventually became curious as to what had been written about them. I had never taken a course in American history and was preserved thereby (providentially) from the prejudices of the historians. Albert J. Beveridge had set the course for American scholars (the Englishman Lord Charnwood, in 1917, differing) when he wrote, in the first of the great Lincoln biographies (1928), that "solely on their merits, the debates themselves deserve little notice." And in all the years that followed, until I wrote *Crisis of the House Divided*, the debates had little notice.[2]

When *Crisis* was published in 1959, I sent a copy to Roy Nichols, then president of the American Historical Association. He made a gracious reply, in which he said I had done something no American historian had ever done: I had read through the Lincoln-Douglas debates.

At the time of the breakup of the Soviet Union, a letter of mine was published in the *Wall Street Journal* in which I praised one of its editorial writers for differing with the president of the United States as to the desirability of the Ukraine and the Baltic states seceding from the Soviet Union. It was not uncommon in 1989 to compare secession from the Soviet Union with the secession in 1860 and 1861 from our own American union. The implication was that secession from political unions, whether theirs or ours, was a bad thing. The editorial writer had, however, insisted that seceding *from slavery* was morally justified, while seceding *for the sake of slavery* was not. Seceding from the USSR, following the collapse of Communism, was seceding from slavery. Seceding from the American union, following the election of Abraham Lincoln, was seceding to preserve and extend human slavery. There was accordingly the same justification for promoting the breakup of the Soviet Union as there was for preventing the breakup of the Union that had elected Abraham Lincoln.

I added to what the *Journal* writer had said, that the seceding states in America in 1860 and 1861 justified their withdrawal from the Union by what they called states' rights. But the doctrine of states' rights to which they appealed was a doctrine of the collective rights of the states as political communities. But the states' rights of the Founding period, upon which the Constitution was based, were rights derived from the more fundamental rights of individuals, individuals "endowed by their Creator with certain unalienable rights." In the political theory of the Revolution and of the Founding, only those rights consistent with the prior and more fundamental rights of individuals might become the rights of states. For the Revolutionary generation, the rights of states, or of any legitimate political community, were derived from the voluntary action of individuals. The voluntary action by which free and independent individuals transformed themselves into fellow citizens bound by a law common to them all was called the social contract, or compact. James Madison repeated as a mantra that "compact is the basis of all free government." Compact as the basis of free government means neither more nor less than what Lincoln understood himself to mean when he said at Gettysburg that all men are created equal. We must then try to understand as precisely as possible what Madison meant. For this is what Lincoln inherited for the sake of which the Union had to be preserved and slavery destroyed. The doctrine of individual rights, as the basis of states' rights, is something the rebelling Southerners did not want their slaves to hear, because it would have justified a slave revolt as much as it justified the revolt against Great Britain in 1776.

A short time after my letter was published, I heard from someone who complained that the *Journal* had preferred a bad letter from a famous writer (me) to a good letter from one (himself) who was not famous. In the ensuing correspondence, I assured him that this was my first inkling that I was famous. He replied that I was famous "in Texas proslavery circles." He also sent me a copy of a handbill, advertising that he and his proslavery circle celebrated the birthday and honored the memory of John Wilkes Booth. I mention this to share with you that there are indeed proslavery circles here today and that there is a vigorous subculture devoted, not merely to preserve the memory of the glories of a regime dedicated to human slavery, but to join in political activity embodying that cause. Recently there was a best-selling book by a *New York Times* reporter called *Confederates in the Attic*.[3] It records a year-long adventure in pursuit of dedicated reenactors of Civil War battles. These reenactors are not necessarily political partisans, but they are people whose whole souls are absorbed into the being of their Confederate ancestors. But the Confederates in the attic are not confined to the attic. They are a largely concealed—from the general public—but nonetheless vigorous presence within the American polity. Less important than this presence is the extent to which doctrines derived from the Confederate cause have passed over into the opinions of our governing elites.

I have known of course of a journal called the *Southern Partisan*, which is unabashedly pro-Confederate and which does not hesitate to justify slavery. Russell Kirk, the late author of the *Conservative Mind* and a hero of the conservative movement that took shape in the 1950s, notably around Bill Buckley's *National Review*, contributed an article on John C. Calhoun to it.[4] Calhoun was the philosopher-king of slavery and of Southern independence. Nearly a century and a half after the defeat of the Confederacy, the example of Kirk illustrates how Calhoun remains a major influence on our political elites, while Abraham Lincoln is seldom mentioned in these circles, except for scorn and derision. So influential was Calhoun in the Civil War era that in 1861 the great English liberal Lord Acton judged him—in the *Disquisition on Government*—to be a major theoretician of minority rights in free constitutions. He considered Southern secession and Southern independence to be in vindication of Calhoun's defense of minority rights.

I believe I have dealt definitively with Calhoun's political theory in chapter 7 of *A New Birth of Freedom*.[5] I am not so vain, though, as to think that I have convinced anyone else of this. However, until I wrote for the *National Review*, no good word ever appeared in it for Lincoln, Jefferson, the Declaration of Independence, or the idea of equality. In corresponding with my unabashedly proslavery Texan, I quoted to him Lincoln's observation concerning the positive good theory of slavery, that slavery was the only good thing he had ever heard of that no one wanted the good of for himself. I invited him, as a gesture of his sincerity, to find someone who was clearly his superior, whether black or white, and offer himself up as a slave. That was, I said, the way he could refute Lincoln, by taking the good of slavery for himself. He replied by citing with surprising sophistication Plato's *Republic*, with its tripartite class division, allegedly corresponding with the allegedly natural differences of human souls. Plato's unequal division within man's humanity, he said, was the "true" nature of man's humanity and not the false universal equality of all human persons in the Declaration of Independence. In the course of the nineteenth century, Darwinism also confirmed (against the

Declaration) the diversity in the origins of human natures. George Fitzhugh had in 1856 published a book called *Cannibals All: Slaves without Masters*, which became a master work in the proslavery cause. It delighted Lincoln, because the argument for slavery in it—like the citing of Plato's *Republic*—had nothing that confined it to blacks. Lincoln always warned that there was no argument that justified the enslavement of blacks that could not equally justify the enslavement of whites.

The mainstream of nineteenth-century European thought, from which Southern conservatism is descended and which remains, however deeply concealed, within American conservatism to this day, is derived from the Holy Alliance that defeated Napoleon and that tried to roll back the French Revolution and restore the ancien régime. This reactionary politics was, however, based upon political thought more radically modern than what it was intended to supplant. The thought of our Declaration, which was the core of the antislavery movement led by Lincoln, was based upon the idea of nature, of the "Laws of Nature and of Nature's God." Lincoln said that the Declaration incorporated "an abstract truth applicable to all men and all times."[6] A truth applicable to all times would itself be independent of time. The underlying premise of the Declaration and of the thought of the Founding generally was of a truth outside of time, accessible to the human mind, by which human action in time, and within our mortal existence, might be guided. The Declaration indicates this when the Signers, in the name of the American people, appeal to the "Supreme Judge of the world" for the rectitude of their intentions. The standard of nature, and of a natural theology, was replaced in the nineteenth century by History, especially in the thought of Hegel, which was later merged with evolutionary theory derived from Darwin. History, thus conceived, became the standard by which man within History was to be judged. This standard, like man himself, evolved within time and was itself a product of time. Unlike Lincoln's Declaration, there was nothing outside of History by which events within History might be judged. The historical process had led to freedom for some and to slavery for others. Judgment of the justice of this historical allocation of slavery for some and of freedom for others had to be made within the same time-bound reality that had produced slavery and freedom. This led to the conclusion that those who were slaves deserved to be slaves and that those who were free deserved to be free. In short, the "Is" became the "Ought." This was, incidentally, the conclusion of my John Wilkes Booth correspondent.

The slavery controversy flared up in the United States, first in 1820 over Missouri and again in 1830 over South Carolina's attempt to nullify the tariff of 1828. Nullification and secession first made their presence in American politics in 1830. At virtually the same moment, abolitionism and the positive good theory of slavery made their appearance. Throughout the Founding period, American slavery had been regarded as at best a necessary evil but never as a positive good. When the political theory of the Holy Alliance crossed the water, it substituted the defense of slavery for the defense of the ancien régime, a society of rank, inherited privilege, and religious conformity. Clearly, a modified form of the ancien régime, something that might be called up-to-date feudalism, remains the ideal of those conservatives (for example, Russell Kirk) who reject the idea of equality in the Declaration of Independence.

The reputation and regard in which Abraham Lincoln has been held by the American people as a whole is represented by the Lincoln Memorial, which, together with the Washington Monument, dominates the nation's consciousness of itself in the nation's capital. Within the Memorial are these words:

> In this Temple,
> As in the hearts of the people,
> For whom he saved the Union,
> The memory of Abraham Lincoln
> Is enshrined forever.

That sentiment has never succumbed to the changing intellectual fashions that have swept over our elites. But the work of these elites has dangerously undermined what Lincoln sought to achieve. In 1856, Lincoln observed that public opinion always had a central idea, from which all its minor thoughts radiated. The central idea of our Founding was the equality of man. Seven years later, Lincoln would reassert this central idea when, at Gettysburg, he said that the nation at its birth had been dedicated to the proposition that all men are created equal. In Independence Hall, on his way to Washington in February 1861, Lincoln said that he had never had a political sentiment that did not come from the Declaration of Independence.

ALL MEN ARE CREATED EQUAL

Let us now turn to the great self-evident proposition, that all men are created equal. I think I can best begin by repeating an incident that occurred some years ago, at a Philadelphia Society meeting. I was lecturing on the Declaration and had come to the subject of self-evident truth. A very distinguished conservative—one who, I think, may in our time have contributed more signed articles to conservative journals that any other single individual— stood up and declared that there were no self-evident truths. I then asked him if it was not self-evident that he was not a dog. He said, "No." Then I asked him if he did not know that he was not a dog. He again said, "No." I then said perhaps he did not know that I was not a fire hydrant, implying that I wanted to keep a convenient distance between us. Now this famous scholar was obviously a victim of the radical nihilism that is the culmination of modern philosophy. He was a victim of an ideological conviction that overrode what was plainly true on the basis of ordinary sense perception. He certainly knew that he was not a dog, but he was not prepared to believe what he knew in the face of a theory that told him not to believe it. Both the Communists and the Nazis believed things about the world—for example, that capitalists were the enemies of the workers and thereby of the human race and that there was a Jewish conspiracy to take over the world—for which there was no evidence whatever, but their ideology overrode whatever did not agree with it. In Arthur Koestler's *Darkness at Noon,* the central character accepts his condemnation by the Stalinist court, although he knows he is innocent. But he has been condemned by the Party, and he has committed his life to the Party, and its judgments are the judgments of History, which is the highest authority for what is true. The Party's truth is the highest truth, and so he accepts its pronouncement of his guilt. We see at work—within American conservatism—the same abnegation of responsibility for theoretical and practical judgment.

I trust, however, that everyone reading these words will agree that the man was lying. He knew he was not a dog. Everyone who knew of his existence knew that he was not a dog. That he was not a dog was a self-evident truth. It was not something that had to be proved, because any attempt to prove it would have involved assertions less evident than the fact of his being a human being and not a dog, or any other species. The difference between human and canine nature may be such as to warrant extensive and complicated analysis and exposition. But such can take place only within a framework within which human and canine natures, on the most general level, are distinguished. On this level, when man meets dog, natural ruler meets natural servant. When man rides horse, which is the rider and which is the horse is immediately apparent: the difference is self-evident. But there is no such difference between one human being and another such as there is between man and dog, or man and horse, to make one necessarily the master and the other necessarily the servant. Slavery is morally wrong in that it endows upon one human being the right to command another, as if there was a difference in species.

All of the very elaborate political theory implicit in the Declaration of Independence, which guided Lincoln's thought and action, can be elucidated from the basic distinction between man and beast on the one hand and from the corresponding distinction between man and God on the other. For it is no less true that there is a difference between man and God, such that God may rule man by virtue of his superiority, as man can rule beast by virtue of his superiority. Man is superior to beast because of his reason. Beasts are ruled within themselves by instinct and passion. Passion in humans frequently distorts or subverts reason. The essence of virtue in human beings is the subjection of passion by reason. Aristotle defines the rule of law as the rule of reason undistorted by passion. The rule of law is in essence the attempt to bring God's rule so far as possible within the scope of human institutions. It may be objected that we do not know of the existence of God in the same self-evident way that we know of man and beast. But we do know, in a perfectly objective way, that no man is God and that the attempt to govern other human beings as if they were an inferior species is to assume one's self-prerogatives that might belong to one only if one were God. Lincoln reduced all assumptions of authority that implied an original superiority of the governors to the governed to the doctrine of the divine right of kings. Such kings played God to their subjects. But no man has the right to play God. Whether or not the God of the Declaration actually exists, we know that no man claiming the prerogatives of God has any right to such a claim. In point of fact, there was no government before 1776 that did not, in whole or in part, depend for its authority upon claims, whether of an individual, an individual family, or an aristocratic class, that made the rulers superior by birth to the many they ruled.

EQUALITY OF HUMAN BEINGS

We must now turn to how the equality of human beings—that is to say, the equality in "dominion," the equality in the right to rule—is transformed into political community, in which there are rulers and ruled. For the state in which natural equality rules is what is called a state of nature, no one having more authority over another than the other has over him. Although in the state of nature, no one has authority over another, neither can anyone command the person or property of another in defense of his own person or property. The insecurity of the state of nature makes it imperative that security be sought by means of political community.

The transformation of the state of nature into the political state is accomplished by means of the social contract (or as Madison called it, "compact"). We must attend to this with the greatest care and precision. The contract takes place when a number of free and equal humans agree with each other to form a political community. The agreement must reflect the equality and freedom that preceded it. The government they form must be dedicated to the equal protection of the persons and property of each. All must place themselves at whatever risk is necessary for the protection of any one of them. Every one of them must be prepared to take whatever risk is necessary to join with others in protecting each of them. In the original form of civil society, every adult is in principle a member of the militia of his community.

Let us imagine a group of families on the frontier building a stockade into which one can take shelter from Indians or wild animals. If the stockade is under assault, everyone must take whatever part they can in the defense of the stockade. No one can opt out under the pretense that they sought only safety, and not danger, in joining the community. The equal protection of the laws allows no exemption from equal responsibility to the laws. Similarly, everyone is bound to be taxed in whatever manner is deemed equal. This reciprocality in the equal entitlement to the protection of the laws, and the equal responsibility to enable the government to offer that protection, is the essence of the social contract. This understanding is moreover unanimous among the contracting partners, who by contracting become fellow citizens. To repeat: this is a unanimous decision, not a majority decision. But it is this unanimous decision that becomes the basis of majority rule.

It is essential that we understand correctly this relationship between unanimity and majority. Civil society cannot function by unanimity. If it could, then government would be possible in the state of nature. Majority rule is the practical means whereby the community, unanimous in its desire for security of person and of property, may act to gain that security. It is impossible to exaggerate the importance of the unanimous consent by which the political community is first formed and the majority rule that follows upon that unanimity. Majority rule, apart from this underlying unanimity, has no moral obligation whatever. Yet in the world today, demands are constantly made in the name of the authority of the majority. No less a personage than Supreme Court justice Antonin Scalia has declared that the whole theory of democracy is majority rule. When asked about the minority, he replied, "They lose," unless the majority decides to accord them certain rights. He also said that if a people decide they want abortion to be legal, then abortion should be legal. If, on the contrary, they want abortion to be illegal, then it should be illegal.

If one substitutes "slavery" for "abortion," one might be quoting Senator Stephen A. Douglas in his debates with Abraham Lincoln. Douglas held to what he called "popular sovereignty." He did not care, he said, whether slavery in the territories was voted up or down. He cared only for the sacred right of the people to decide. Lincoln responded by saying that if slavery was a matter of moral indifference, then it would be perfectly correct to let the majority decide. But if slavery was wrong, then the people had no right to vote for what was wrong. A people, properly so called, is itself formed by the moral law. The people does not form the moral law; the moral law forms the people. This is certainly implied in the Declaration of Independence, when the Congress appeals to the Supreme Judge of the world for the righteousness of their intentions. Majority rule begins only after the unanimous consent forms a moral bond between any possible majority and any possible minority. The foundation of majority rule is the individual rights that are transferred from the individual in the state of nature to the same individual, as civil rights, within civil society. However, in civil society, the individual seeks protection for those rights not from his or her individual exertion but from the government, acting by the majority, but acting always in the name of the people whose unanimity authorized the majority. Strictly speaking, there are no minority rights or majority rights; there are only individual rights, the rights with which we have been endowed by our Creator, for the security of which all legitimate governments are instituted.

The great difficulty with the theory we have outlined is that, in its perfection, human beings are bound to recognize each other's humanity as the foundation of the social contract. But human beings, by and large, form their loyalties to family, clan, tribe, city, and nation. Differences in ethnicity issue in differences in religion, since all (or nearly all) human religions have their origin in the worship of ancestors. To enslave those who worship strange gods seems altogether more "natural" than to accept them as partners in the social contract. The core of Lincoln's political struggle was to gain simple recognition of the Negro's humanity. Such recognition would mean that the Negro was endowed by the Creator with the same rights as the white man and that denial of these rights to Negroes would justify denying them to whites.

Much has been made of the fact that, before 1860, Lincoln denied seeking any of the privileges of citizenship for Negroes. He did not do so because he was waging political war against the spread of slavery. To seek more than the prevention of the spread of slavery to new territories would only divide those he sought to lead and render him completely ineffective. He was most effective when he said of a Negro man that he might not perhaps be his equal in many respects, but in the right to put into his mouth the bread that his own hand had earned, he was his equal, the equal of Judge Douglas, and the equal of any man.[7] But Lincoln knew that the black man would never be able to defend the right to put that bread into his mouth until he not only was free but possessed the power coming from full citizenship. He once said, "Allow all the governed an equal voice in the government, and that alone is self-government." Such perfection of the idea of equality was not, however, to be expected in any foreseeable future. Yet Lincoln quoted from the New Testament, "Be ye perfect as your Father in Heaven is perfect." "No one," he said, "could be as perfect as God in Heaven." But God's perfection was the assurance that striving toward it was the right direction to human life. So it was with the perfection of the regime of equal rights. However imperfectly, we must strive toward it. But we must strive toward it with the means already authorized by the regime of equality.

CONCLUSION

Lincoln knew that Napoleon had claimed to advance the ends of equality but had done so with the means of tyranny. Lincoln did not want to free the slaves by enslaving the free. Only by the laborious process of free constitutional government, persuading the people to recognize their own better natures, could the ends of the regime of equality be realized. For the regime of equality was itself possessed of this paradoxical nature. It could advance only by the consent of the governed. But the governed would often stubbornly refuse that very equality that was the ground of their own authority. The abolitionists would not have hesitated, like Napoleon, to have used tyrannical means against the tyranny of slavery. But Lincoln would not. Unlike his critics, Lincoln's patience was grounded in a sound theoretical understanding of the politics to which his whole soul was committed—as ours ought to be.

NOTES

1. *The Collected Works of Abraham Lincoln*, ed. Roy P. Basler, 9 vols. (New Brunswick, N.J.: Rutgers University Press, 1953–55), 2:273.

2. Henry V. Jaffa, *Crisis of the House Divided: An Interpretation of the Issues in the Lincoln-Douglas Debates* (1959; Chicago: University of Chicago Press, 1998).

3. Tony Horwitz, *Confederates in the Attic: Dispatchers from the Unfinished Civil War* (New York: Vintage, 1999).

4. Russell Kirk, *The Conservative Mind: From Burke to Eliot* (Washington, D.C.: Regnery Publishing, 2001).

5. Henry V. Jaffa, *A New Birth of Freedom: Abraham Lincoln and the Coming of the Civil War* (Lanham, Md.: Rowman and Littlefield, 2000).

6. *Collected Works*, 3:376.

7. Ibid., 3:16.

*Lincoln through the Eyes of a Civil War
and Civil Rights Historian*

My acquaintance with Abraham Lincoln has been gradual through my education, my research and writing, and my adult life in the South. Born in 1939 into a family of first-generation Polish Americans, I spent my early years in an ethnic neighborhood in Buffalo, New York. In this environment, Abraham Lincoln was not a household word. I could never have imagined then that someday I would be teaching classes on the Civil War and writing books about individuals variously associated with the sixteenth president of the United States.

In elementary school, I heard all the usual stories about Lincoln: the log cabin, Honest Abe, and reading by the light of a fireplace. I found such tales interesting enough, but they had little impact on me. By the time I entered the fifth grade, my family had moved to a then sparsely populated area of the Buffalo suburbs, where my parents purchased a general store, selling everything from meat freshly cut from a side of beef to needles and thread stocked in a glass showcase. I helped work in the store, but my father did not use the story about Lincoln's honesty as a clerk to teach me how to behave properly behind the counter. My childhood heroes were professional athletes Joe Louis and Stan Musial, not President Abraham Lincoln.

I attended a school that was so small that each classroom housed two grades. Memorizing poetry was one of our regular chores, and it was in this way that I learned Walt Whitman's poem "O Captain! My Captain!"[1] To this day, I can still remember lines from it, and they continue to send a chill through me: "the bleeding drops of red," the Captain lying on the deck "[f]allen cold and dead." Who was this captain who had guided his ship into port so skillfully, yet had died mysteriously and awfully just at its arrival? I did not know then that Whitman was eulogizing the victorious but tragically assassinated Abraham Lincoln. The poem was mesmerizing to me, but I did not really understand its significance.

During my high school and college years, numerous teachers opened my eyes to the thrill of historical discovery. However, it was Franklin D. Roosevelt and Andrew Jackson, not Abraham Lincoln, who first caught my attention. At Canisius College, I read the classic biography of Lincoln by Lord Charnwood.[2] I thought it was a wonderful book and remember one of my teachers saying that sometimes it takes someone from another country to understand and explain American icons to us. Yet, I was not drawn to Lincoln.

He first began to emerge for me when I was in graduate school and especially when John F. Kennedy was assassinated. Grieving with the rest of the nation, I saw in the newspaper an image that expressed my feelings. It was a Bill Mauldin political cartoon that showed the familiar Lincoln Memorial scene of the sitting Lincoln. In this drawing, however, Lincoln was bent over with his face in his hands, in deep mourning.[3] As Whitman had mourned Lincoln's assassination, Lincoln himself was mourning the death of the president of my day. It was a powerful representation that I have never forgotten.

Then, of course, the number of coincidences between Lincoln and Kennedy became part of public folklore: both were elected in a year that contained "60"—1860 and 1960; both were succeeded by a man named Johnson; their remains were both carried on the same caisson; and on and on.[4] Somehow the nineteenth-century Abraham Lincoln provided comfort at a time of twentieth-century tragedy.

It was Civil War general William T. Sherman who drew me closer to Lincoln. When I arrived at the University of Notre Dame in the fall of 1961, I had hoped to write my doctoral dissertation on Andrew Jackson. My senior paper in college had been on the Eaton Affair, and I wanted to expand that research into a dissertation and eventually a book. All of my professors warned me against it, however. Trying to research this elusive topic might very well delay my dissertation, they warned, and if I wanted a teaching position, I'd better have that Ph.D. in hand.

One of those persons was the university archivist, who told me that the archives had received, on loan, the family papers of General Sherman. He thought that if he could tell the donor, a Sherman granddaughter, that someone was using these manuscripts for a dissertation, she might be willing to donate them permanently. Do a paper for a seminar, he advised, and see what you think.

I took this advice, and I immediately was taken with Sherman. I eventually wrote a paper on him and his problems in Kentucky and Missouri in the fall of 1861. He believed that newspaper reporters were spies for the enemy and regularly threatened them with hanging. In response, reporters decided he was crazy and said so in print.

As I dug into what I came to see was a very personal struggle between freedom of the press and national security, President Lincoln played an important role. General Sherman's wife, Ellen, and her family battled to restore Sherman's reputation after the insanity charge surfaced. In the process, Ellen visited the White House, ready to pounce on Lincoln for any perception of unfairness to her husband. Lincoln was soothing throughout the interview, so charming this irate wife that she calmed down. From that point on, she always considered the president to be a fair-minded supporter of her husband. My respect for Lincoln grew. He faced a difficult situation of human relations, and he turned it into a positive result for himself and the nation. In this tiny matter, he showed himself to be a political genius of the first order.

I eventually completed a dissertation on Sherman and the press.[5] (And, Notre Dame did receive permanent possession of the Sherman Family Papers.) In 1968, I accepted a teaching position at Gannon College (now University), Erie, Pennsylvania. I immediately began doing further research on Sherman and came across the amazing story of a black West Point cadet named Johnson C. Whittaker. In 1880, he was assaulted in the night by three masked men and told to leave the military academy or be killed. The result of the episode was a lengthy court of inquiry and an even lengthier army court-martial, both of which found Whittaker guilty of self-mutilation to avoid an examination two months into the future. Sherman was commanding general of the army at the time, Rutherford B. Hayes was president, and a host of other famous Americans of the day were involved. One of these was the secretary of war, Robert T. Lincoln, the president's son. It was this Lincoln who permanently separated Whittaker from West Point, even though the army judge advocate general had thrown out the court-martial decision on both procedural and factual grounds. Robert Lincoln accepted the West Point faculty's verdict in failing Whittaker on an oral examination taken at the same time that the earlier judicial proceedings were taking place. Lincoln separated him from the academy, despite the favorable legal ruling.[6]

Abraham Lincoln had been dead for over fifteen years when his son made this shocking decision, reflecting and enforcing the anti-black racism demonstrated in the assault and subsequent court actions. I found Robert Lincoln's action unsettling. Somehow I expected more from the son of the "Great Emancipator." I wondered what Lincoln would think. He had supported the use of "colored troops" in the Civil War; he was friends with Frederick Douglass; his Gettysburg Address had spoken of "a new birth of freedom." Was his thinking so far in advance of American society that his own son could reflect anti-black prejudice and forget what his father had done just a few years previously? I repeatedly mulled these thoughts over in my mind, and the result was additional respect for Lincoln. He had been able to transcend the white superiority attitudes that he had once shared with other Americans and that his own son retained some fifteen years later. Lincoln provided a sterling example, but even his own son did not accept it. Racism seemed impervious to elimination, even in Lincoln's family.

As I studied in graduate school, began my teaching career, and researched and wrote a book on racial injustice, I saw the racism of my own age and experienced the civil rights movement that was attempting to transform it. The 1963 March on Washington was one of the crystallizing events of this movement. It consisted of major leaders and average black and white Americans publicly calling on their government to end the prejudice against black people. In my eyes, Abraham Lincoln seemed to be there. As Martin Luther King Jr. made his famous "I Have a Dream" speech, he stood in front of the Lincoln Memorial, highlighting it again as a shrine of freedom. There sat the marble Lincoln, seemingly taking in the powerful words and appreciating King's biblical allusions and cadences that Lincoln himself had used in his own speeches and writings. Listening to Dr. King's words and considering the spot where he stood was overwhelming. One of the greatest of America's white leaders and one of its greatest black leaders seemed merged.

This melding was particularly obvious at the beginning of King's speech, when he reminded the nation and the world of Lincoln's earlier leadership in race relations. "Five score years ago," he said, "a great American, in whose symbolic shadow we stand today, signed the Emancipation Proclamation. This momentous decree came as a great beacon light of hope to millions of Negro slaves, who had been seared in the flames of withering injustice. It came as a joyous daybreak to end the long night of their captivity."[7] As a 1963 black American called for justice, he began by reminding his integrated audiences—those at the scene and those, like me, watching on television—that it was the 1863 Abraham Lincoln who had provided the first spark of equality to a downtrodden people. Lincoln was truly a symbol of freedom, not just a marble monument.

Like the Emancipation Proclamation, which he cited, Martin Luther King's "I Have a Dream" speech did not solve the problem of race in America. King was trying to bring Lincoln's earlier actions to their logical conclusion, and he too suffered the assassin's bullet. In many a black home, there had long hung Abraham Lincoln's picture. Now Martin Luther King's likeness took its place alongside Lincoln's as another symbol of hope for a better future for all people.

As a historian, I knew I was living through historic times, and I was alternately encouraged and then appalled by what I witnessed. Gannon College, where I taught, had few black students and fewer black faculty. When the school, to its credit, actively recruited African Americans to its student body, almost all came from Pennsylvania's urban areas, and they were not Gannon's typical students. These new students reacted sharply to what they encountered: paternalism at best and prejudice at worse. They forthrightly demanded justice.

A group of these young people came to the history department one day, calling on us to introduce a course in African American history (and it was to be taught by a person with black skin). I am not a black man and had no training in the field, but I was, at that time, writing my book on the black West Point cadet, and my field in the Civil War and my ever-increasing interest in Abraham Lincoln gave me hope that I might be able to teach the class. In fact, there was no one else, black or white, able or willing to do it. I volunteered. I taught an integrated undergraduate class and later taught a graduate class for high school teachers.

To the students, it was all so new. A black presence in American history was not their usual experience. White students had the most difficult time. The existence of 1960s discrimination was not a reality to many of them. They saw run-down black neighborhoods as the sole fault of blacks themselves. To some, the mere presence of black students in the college and especially their insistence on change was threatening and unacceptable. My classes were a microcosm of the turmoil in American society over race. Once again, Abraham Lincoln was never far away; he provided one of the few focuses of unity. Both black and white students accepted him as someone who had saved the Union and eliminated slavery. He had died because of the good he had done for race relations, they agreed.

In 1973, my family and I moved to Mississippi, then only a few years away from the violence of the civil rights movement. My new home town of Starkville had not integrated its public schools until 1970, and that same year a private academy was opened for those white families who refused to have their children attend school with members of the other race. When I arrived at Mississippi State University, which had been integrated since 1965, a black graduate student was teaching a course in black history, and the football and basketball teams had a sprinkling of black faces.

As I began teaching students at the university and meeting people in town, the civil rights movement was frequently discussed in the context of the Civil War and Reconstruction. After all, these events had affected Mississippi. Abraham Lincoln was frequently discussed. If only he had not died in 1865, Reconstruction would not have been so awful, I regularly heard. He was the tyrant, I was told, who had brought on war and cruelly invaded the innocent South, but, at war's end, he was the individual who believed in "malice toward none" and "charity for all." Had he lived, the story continued, he would have left the South alone in the years after the war; he would have set things right. During Reconstruction it was all those carpetbaggers, those outsiders, who had created problems that white Southerners would have solved without such interference. I sensed that my students and neighbors believed that, had Abraham Lincoln lived, not only would there not have been a Reconstruction, but there would never have been a need for the civil rights movement. Lincoln would have solved all of the problems without any need for either. It was an amazing perception, and once again it demonstrated the power of Lincoln, this time even in the minds of those who were critical of his actions during the Civil War.

It was in my new Mississippi home that I published several books on William T. Sherman, a diary of a Confederate white woman, a couple of books on local civil rights leaders, an encyclopedia of national civil rights, an account of a sex scandal in the administration of Andrew Jackson, and a biography of Union general Henry W. Halleck.[8] In every one of these books, with the exception of the monograph on the Jackson administration, Abraham Lincoln was never far from the text. The books I published on civil rights did not deal with Lincoln directly, but he would often appear. Sometimes, modern-day civil rights spokesmen castigated Lincoln for not doing enough, or writers insisted that he was a racist who believed in white supremacy above all else. More often, Lincoln was the recipient of admiration from black leaders who, like Martin Luther King, credited him with beginning the movement that they were trying to bring to fruition.

My extended work on Halleck and Sherman put me directly in touch with Lincoln. He and Sherman saw each other only a few times during the war, in the White House early in the conflict and on the *River Queen* at City Point, Virginia, at its end. Still, they influenced each other, and I learned more about the president. In my biography of Sherman, I noted how the general at first thought little of the president but slowly grew in admiration of him. Lincoln was similarly unsure about Sherman. When Sherman court-martialed a reporter in February 1863, Lincoln clearly did not agree with the action, but he recognized the possible military repercussions if he overturned the sentence and allowed the reporter back into Sherman's area. Cleverly, he told the reporter's friends that the ouster order would be lifted if General Grant allowed it. Grant said it was all up to Sherman, who then excoriated the reporter and refused to let him return. Lincoln allowed Sherman's decision to stand. Still, reporters were happy with what they saw as Lincoln's support, and Sherman was happy with the president's willingness to let him make the decision. Lincoln had somehow been able to please both sides in the complicated, contentious issue that could have created major war problems but for his talents.

When Sherman captured Atlanta in September 1864, Lincoln sent a letter of profuse thanks, recognizing the positive effect this military victory would have on his presidential campaign. When Sherman proposed the march to the sea, however, Lincoln was worried. Still, he went along with the proposal because of his respect for Sherman. Arriving in Savannah in December at the end of the march, Sherman presented the city to the president as a Christmas gift, exciting both Lincoln and the nation. When Sherman made his agreement with Joe Johnston to end the war, he based it on what he thought were Lincoln's wishes. In the postwar years, whenever Sherman mentioned Lincoln, he did so positively, demonstrating how Lincoln had become an admired figure in his life. He had grown in Sherman's estimation because of his successful handling of the war effort and the people involved in it.

Lincoln's relationship with another famous Civil War general provided me with a diametrically opposite perception. At first, Lincoln had the highest respect for Henry W. Halleck. The general had been a huge success in his pre–Civil War life as a San Francisco attorney/entrepreneur, and he and West Point professor Dennis Hart Mahan were considered the leading military theorists in the nineteenth-century U.S. military. Lincoln demonstrated his admiration for Halleck's military prowess when he became president and wanted to make up for his own lack of military knowledge. He turned to Halleck's famous book on military theory, *Elements of Military Art and Science*, and read it cover to cover. He came close to naming Halleck commanding general in late 1861 to replace the aging Winfield Scott, but he chose George B. McClellan instead because "Little Mac" was on the scene while Halleck was traveling east from California. When McClellan failed and Lincoln and Secretary of War Edwin Stanton were unhappy with their own handling of the war effort, Lincoln called Halleck, the successful general in the western theater of the war, to come to Washington to take over the post. Lincoln was sure that Halleck had the knowledge and ability to provide the leadership that the Union army required.

It did not prove to be so. Because of a myriad of psychological and medical problems, Halleck did not demonstrate that leadership. He suggested, cajoled, counseled, and encouraged, but he seldom ordered. The result was a Union war effort that, except in the area of logistics, did not have the centralized organization it required. Lincoln grew increasingly exasperated with Halleck, eventually referring to him as a mere "clerk."

Despite his recognition of Halleck's shortcomings, Lincoln continued working with him. He had shown no compunction about firing other generals, but he kept Halleck as commanding general because he could see no one else capable of handling the job, and he kept hoping that the learned Halleck would still take hold. It was only when Lincoln believed that Ulysses S. Grant was ready for the task that he hired him. Continuing to show his respect for Halleck's ability, however, he created a new post, "chief of staff," for him. Despite Lincoln's support, Halleck did not develop warm feelings for the president. He was in the room with many others when Lincoln died, but, unlike Edwin Stanton, who said that now Lincoln "belongs to the ages," Halleck was mute. To him, Lincoln remained a mediocre politician, unable, as he did with so many others, to convince Halleck of his greatness.

The opposite attitudes of Sherman and Halleck toward Lincoln indicated to me the well-known fact that Lincoln's image was never universally positive. When I edited the Civil War diary of Emma Holmes, a white Charlestonian, her view of Lincoln was distinctly negative. He was a tyrant of the worst order who had invaded a blameless South without justification and tried to destroy an ideal social system. When Lincoln was assassinated, Holmes displayed no sorrow for the fallen president but expressed concern for the white South, which she feared might suffer unfairly for the deed. I realized that, to concentrate only on the positive reactions to Lincoln, whether during the Civil War or later, was to miss an essential part of the Lincoln legacy. He was too complicated and human, and he was part of something too complex, to elicit only praise and adulation. Yet in my mind, he continued to grow in stature as I learned more about his handling of important problems and difficult personalities around him.

Lincoln has always been present to me from my early life to my later research and writing. As a writer, I have repeatedly been impressed with his ability to write, his talent to express himself in ways that conveyed his meaning poetically and clearly. As a historian of the Civil War, I have found him at the center of everything that happened during those years. As a historian of civil rights, I have marveled at his basic humanity, his ability to inspire, and his capacity to grow out of a racism so prevalent among his fellow Americans, even his own son. He inspired me and so many other Americans, providing hope for the United States during the darkest days of twentieth-century racial turmoil.

As I've become acquainted with Lincoln, I've learned that when he was seemingly caught in unsolvable problems, he would somehow reach deep into his being and find solutions that brought peace out of chaos. His Emancipation Proclamation took the difficult moral issue of slavery and dealt with it politically in a way that helped lead to its eventual demise. That document then continued to inspire brave men and women in later days to continue the struggle, to overcome the modern vestiges of that horrible institution.

When I think of Lincoln today, I still mourn his death. I wonder what modern-day America would be like had he lived to complete his second term. The application of his talents to the post–Civil War world might very well have brought greater interracial healing than was accomplished in his absence. He would have used his vast political skills against the white South's desire to maintain white supremacy despite the end of slavery. He would have attempted to put into practice the theme of the Gettysburg Address, "a new birth of freedom." He would have demonstrated by act and example that all men were "created equal" and indeed deserved an equal chance at "Life, Liberty, and the pursuit of Happiness." How successful he would have been is impossible to say, but certainly his great political skills would have given him the tools to make progress that so long evaded those who followed him. Believing this, Whitman's poem influences me today more than when I first memorized it. Then I did not understand its meaning. Now I know about the man it is eulogizing, and the words of rhyme draw deeper emotions from me than they did before. Abraham Lincoln has remained at the center of the major issue of twentieth-century America—black-white race relations—and he continues to influence the modern world of the twenty-first century as no other human beings do. Rethinking Whitman's "O Captain! My Captain!," Mauldin's cartoon, Martin Luther King's "I Have a Dream" speech, the experience of black West Point cadet Johnson C. Whittaker, and Sherman, Halleck, and Emma Holmes, I wonder and grieve for what might have been Abraham Lincoln's greater example and influence had his life extended only one more score.

NOTES

1. Walt Whitman, "O Captain! My Captain!," in *The Columbia Book of Civil War Poetry*, ed. Richard Marius (New York: Columbia University Press, 1994), 345–47.

2. Lord Geoffrey Rathbone Benson Charnwood, *Abraham Lincoln* (London: Constable, 1916).

3. *Chicago Sun-Times*, November 22, 1963.

4. "Linkin' Kennedy," *Snopes.com*, www.snopes.com/history/american/lincoln-kennedy.asp.

5. John F. Marszalek, "William T. Sherman and the Press, 1861–1854" (Ph.D. diss., University of Notre Dame, 1968); Marszalek, *Sherman's Other War: The General and the Civil War Press* (Memphis: Memphis State University Press, 1981; rev. paperback ed., Kent, Ohio: Kent State University Press, 1999).

6. John F. Marszalek, *Court Martial: A Black Man in America* (New York: Charles Scribner's Sons, 1972), reprinted with an afterword as *Assault at West Point* (New York: Collier, 1994). A motion picture based on this book was first aired on Showtime in 1994 and is regularly replayed on a variety of cable television stations.

7. Martin Luther King Jr., "I Have a Dream" audio and transcript, *History and Politics Out Loud*, www.hpol.org/transcript.php?id=72.

8. John F. Marszalek, *Sherman: A Soldier's Passion for Order* (New York: Free Press, 1993); *Sherman's Other War: The General and the Civil War Press*; *Sherman's March to the Sea* (Abilene, Texas: McWhiney Foundation Press, 2005); *The Diary of Miss Emma Holmes, 1861–1866* (Baton Rouge: Louisiana State University Press, 1979; paperback ed., 1994); Sadye H. Wier with Marszalek, *A Black Businessman in White Mississippi, 1886–1974* (Jackson: University Press of Mississippi, 1977); Douglas

L. Conner with Marszalek, *A Black Physician's Story: Bringing Hope in Mississippi* (Jackson: University Press of Mississippi, 1985); Charles D. Lowery and Marszalek, eds., *Greenwood Encyclopedia of African American Civil Rights, from Emancipation to the Twenty-First Century*, 2 vols. (Westport, Conn.: Greenwood, 2003; original one-volume ed., 1992); *The Petticoat Affair: Manners, Mutiny, and Sex in Andrew Jackson's White House* (New York: Free Press, 1998; paperback ed., Baton Rouge: Louisiana State University Press, 2000); *Commander of All Lincoln's Armies: A Life of General Henry W. Halleck* (Cambridge: Harvard University Press, 2004).

Lincoln's Legacy for Our Time

Editors' note: Professor McPherson first encountered Abraham Lincoln in Freeborn, Minnesota, where he attended school from the third through the eighth grade. He developed a serious interest in him while in graduate school during the late 1950s. One important personal lesson that he has learned from studying Lincoln "is to examine all sides of an issue carefully before making a judgment or decision, but once having made it, stick with it without waffling or wavering."

W hen Abraham Lincoln breathed his last at 7:22 A.M. on April 15, 1865, Secretary of War Edwin M. Stanton intoned: "Now he belongs to the ages."

Stanton's remark was more prescient than he knew, for Lincoln's image and his legacy became the possessions not only of future ages of Americans but also of people of other nations. On the centenary of Lincoln's birth in 1909, Leo Tolstoy described him as "a Christ in miniature, a saint of humanity." An Islamic leader projected a more militant image of Lincoln, declaring that America's sixteenth president "spoke with a voice of thunder . . . and his deeds were as strong as the rock." When Jacqueline Kennedy lived in the White House, she sought comfort in the Lincoln Room in times of trouble. "The kind of peace I felt in that room," she recalled, "was what you feel when going into a church. I used to feel his strength, I'd sort of be talking to him."[1]

Martin Luther King Jr. tried to persuade Jacqueline Kennedy's husband to issue a second Emancipation Proclamation on the hundredth anniversary of the first. John Kennedy demurred. So King went ahead on his own. When he stood on the steps of the Lincoln Memorial in August 1963 to deliver his "I Have a Dream" speech, King declared: "Fivescore years ago, a great American, in whose shadow we stand today, signed the Emancipation Proclamation. This momentous decree came as a great beacon of hope to millions of Negro slaves who had been seared in the flames of withering injustice."[2]

Lincoln could not have anticipated the reverence that millions would feel for him in future ages. But he *was* intensely aware, as he told Congress in December 1861 when America was engulfed in a tragic Civil War, that this struggle to preserve the Union "is not altogether for today—it is for a vast future also."[3] More than any other president of the United States, except perhaps Thomas Jefferson, Abraham Lincoln had a profound sense of history. He did not acquire it from formal education. Unlike Woodrow Wilson, Lincoln did not have a Ph.D. He did not study history in college or high school; indeed, he did not study it in school at all, for he had less than a year of formal schooling, which included no history courses. The only work of history Lincoln seems to have read as a boy was "Parson" Weems's famous filiopietistic biography of George Washington, with its apocryphal story of the hatchet and cherry tree.

That book made a lasting impression on Lincoln. Forty years after he first read it, president-elect Lincoln addressed the New Jersey legislature in Trenton, near the spot where Washington's ragged troops had won the victory the day after Christmas 1776 that saved the American Revolution from collapse. Lincoln told the legislators: "I remember all the accounts" in Weems's book "of the battle-fields and struggles for the liberty of the country, and none fixed themselves upon my imagination so deeply as the struggle here at Trenton. . . . The crossing of the river; the contest with the Hessians; the great hardships endured at that time, all fixed themselves on my memory more than any simple revolutionary event. . . . I recollect thinking then, boy even though I was, that there must have been something more than common that those men struggled for."[4]

These words were not merely an exercise in nostalgia. As always, Lincoln invoked the past for a purpose. On this occasion, he shifted from the Revolution to the present and future. Prospects for the United States in that present and future were dark. The country of which Lincoln would become president eleven days later was no longer the United States but the *dis*-United States. Seven slave states, fearing for the future of their "peculiar institution" in a nation governed by the new antislavery Republican Party, had seceded from the Union in response to Lincoln's election. Several more slave states were threatening to withdraw. Even as Lincoln spoke in Trenton, delegates from those first seven states were meeting in Montgomery, Alabama, to form the independent nation of the Confederate States of America. Civil war, or a permanent division of the country with its dire precedent for further divisions, or both, loomed on the horizon. Thus, it is not surprising that when Lincoln shifted from his discussion of the Revolution to the present, he began: "I am exceedingly anxious" that what those men fought for, "that something even more than National Independence; that something that held out a great promise to all the people of the world [for] all time to come; I am exceedingly anxious that this Union, the Constitution, and the liberties of the people shall be perpetuated in accordance with the original idea for which that struggle was made."[5]

The next day, Washington's Birthday, Lincoln spoke at Independence Hall in Philadelphia, where he spelled out more clearly what he believed was at stake both in the Revolution and in the crisis of 1861. "I have often inquired of myself," said Lincoln, "what great principle or idea it was that kept this [Union] so long together. It was not the mere matter of the separation of the colonies from the motherland, but that sentiment in the Declaration [of Independence] which gave liberty, not alone to the people of this country, but hope to the world for all future time." At this point in Lincoln's remarks, the newspaper text indicated "Great applause" from the audience, which included the city council and leading citizens of Philadelphia. Lincoln told them: "I have never had a feeling politically that did not spring from the sentiments embodied in the Declaration of Independence" ("Great cheering," according to the press). The ringing phrases that "all men are created equal, that they are endowed by their Creator with certain unalienable Rights, that among these are Life, Liberty, and the pursuit of Happiness," said Lincoln in 1861, not only "gave promise" to Americans but also "hope to the world" that "in due time the weights should be lifted from the shoulders of all men, and that *all* should have an equal chance. (Cheers.)"[6]

The sincerity of some in the audience who cheered Lincoln's egalitarian sentiments might be questioned. But Lincoln was quite sincere in his endorsement of them. He was, of course, painfully aware that many Americans enjoyed neither liberty nor equality. Four million were slaves, making the United States—the self-professed beacon of liberty to oppressed masses everywhere—the largest slave-holding country in the world. Lincoln grasped this nettle. "I hate . . . the monstrous injustice of slavery," he had said in his famous Peoria speech of 1854. "I hate it because it deprives our republican example of its just influence in the world—enables the enemies of free institutions, with plausibility, to taunt us as hypocrites."[7]

As for equality, said Lincoln on another occasion, the author of the Declaration of Independence and the Founding Fathers who signed it clearly "did not intend to declare all men equal *in all respects*." They did not even "mean to assert the obvious untruth" that all men in 1776 were equal in rights and opportunities. Rather, "they meant to set up a standard maxim for free society, which should be . . . constantly looked to, constantly labored for, and even though never perfectly attained, constantly approximated, and thereby constantly spreading and deepening its influence, and augmenting the happiness and value of life to all people of all colors everywhere."[8]

Like Thomas Jefferson, Lincoln asserted a universality and timelessness for the principles of liberty, equal rights, and equal opportunity on which the nation was founded. And Lincoln acknowledged his intellectual debt to Jefferson—not Jefferson the slaveholder, not Jefferson the author of the

Kentucky resolutions of 1799 asserting the superiority of state over federal sovereignty, not even Jefferson the president, but Jefferson the philosopher of liberty, author of the Northwest Ordinance that kept slavery out of future states comprising 160,000 square miles at a time when most existing states of the Union still had slavery, and the Jefferson who, though he owned slaves, said of the institution that "he trembled for his country when he remembered that God was just." This was the Jefferson, said Lincoln in 1859, who "in the concrete pressure of a struggle for national independence by a single people had the coolness, forecast, and capacity to introduce into a merely revolutionary document"—the Declaration of Independence—"an abstract truth, applicable to all men and all times."[9]

Universal and timeless this truth may be, but in Jefferson's time, it remained mostly as Lincoln described it—abstract. Fate decreed that it fell to Lincoln, not Jefferson, to give substance and meaning to what Jefferson had called a self-evident truth. Ironically, it was the slaveholders who provided Lincoln the opportunity to do so, for by taking their states out of the Union, they set in train a progression of events that destroyed the very social and political order founded on the slavery that they had seceded to preserve.

Secession transformed the main issue before the country from slavery to disunion. When Lincoln became president, he confronted not the question of what to do about slavery but of what to do about secession. On this question, Lincoln did not hesitate. Branding secession as "the essence of anarchy," he insisted in 1861 that "the central idea pervading this struggle is the necessity that is upon us, of proving that popular government is not an absurdity. We must settle this question now, whether in a free government that minority have the right to break up the government whenever they choose. If we fail it will go far to prove the incapability of the people to govern themselves."[10]

Lincoln had come a long way in his understanding of history since his boyhood reading of Weems's biography of Washington. Like other thoughtful Americans, he was acutely conscious of the unhappy fate of most republics in the past. The United States stood almost alone in the mid-nineteenth century as a democratic republic in a world bestrode by kings, queens, emperors, czars, petty dictators, and theories of aristocracy. Some Americans alive at midcentury had seen two French republics rise and fall. The hopes of 1848 for the triumph of popular government in Europe had been shattered by the counterrevolutions that brought a conservative reaction in the Old World. Would the American experiment in government of, by, and for the people also be swept into the dustbin of history?

Not if Lincoln could help it. "Our popular government has often been called an experiment," he told a special session of Congress that met on July

4, 1861. "Two points in it, our people have already settled—the successful *establishing*, and the successful *administering* of it. One still remains—its successful *maintenance* against a formidable internal attempt to overthrow it." If that attempt succeeded, said Lincoln, the forces of reaction in Europe would smile in smug satisfaction at this proof of their contention that the upstart republic launched in 1776 could not last.[11]

Many in the North shared Lincoln's conviction that democracy was on trial in this war. "We must fight," proclaimed an Indianapolis newspaper two weeks after Confederate guns opened fire on Fort Sumter. "We must fight because we *must*. The National Government has been assailed. The Nation has been defied. If either can be done with impunity neither Nation nor Government is worth a cent. . . . War is self preservation, if our form of Government is worth preserving. If monarchy would be better, it might be wise to quit fighting, admit that a Republic is too weak to take care of itself, and invite some deposed Duke or Prince of Europe to come over here and rule us. But otherwise, *we must fight*."[12]

The outbreak of war brought hundreds of thousands of Northern men to recruiting offices. A good many of them expressed a similar sense of democratic mission as a motive for fighting. "I do feel that the liberty of the world is placed in our hands to defend," wrote a Massachusetts soldier to his wife in 1862, "and if we are overcome then farewell to freedom." In 1863, on the second anniversary of his enlistment, an Ohio private wrote in his diary that he had not expected the war to last so long, but no matter how much longer it took, it must be carried on "for the great principles of liberty and self government at stake, for should we fail, the onward march of Liberty in the Old World will be retarded at least a century, and Monarchs, Kings, and Aristocrats will be more powerful against their subjects than ever."[13]

Some foreign-born soldiers appreciated the international impact of the war more intensely than native-born men who took their political rights for granted. A young British immigrant in Philadelphia wrote to his father back in England explaining why he had enlisted in the Union army. "If the Unionists let the South secede," he wrote, "the West might want to separate next Presidential Election. . . . [O]thers might want to follow and this country would be as bad as the German states." Another English-born soldier, a forty-year-old corporal in an Ohio regiment, wrote to his wife in 1864 explaining why he had decided to reenlist for a second three-year hitch. "If I do get hurt I want you to remember that it will be not only for my Country and my Children but for Liberty all over the World that I risked my life, for if Liberty should be crushed here, what hope would there be for the cause of Human Progress anywhere else?" An Irish-born carpenter, a private in the Twenty-eighth Massachusetts Infantry of the famous Irish Brigade, rebuked both his wife in Boston and his father-in-law back in Ireland for questioning his judgment in risking his life for the Union. "This is the first test of a modern free government in the act of sustaining itself against internal enemys," he wrote almost in echo of Lincoln. "If it fails then the hopes of millions fall and the designs and wishes of all tyrants will succeed the old cry will be sent forth from the aristocrats of Europe that such is the common lot of all republics."[14] It is worth noting that both this Irish-born private and the English-born Ohio corporal were killed in action in 1864.

The American sense of mission invoked by Lincoln and by these soldiers—the idea that the American experiment in democracy was a beacon of liberty for oppressed people everywhere—is as old as the Mayflower Compact and as new as the American victory in the Cold War. In our own time, this sentiment sometimes comes across as self-righteous posturing that inspires more resentment than admiration abroad. The same was true in Lincoln's time, when the resentment was expressed mainly by upper-class conservatives, especially in Britain. But many spokesmen for the middle and working classes in Europe echoed the most chauvinistic Yankees. During the debate that produced the British Reform Act of 1832, the London Working Men's Association pronounced "the Republic of America" to be a "beacon of free for all mankind," while a British newspaper named the *Poor Man's Guardian* pointed to American institutions as "the best precedent and guide to the oppressed and enslaved people of England in their struggle for the RIGHT OF REPRESENTATION FOR EVERY MAN."[15]

In the preface to the twelfth edition of his *Democracy in America*, written during the heady days of the 1848 democratic uprisings in Europe, Alexis de Tocqueville urged the leaders of France's newly created Second Republic to study American institutions as a guide to the "approaching irresistible and universal spread of democracy throughout the world." When instead of democracy France got the Second Empire under Napoleon III, the republican opposition to his regime looked to the United States for inspiration. "Many of the suggested reforms," wrote the historian of the French opposition, "would have remained utopic had it not been for the demonstrable existence of the United States and its republican institutions." The existence of the United States remained a thorn in the side of European reactionaries, according to a British radical newspaper, which stated in 1856 that "to the oppressors of Europe, especially those of England, the [United States] is a constant terror, and an everlasting menace," because it stood as "a practical and triumphant refutation of the lying and servile sophists who maintain that without kings and aristocrats, civilized communities cannot exist."[16]

Once the war broke out, some European monarchists and conservatives did indeed make no secret of their hope that the Union would fall into the dustbin of history. The powerful *Times* of London considered the likely down-fall of "the American colossus" a good "riddance of a nightmare.... Excepting a few gentlemen of republican tendencies, we all expect, we nearly all wish, success to the Confederate cause." The Earl of Shrewsbury expressed his cheerful belief "that the dissolution of the Union is inevitable, and that men before me will live to see an aristocracy established in America."[17] In Spain, the royalist journal *Pensamiento Español* found it scarcely surprising that Americans were butchering each other, for the United States, it declared editorially, "was populated by the dregs of all the nations of the world. . . . Such is the real history of the one and only state in the world which has suc-ceeded in constituting itself according to the flaming theories of democracy. The example is too horrible to stir any desire for emulation." The minister to the United States from Czar Alexander II echoed this opinion in 1863. "The republican form of government, so much talked about by the Europeans and so much praised by the Americans, is breaking down," he wrote. "What can be expected from a country where men of humble origin are elevated to the highest positions?" He meant Lincoln, of course. "This is democracy in practice, the democracy that European theorists rave about. If they could only see it at work they would cease their agitation and thank God for the government which they are enjoying."[18]

French republicans, some of them in exile, supported the North as "de-fenders of right and humanity." In England, John Stuart Mill expressed the conviction that the American Civil War "is destined to be a turning point, for good and evil, of the course of human affairs." Confederate success, said Mills, "would be a victory for the powers of evil which would give courage to the enemies of progress and damp the spirits of its friends all over the civilized world."[19]

Clearly, opinion in Europe supported Lincoln's conviction that the very survival of democracy was at stake in the Civil War. But in the first year and a half of the war, the problem of slavery muddied the clarity of this issue. The Confederacy was a slave society, which should have strengthened the Union's image abroad as the champion of liberty and equal rights. As Lincoln put it in a private conversation in January 1862: "I cannot imagine that any European power would dare to recognize and aid the Southern Confederacy if it became clear that the Confederacy stands for slavery and the Union for freedom." The problem was, at that time the Union did not yet stand for the freedom of slaves. Constitutional constraints plus Lincoln's need to keep Northern Democrats and the border slave states in his war coalition inhibited efforts to make it a war against slavery. This restraint puzzled and alienated many potential European friends of the Union cause. An English observer asked in September 1861: Since "the North does not proclaim abolition and never pretended to fight for anti-slavery," how "can we be fairly called upon to sympathize so warmly with the Federal cause?"[20]

Lincoln recognized the validity of this question. In September 1862, he agreed with a delegation of antislavery clergymen that "emancipation would help us in Europe, and convince them that we are incited by something more than ambition." When he said this, Lincoln had made up his mind to issue an emancipation proclamation. The balance of political forces in the North and military forces on the battlefield had shifted just enough to give this decision the impetus of public support. Basing his action on the power of the commander in chief to seize enemy property being used to wage war against the United States—slaves were property and their labor was essential to the Confederate war economy—Lincoln issued a preliminary emancipation proclamation in September 1862 and the final one on January 1, 1863, justifying it as both a "military necessity" and an "act of justice."[21]

The Emancipation Proclamation not only laid the groundwork for the total abolition of slavery in the United States, which was accomplished by the Thirteenth Amendment to the Constitution in 1865, but it also emancipated Lincoln from the contradiction of fighting a war for democratic liberty without fighting a war against slavery. Emancipation deepened Lincoln's sense of history. As he signed the proclamation on that New Year's Day 1863, he said to colleagues who gathered to witness this historic occasion: "I never, in my life, felt more certain that I was doing right than I do in signing this paper. If my name ever goes into history it will be for this act, and my whole soul is in it."[22]

Lincoln here connected the act of emancipation with the future; as he had earlier connected the war for the Union with a past that had given Lincoln's generation the legacy of a united country. Just as the sacrifices of those who had fought for independence and nationhood in 1776 inspired Lincoln and the people he led, their sacrifices in the Civil War would leave a legacy of democracy and freedom to future generations. In his first annual message to Congress—we call it today the State of the Union address—Lincoln declared that "the struggle of today is not altogether for today—it is for a vast future also." Lincoln sent his second annual message to Congress in December 1862, just before he issued the final Emancipation Proclamation. On this occasion, he defined the war's meaning by linking past, present, and future in a passage of unsurpassed eloquence and power. "Fellow-citizens, we cannot escape history," he said. "We of this Congress and this administration, will be remembered in spite of ourselves. . . . The fiery trial through which we pass, will light us down, in honor or dishonor, to the latest generation. . . . We shall nobly save, or meanly lose, the last best, hope of earth. . . . The dogmas of the quiet past, are inadequate to the stormy present. . . . In *giving* freedom to the *slave*, we *assure* freedom to the *free*. . . . We must disenthrall ourselves, and then we shall save our country."[23]

Lincoln's eloquence in this passage was unsurpassed, but he did surpass himself nearly a year later, in the prose poem of 272 words that we know as the Gettysburg Address. In this elegy for Union soldiers killed at the battle of Gettysburg, Lincoln wove together past, present, and future with two other sets of three images each: continent, nation, battlefield, and birth, death, rebirth. The Gettysburg Address is so familiar that, like other things we can recite from memory, its meaning sometimes loses its import. At the risk of destroying the speech's poetic qualities, let us disaggregate these parallel images of past, present, future; continent, nation, battlefield; and birth, death, rebirth. To do this will underscore the meaning of the Civil War not only for Lincoln's time but also for generations into the future, indeed for the new millennium we have recently entered.

Four score and seven years in the *past*, said Lincoln, our fathers *brought forth* on this *continent* a *nation* conceived in liberty. *Today*, he continued, our generation faces a great test whether a nation so conceived can survive. In dedicating the cemetery on this *battlefield*, the living must take inspiration to finish the task that those who lie buried here "so nobly advanced" by giving their "last full measure of devotion." Life and *death* in this passage have a paradoxical but metaphorical relationship: men died that the nation might live, yet metaphorically the old Union also died, and with it would die the institution of slavery. After these deaths, the nation must have a *"new birth* of freedom" so that the government of, by, and for the people that our fathers conceived and brought forth in the past "shall not perish from the earth" but live into the vast *future*, even unto the next millennium.

Although Lincoln gave this address at the dedication of a cemetery, its rhetoric was secular. As the war went on, however, Lincoln's efforts to come to grips with the mounting toll of death, destruction, and suffering became more infused with religious inquiry. Perhaps God was punishing Americans with "this terrible war" for some great sin. By the time of his inauguration for a second term, Lincoln believed he had identified that sin. "Fondly do we hope—fervently do we pray—that this mighty scourge of war may speedily pass away," said Lincoln in his second inaugural address. "Yet, if God wills that it continue, until all the wealth piled by the bond-man's two hundred and fifty years of unrequited toil shall be sunk, and until every drop of blood drawn with the lash, shall be paid by another drawn with the sword, as was said three thousand years ago, so still it must be said 'the judgments of the Lord, are true and righteous altogether.'"[24]

Fortunately, the war lasted only another few weeks after Lincoln's second inauguration. In this new millennium, we may well wonder if we are still paying for the blood drawn with the lash of slavery. But the impact abroad of Union victory was almost immediate. In Britain, a disgruntled Tory member of Parliament expressed disappointment that the Union had not broken in "two or perhaps more fragments," for he considered the United States "a menace to the whole civilized world." A Tory colleague described this menace as "the beginning of an Americanizing process in England. The new Democratic ideas are gradually to find embodiment." Indeed they were. In 1865, a liberal political economist at University College London, Edward Beesly, who wanted the expansion of voting rights in Britain, pointed out the moral of Union victory across the Atlantic. "Our opponents told us that Republicanism was on trial" in the American Civil War, said Beesly. "They told us that it was forever discredited in England. Well, we accepted the challenge. We staked our hopes boldly on the result.... Under a strain such as no aristocracy, no monarchy, no empire could have supported, Republican institutions have stood firm. It is we, now, who call upon the privileged classes to mark the result.... A vast impetus has been given to Republican sentiments in England."[25]

Queen Victoria's throne was safe. But a two-year debate in Parliament, in which the American example figured prominently, led to enactment of the Reform Bill of 1867, which nearly doubled the eligible electorate and enfranchised a large part of the British working class for the first time. With this act, the world's most powerful nation took a long stride toward democracy. What might have happened to the Reform Bill if the North had lost the Civil War, thereby confounding liberals and confirming Tory opinions of democracy, is impossible to say.

The end of slavery in the re-United States sounded the death knell of the institution in Brazil and Cuba, the only other places in the Western Hemisphere where it still existed. Commending the Brazilian government's first steps toward abolition of slavery in 1871, an abolitionist in that country was glad, as he put it, "to see Brazil receive so quickly the moral of the Civil War in the United States."[26]

Even without Northern victory in the war, slavery in the United States, Brazil, and Cuba would have been unlikely to survive into the next millennium. But it might well have survived into the next century. And without the Fourteenth and Fifteenth Amendments to the U.S. Constitution, which, like the Thirteenth, were a direct consequence of the war and which granted equal civil and political rights to African Americans, the United States might have developed into even more of an apartheid society in the twentieth century than it did.

These amendments consummated a new interpretation of liberty in the American polity, an interpretation that may be the most important legacy of the Civil War for the new millennium. Lincoln played a crucial role in the evolution of this new concept of liberty. In April 1864, he chose the occasion of a public speech in Baltimore to define the difference between two meanings of this word that is so central to America's understanding of itself. "The world has never had a *good* definition of the word liberty," Lincoln declared in that state of Maryland, which still had slavery but was about to abolish it. "We all declare for liberty, but in using the same *word* we do not mean the same *thing*. With some the word liberty may mean for each man to do as he pleases with himself, and the product of his labor; while with others the same may mean for some men to do as they please with other men, and the product of other men's labor. Here are two, not only different, but incompatible things, called by the same name—liberty." As he often did, Lincoln went on to illustrate his point with a parable. One of the first books he had read as a child was *Aesop's Fables*, and throughout his life Lincoln told apparently simple stories about animals to make subtle and profound points about important matters. "The shepherd drives the wolf from the sheep's throat," he said, "for which the sheep thanks the shepherd as a *liberator*, while the wolf denounces him for the same act as a destroyer of liberty, especially as the sheep is a black one. Plainly the sheep and the wolf are not agreed upon a definition of the word liberty; and precisely the same difference prevails to-day among us human creatures, even in the North, and all professing to love liberty. Hence we behold the processes by which thousands are daily passing from under the yoke of bondage, hailed by some as the advance of liberty, and bewailed by others as the destruction of all liberty."[27]

The shepherd in this fable was, of course, Lincoln himself; the black sheep was the slave; and the wolf was the slave's owner. The point of the fable was similar to a barbed comment Lincoln had made a decade earlier about Southern rhetoric professing a love of liberty. "The perfect liberty they sight for," said Lincoln on that occasion, "is the liberty of making slaves of other people."[28]

More suitably, Lincoln in this parable was drawing a distinction between what philosopher Isaiah Berlin described as "negative liberty" and "positive liberty."[29] The concept of negative liberty is perhaps more familiar. It can be defined as the absence of restraint, a freedom from interference by outside authority with individual thought or behavior. Laws requiring automobile passengers to wear seatbelts or motorcyclists to wear helmets are a violation of their liberty to go without seatbelts or helmets. Negative liberty, therefore, is best described as freedom *from*. Positive liberty can be defined as freedom *to*—freedom to live longer and better because wearing a seatbelt or helmet has saved one from death or injury.

The example of freedom of the press perhaps provides a better illustration. This freedom is usually understood as a negative liberty—freedom from interference with what a writer writes or a reader reads. But an illiterate person suffers from a denial of positive liberty. He is unable to enjoy the freedom to read or write whatever he pleases, not because some authority prevents him from doing so but because he cannot read or write anything. The remedy lies not in removal of restraint but in achievement of the capacity to read and write—positive liberty.

Another way of defining the difference between these two concepts of liberty is to describe their relation to power. Negative liberty and power are at opposite poles; power is the enemy of liberty, especially power in the hands of a central government. Negative liberty was the preeminent concern of Americans in the eighteenth and first half of the nineteenth centuries. Many feared the federal government as the main threat to individual liberty; some still do today. Americans fought their Revolution against the overweening power of King and Parliament. In the Constitution, they fragmented power among the three branches of the federal government, between the two houses of Congress, and between the national and state governments. But even this was not enough, in James Madison's words, to prevent the "tendency in all Governments to an augmentation of power at the expense of liberty."[30] So the founders wrote a Bill of Rights that, in the first ten amendments to the Constitution, imposed limits on the power of the federal government.

Throughout early American history, political leaders remained vigilant against concentrations of power. Andrew Jackson vetoed the charter renewal of the Second Bank of the United States in 1832 because, he said, such a combination of private wealth and government power would cause "our liberties to be crushed." In 1854, the famous reformer of mental hospitals, Dorothea Dix, persuaded Congress to pass a bill granting public lands to the states to subsidize improved facilities for the mentally ill. President Franklin Pierce vetoed the bill because, he wrote in his veto message, if Congress could enact such a law, "it has the power to provide for the indigent who are not insane, and thus . . . the whole field of public beneficence is thrown open to the care and culture of the Federal Government." This would mean "all sovereignty vested in an absolute consolidated central power, against which the spirit of liberty has so often and in so many countries struggled in vain." Therefore, a law to improve mental hospitals, concluded Pierce, would be "the beginning of the end . . . of our blessed inheritance of representative liberty."[31]

Owners of slaves also relied on this bulwark of negative liberty to defend their right of property in human beings. John C. Calhoun and other Southern political leaders constructed an elaborate structure of state sovereignty and limitations on national power. No exercise of federal power escaped the censure of these proslavery libertarians. As Senator Nathaniel Macon of North

Carolina explained: "If Congress can make banks, roads, and canals under the Constitution, they can free any slave in the United States."[32]

The ultimate manifestation of negative liberty was secession. Southern states left the Union in 1861 because they feared that sometime in the future, the growing Northern antislavery majority embodied in the Republican Party would exercise its power to free the slaves—a form of positive liberty that might even go so far as to empower them to read and write, to vote, and to aspire to equality with whites, a truly frightening scenario of positive liberty. Yet ironically, by seceding and provoking a war, Southern whites hastened the very achievement of positive liberty they had gone to war to prevent. By 1864, when Lincoln told his parable about the shepherd protecting the black sheep from the wolf, that shepherd wielded a very big staff as commander in chief of the largest army yet known in the United States. It took every ounce of this power to accomplish the "new birth of freedom" that Lincoln invoked at Gettysburg.

Tragically, Lincoln did not live to oversee advancement toward that goal. His earlier definition of equality as a "maxim for free society . . . constantly labored for . . . even though never perfectly attained . . . and thereby constantly spreading and deepening its influence, and augmenting the happiness and value of life to all people of all colors" suggests the policies of positive liberty he would have pursued had he lived. But at Ford's Theatre, John Wilkes Booth ended that possibility as he shouted Virginia's state motto, "sic semper tyrannis" (thus always to tyrants)—the slogan of negative liberty.

But Lincoln's party carried on the tradition of positive liberty with its efforts to legislate and enforce equal civil rights, voting rights, and education during Reconstruction. As Republican congressman George Julian noted in 1867, the only way to achieve "justice and equality . . . for the freedmen of the South" was by "the strong arm of *power*, outstretched from the central authority here in Washington." Or as Congressman James Garfield, a future Republican president, also put it in 1867, "We must plant the heavy hand of . . . authority upon these rebel communities, and . . . plant liberty on the ruins of slavery."[33]

That is what the Thirteenth, Fourteenth, and Fifteenth Amendments to the Constitution tried to do. These amendments radically transformed the thrust of the Constitution from negative to positive liberty. Instead of the straitjacket of "thou shalt nots" imposed on the federal government by the Bill of Rights, the Civil War amendments established a precedent whereby nine of the next fourteen Constitutional amendments contained the phrase "Congress shall have the *power*" to enforce the provisions. Lincoln himself set this precedent by helping to draft the Thirteenth Amendment, which was the centerpiece of the platform on which he was reelected in 1864.

Lincoln's party continued its commitment to positive liberty at least through the presidency of Theodore Roosevelt. In the twentieth century, however, the two major parties gradually reversed positions. The Democratic Party, once the bastion of negative liberty, states' rights, and limited government, donned the mantle of positive liberty, while most Republicans invoked the mantra of negative liberty. How these matters will play out in the new millennium remains to be seen. But whatever happens, Lincoln's legacy of one nation, indivisible, with freedom for four million slaves and their descendants seems likely to persist far into the millennium.

A few years ago, the Huntington Library sponsored an essay contest on Lincoln for high school students in connection with its major Lincoln exhibit. One of the finalists was a seventeen-year-old girl from Texas, whose forebears had immigrated to the United States from India. She wrote that "if the United States was not in existence today, I would not have the opportunity to excel in life and education. The Union was preserved, not only for the people yesterday, but also for the lives of today."[34]

Lincoln would surely have applauded this statement. In 1861, he said that the struggle for the Union involved not only "the fate of these United States" but also that of "the whole family of man."[35] It was a struggle "not altogether for today" but "for a vast future also." We are living in that vast future. Lincoln's words resonate in the twenty-first century with as much relevance as they did seven score years ago.

NOTES

1. All quoted in Merrill D. Peterson, *Lincoln and American Memory* (New York: Oxford University Press, 1994), 185, 342n.

2. Ibid., 355–56.

3. *The Collected Works of Abraham Lincoln*, ed. Roy P. Basler, 9 vols. (New Brunswick, N.J.: Rutgers University Press, 1953–55), 5:53. Hereafter *CWL*.

4. Ibid., 5:235–36.

5. Ibid., 4:236.

6. Ibid., 240.

7. Ibid., 2:255.

8. Ibid., 405–6.

9. Ibid., 3:376.

10. Ibid., 4:268; Michael Burlingame and John R. Turner Ettlinger, eds., *Inside Lincoln's White House: The Complete Civil War Diary of John Hay* (Carbondale: Southern Illinois University Press, 1997), 20.

11. *CWL*, 4:439.

12. *Indianapolis Daily Journal*, April 27, 1861.

13. Josiah Perry to Phebe Perry, October 3, 1862, Josiah Perry Papers, Illinois State Historical Library, Springfield; Robert T. McMahan diary, entry of September 3, 1863, State Historical Society of Missouri, Columbia.

14. Titus Crenshaw to father, November 10, 1861, in Charlotte Erickson, *Invisible Immigrants: The Adaptation of English and Scottish Immigrants in Nineteenth Century America* (Coral Gables: University of Miami Press, 1972), 348; George H. Cadman to Esther Cadman, March 6, 1864, Cadman Papers, Southern Historical Collection, University of North Carolina, Chapel Hill; Peter Welsh to Mary Welsh, February 3, 1863, and Peter Walsh to Patrick Prendergast, June 1, 1863, in *Irish Green and Union Blue: The Civil War Letters of Peter Welsh*, ed. Laurence Frederick Kohl and Margaret Cosee Richard (New York: Fordham University Press, 1986), 65–66, 102.

15. Quoted in G. D. Lillibridge, *Beacon of Freedom: The Impact of American Democracy upon Great Britain 1830–1870* (Philadelphia: University of Pennsylvania Press, 1955), 5, 28.

16. Alexis de Tocqueville, *Democracy in America*, 12th ed., trans. George Lawrence, ed. J. P. Mayer (New York: Harper and Row, 1966), xiii; Serge Gavronsky, *The French Liberal Opposition and the American Civil War* (New York: Humanities Press, 1968); Lillibridge, *Beacon of Freedom*, 80.

17. *Times* quoted in Frank L. Owsley, *King Cotton Diplomacy: Foreign Relations of the Confederate States of America*, 2nd ed., rev. by Harriet C. Owsley (Chicago: University of Chicago Press, 1959), 186; Earl of Shrewsbury quoted in Ephraim D. Adams, *Great Britain and the American Civil War*, 2 vols. (New York: Russell and Russell, 1925), 2:282.

18. *Pensamiento Español*, September 1862, quoted in Belle Becker Sideman and Lillian Friedman, eds., *Europe Looks at the Civil War* (New York: Orion Press, 1960), 173–74; Eduard de Stoeckl quoted in Albert A. Woldman, *Lincoln and the Russians* (Cleveland: World Publishing, 1952), 216–17.

19. *Revue des Deux Mondes*, August 15, 1861, and John Stuart Mill, *Autobiography*, both quoted in Sideman and Friedman, *Europe Looks at the Civil War*, 81, 117–18.

20. Lincoln quoted in *The Reminiscences of Carl Schurz*, 3 vols. (New York: McClure, 1907–8), 2:309; *Saturday Review*, September 14, 1861, quoted in Adams, *Great Britain and the American Civil War*, 1:181; *Economist*, September 1861, quoted in Karl Marx and Friedrich Engels, *The Civil War in the United States*, ed. Richard Enmale (New York: International Publishers, 1937), 12.

21. *CWL*, 5:423, 6:30.

22. Quoted in Frederick W. Seward, *Seward at Washington as Senator and Secretary of State* (New York: Derby and Miller, 1891), 151.

23. *CWL*, 5:53, 537.

24. Ibid., 8:333.

25. Sir Edward Bulwer-Lytton to John Bigelow, April 2, 1865, quoted in Sideman and Friedman, *Europe Looks at the Civil War*, 282; Beesly quoted in Harold M. Hyman, ed., *Heard Round the World: The Impact Abroad of the Civil War* (New York: Alfred A. Knopf, 1969), xi, 73.

26. Quoted in Hyman, *Heard Round the World*, 323.

27. *CWL*, 7:301–2.

28. Ibid., 2:250.

29. Isaiah Berlin, *Four Essays on Liberty* (New York: Oxford University Press, 1974), 118–72.

30. Quoted in Gordon S. Wood, *The Creation of the American Republic, 1776–1787* (Chapel Hill: University of North Carolina Press, 1969), 413.

31. Jackson quoted in Robert Remini, *Andrew Jackson and the Bank War* (New York: Norton, 1967), 45; Pierce quoted in James D. Richardson, comp., *Messages and Papers of the Presidents*, 20 vols. (Washington, D.C.: Government Printing Office, 1897), 2780–84.

32. Quoted in Norman K. Risjord, *The Old Republicans: Southern Conservatism in the Age of Jefferson* (New York: Columbia University Press, 1965), 242.

33. *Congressional Globe*, 39th Cong., 2nd sess., January 28, 1867, appendix, 78; *The Works of James Abram Garfield*, ed. Burke A. Hinsdale, 2 vols. (Boston: J. R. Osgood, 1882), 1:249.

34. Reena Mathew, "One Set of Footprints," essay in author's possession.

35. *CWL*, 4:426.

Lincoln and African American Memory

A mericans have long held a passionate interest in and warm regard for Abraham Lincoln. The vast array of books written about him, the frequency with which he is quoted by politicians, and the invoking of his name to sell goods and services exceed the degree of attention given to other men and women of national stature. Of course, it is characteristically American to transform mere mortals into mythic figures, but the national fascination with Lincoln transcends typical hero-worship.

The extent of America's devotion to Lincoln became apparent to me about ten years ago when C-SPAN televised the reenactment of the 1858 senatorial debates between Lincoln and Illinois incumbent Stephen A. Douglas. The telecasts drew large viewing audiences and attracted scores to the seven cities where the reenactments took place. The call-in questions suggested that our sixteenth president, if not equally popular north and south, at least engendered respect throughout the nation. Lincoln garnered similar interest a few years later when C-SPAN hosted the American Presidents Series. When Americans ranked the presidential administrations, it surprised few that Lincoln was favored above the rest.

These telecasts also revealed the extent of the differences between the way white Americans and black Americans remember Lincoln. Not only were African Americans under-represented at the various reenactment sites, but few called into either of the programs, and those who did offered a perspective that was somewhat less celebratory than other viewers. Moreover, their questions tended to focus on Lincoln's views on race, especially on his assessment of black intellectual capacity and fitness for social and political equality.

While I was struck by this obvious racial divide, it did not come as a complete surprise. As an African American child growing up in rural, segregated southeastern Virginia in the 1960s, I had been introduced to the story of Lincoln the "Great Emancipator," but the lesson was without context, except for the simplistic statement that he "freed the slaves." Nor was there a tradition in my community of recognizing Lincoln as a "special friend to the race." To us, he was an American president—doubtless better than most—but not sufficiently different to elicit hero-worship. If we regarded any president as an icon, it was John Kennedy, whom many in my community felt had been assassinated because of a perceived commitment to black equality. His picture and that of Mrs. Kennedy were the only white faces that adorned the walls of my childhood home.

Not until I went off to college did I acquire a greater understanding of Lincoln's significance, but even then, it was primarily in the context of African American history rather than as a figure in the national historical drama. Later, when I entered graduate school, my Lincoln "lessons" dealt primarily with his role in leading and preserving the nation during a devastating civil war, with lesser emphasis on his involvement in shaping the African American experience. It was as though scholars needed to compartmentalize him in order to make sense of his life and his impact on the nation's history.

The tendency is understandable. Any attempt to comprehend the multidimensional Lincoln poses a bit of a challenge. He is no simple historical figure that we can easily categorize. His life, motivations, and actions were complex, often contradictory, and, consequently, controversial. As such, he gives both scholars and Americans in general leave to conclude what they will. Depending on one's perspective, he is sainted or villainous, compassionate or insensitive, pragmatic or idealistic. Rarely is he viewed in shades of gray. And more than any other historical figure, our image of Lincoln is shaped by how we perceive the nation and, concomitantly, our place in it. He symbolizes America's possibilities and its failures, its promise as well as its disappointments. He is so thoroughly recognized as the embodiment of the American character that it is far easier to favor that aspect of the man that confirms our own views of either a noble or shameful nation.

For African Americans, the challenge of understanding Lincoln in his entirety is even greater. One is expected to honor (unconditionally) the memory of the man who historically has been credited with nearly single-handedly ending slavery and, by implication, securing the birthright of future generations of African Americans. And one invites stinging criticism for offering an interpretation of him that challenges the traditional view. After an appearance on a broadcast in which I critiqued Lincoln's early wartime policies of appeasement of the Southern secessionists, an anonymous woman who identified herself only as a person of English birth wrote an especially memorable letter to me. In it she wondered how I could be "so ungrateful when Mr. Lincoln freed" me. Other responses to my "take" on Lincoln have been decidedly less genteel.

My English-born critic failed to understand that one can question Lincoln's motivations and actions without suggesting the extreme position that he is unworthy of respect and acclaim. In fact, many non-black scholars have done just that over the last several decades and have continued to enjoy the respect of their colleagues.[1] Critical assessments from African American scholars have not always met with the same tolerance. Even the suggestion that enslaved people may have played a prominent role in their own liberation has invited an intense debate in recent years, with certain scholars hastening to defend Lincoln's position as the "Great Emancipator."[2] The intensity of that defense has helped to spawn the unfounded suggestion that Lincoln's actions were intended to preserve rather than tear down the institution of slavery.[3] In general, however, blacks simply eschew the debate and absent themselves from associations devoted to the study of Lincoln and from Civil War roundtables as if neither has anything to do with African Americans and their history.[4] I long ago became accustomed to being one of very few African Americans (and frequently the only black woman) present at Lincoln conferences and associations.

My own views of Lincoln have been shaped within the context of these realities. Generally, I have advocated a more nuanced consideration of his role in emancipation and greater attention to the participation of others (including African Americans themselves) in the effort to secure black freedom.[5] Such inquiry neither endangers Lincoln's place in history nor challenges his claim to the honor that Americans have bestowed upon him. Instead, it enhances our understanding of who he was and how he faced the extraordinary challenges of his era.

Perhaps the most significant thing I have learned as a consequence of my study of Lincoln is that he was both a man of his era and one who transcended its most loathsome characteristics. Mid-nineteenth-century America was a place of contradictions and inconsistencies. Americans celebrated democratic values while withholding the franchise from certain segments of the population; they praised rugged individualism but were afraid to venture too far ahead of public opinion; and they espoused a belief in the Declaration of Independence's creed that "all men are created equal" while exhibiting racial intolerance and sanctioning discrimination. In the decade when Lincoln was coming of age, the nation had divested thousands of Native Americans of their lands and demanded their relocation to areas of the country not yet coveted by white men. And even those Americans who detested the South's "peculiar institution" accepted the notion of inherent black inferiority. The North was, as Alexis de Tocqueville observed, as anti-black as the South, if not more so.[6]

For the most part, Lincoln lived comfortably in this environment. He was not an advocate of universal suffrage. Nor did he earn a reputation for taking risks in controversial matters; pragmatism usually guided his actions. And he deemed African Americans intellectually inferior to whites and acceptable subjects for jokes and entertaining stories.

Yet, Lincoln distinguished himself from many of his peers in the degree of his commitment to equality of opportunity. Perhaps influenced by his own humble beginnings, he believed that each individual had the right to the full enjoyment of whatever was acquired by his or her own hands. Hence, slavery was unjust, as was exploitation of the common free laborer.

Coming to terms with this complex man requires no small degree of tolerance, especially for an African American. To us (if I may be so presumptuous as to speak for black people in general, and with the caveat that African Americans are not monolithic in our thinking), Lincoln's inconsistencies are hardly inconsequential or easily explained away. For instance, in 1841, he defended a man accused of reneging on a promissory note involving the sale of a black woman. In *Bailey v. Cromwell,* Lincoln argued successfully that the woman, Nance, was, in fact, free.[7] And in 1857, he intervened on behalf of the luckless John Shelby, a young black man who was caught on the streets of New Orleans without his freedom papers. When Lincoln's appeals to the governor of Illinois proved futile, he assisted in raising funds that secured the man's release.[8] But Lincoln also provided legal representation to a slaveholder, Robert Matson, who sought the return of his runaway property—a family of six, including four children.[9] In the Matson case, he sided with property rights over human rights and in so doing had supported the claims of those who sought to deny the humanity of enslaved people.

As a politician, however, Lincoln had distinguished himself in his arguments against slavery. No abolitionist before the war began, he preferred instead to oppose any attempt at extension of the institution, believing that once contained, it would die a natural death. Hence, he argued against the Kansas-Nebraska Act and the *Dred Scott* decision, both of which threatened to expose heretofore free areas to slavery. And during the Lincoln-Douglas debates, he argued against the institution on moral as well as economic grounds.

With the coming of war, Lincoln's position on slavery did not change as much as it became subsumed under his efforts to preserve the Union. He entered the presidency determined to end the war quickly and reunite the fractured nation through pursuit of a policy of appeasement. This entailed, among other things, a pledge to uphold the laws of the land, even in the states in secession, and to ensure noninterference with domestic institutions, including slavery. This conciliatory posture challenged the ability of black people to seize their freedom and imperiled the lives of those runaways who were returned by Union commanders to their owners, especially to those who were in rebellion against the nation. Congressional measures and the actions of certain commanders in the field served to erode this policy, but the practice did not stop until the spring of 1862 when Congress passed legislation that made it illegal to return fugitives from slavery.

Nor did Lincoln embrace congressional attacks on slavery with much enthusiasm. Both the First and Second Confiscation Acts distressed him, and when Congress abolished slavery in the District of Columbia, he delayed signing the bill into law for six days. Lincoln scholars have noted that such reluctance was guided by his belief in constitutional guarantees in regard to private property and by his belief that any aggressive move on slavery would risk the loyalty of the slave-holding border states. Yet, no similar constitutional or practical concerns seem to have dissuaded him from supporting the denial of civil liberties to certain individuals suspected of engaging in treasonous actions.[10]

Lincoln's initial position on the recruitment and enlistment of black troops has been similarly criticized by African Americans. Having determined that the war's only aim was to save the Union, he rejected the notion of black participation as fighting men. While he welcomed their use in the erecting of breastworks and as cooks and teamsters, he understood that public opinion was against their soldiering in defense of the nation. Moreover, Lincoln doubted that black soldiers could successfully engage white men on the field of battle. He suggested that Union arms might fall into the hands of the enemy because of black cowardice.[11] Military necessity and diplomatic considerations, however, convinced him to permit black men the opportunity to serve. Their performance won Lincoln's respect and confirmed his prediction in 1863 that once peace had been restored, "there will be some black men who can remember that, with silent tongue, and clenched teeth, and steady eye, and well poised bayonet, they have helped mankind on to this great consummation; while . . . there will be some white ones, unable to forget that, with malignant heart and deceitful speech, they have strove to hinder it."[12]

No thornier issue shapes African American memory concerning Lincoln than the one involving colonization. In a speech at Peoria, Illinois, in 1854, he had pondered what he might do with slavery had he the power to determine its future. "My first impulse would be to free all the slaves, and send them to Liberia,—to their own native land," he had indicated, but quickly noted the impracticality of doing that.[13] By the second year of the war, however, trying to find a way to rid the country of slavery and to ensure whites that they would not be overrun by freed blacks, Lincoln was prepared to consider colonization again. He first convinced Congress to appropriate funds for such a venture as part of its larger effort to provide aid to compensate owners in those border states that agreed to abolish slavery. Despite a lack of interest on the part of those states to emancipate, Lincoln proceeded with his plans. He invited a small group of black men, later known as the Committee of Five, to the White House in August 1862 and there attempted to convince them of the reasonableness of his views. The men were then encouraged to return to the black community where they were to persuade their people to depart these shores. Most African Americans remained unconvinced, as they had when the American Colonization Society implemented a relocation program in the half century before the Civil War.[14] A group was sent to Ile à Vache, Haiti, in April 1863, but the scheme met with disaster because of disease and ill-planning on the part of the expedition's white organizers.[15]

In addressing the Committee of Five, Lincoln had suggested that blacks could not hope to gain equality with whites. It was an opinion of long standing, informed by his understanding of his own people as much as it was an indictment of African Americans' social and intellectual capacity. He tactlessly told the men that they and their people were the cause of the war, that both races suffered from the presence of the other, and that the only remedy was separation. "[E]ven when you cease to be slaves," he argued, "you are yet far removed from being placed on an equality with the white race. . . . [O]n this broad continent, not a single man of your race is made the equal of a single man of ours. Go where you are treated the best, and the ban is still upon you."[16] He hinted that Central America, where they could mine coal, might be an ideal site to plant a colony.[17]

Yet, as Benjamin Quarles pointed out decades ago in his still popular study of the president's relationship with African Americans, Lincoln's own political actions and his personal interactions with blacks gave them encouragement that full inclusion in American society might be an attainable goal. He received blacks as visitors to the White House, permitted them access to the mansion grounds for picnics and special observances, and favored certain individuals with special attention. Among his black visitors were the Reverend Daniel A. Payne, bishop of the African Methodist Episcopal Church; Sojourner Truth, a former slave who had spent much of her adult life crusading for freedom; a group of Baltimore ministers, who presented him with a Bible as token of their appreciation for the issuing of the Emancipation Proclamation; the black colonizationist Martin Delany; and the ubiquitous Frederick Douglass. Douglass visited Lincoln in the White House on three occasions, the first time to appeal directly for equal treatment for black soldiers, and the last at the second inaugural ball. Douglass was impressed by Lincoln's reception of him, suggesting that the president greeted him "just as you have seen one gentleman receive another; with a hand and a voice well balanced between a kind cordiality and a respectful reserve."[18] By all accounts, Lincoln treated other people of color with equal dignity and humanity.

Lincoln also won the appreciation of the black community by encouraging the establishment of diplomatic relations with the Haitian and Liberian governments. Haiti's mere existence evoked fear and loathing in some

Americans, as the nation had been founded through slave insurrection. The only black republic in Africa in the nineteenth century, Liberia had been established through the efforts of the American Colonization Society, but heretofore it had not been recognized by official Washington. Lincoln foresaw the potential for trade relationships and hence encouraged association with both nations.[19]

Of course, it was Lincoln's issuing of the Emancipation Proclamation that most endeared the bondman and bondwoman to him. Whichever side one takes in the debate over his deserving the title "Great Emancipator," most would agree that his actions in issuing the decree had a profound impact on the quest for black freedom. While it did indeed have serious limitations, it encouraged black men and women in the effort at self-liberation that they had undertaken from the very beginning of the conflict. Fugitives who had been uncertain of their status when they reached Union lines were now confident that they were free forever.

Free blacks in the North and South had their own reasons for embracing the Emancipation Proclamation. In addition to recognizing its significance for the enslaved, free people of color believed it would transform their own lives as well. They perceived the document as a promise of equality and full citizenship, a guarantee of social justice and economic opportunity. A measure freeing the slaves, they knew, would elevate their own existence.

In the final weeks of his life, Lincoln strengthened his hold on the affections of African Americans. In the address that opened his second term in office, he acknowledged slavery's centrality as the cause of war and the equal complicity of the North and South in the institution's existence. Praying for a speedy end to the war, he nevertheless pledged the nation to fight on until victory was achieved, even if it meant that "all the wealth piled by the bondman's two hundred and fifty years of unrequited toil shall be sunk, and until every drop of blood drawn with the lash, shall be paid by another drawn with the sword."[20] In his last public address on April 11, 1865, Lincoln encouraged the acceptance of the new Louisiana constitution and the readmission of the state into the Union. He was especially pleased with the state's decision to ratify the Thirteenth Amendment and with its efforts to make public school education available to all. However, the matter of the elective franchise was not resolved as Lincoln had wished. In a letter to Louisiana governor Michael Hahn in 1864, Lincoln had privately encouraged granting the vote to certain groups of African Americans—those he considered "the very intelligent" and the soldiers who had aided the Union cause.[21] The new constitution simply empowered the legislature to confer voting rights on black men at some future date. Lincoln now publicly acknowledged his preference. Conceding the limitations in Louisiana's constitution, he argued, however, that it was better to accept it rather than condemn African Americans to an even more uncertain future.[22] The best way to extend rights to black men would be to restore the state to its "practical proper relation" to the Union.

In advocating political rights for any African Americans at all, Lincoln had moved far beyond his stance in 1858 when he had debated the issue with Stephen Douglas. At that time, pragmatism had prevailed. Knowing that few in the audience at Charleston would support the extension of rights to African Americans, Lincoln had declared that he was not "nor ever have been in favor of bringing about in any way the social and political equality of the white and black races . . . nor ever have been in favor of making voters or jurors of negroes."[23] Political realities (and doubtless, personal preferences) did not permit him, even in 1865, to embrace universal suffrage, but his concession to soldiers and elite blacks suggests that he had begun to move forward on the issue of civil rights. One could wish that this growth had come sooner or was more sweeping, but that was not Lincoln's way.

For decades after the war ended, yearly celebrations were held that commemorated the issuing of the Emancipation Proclamation. African Americans used such gatherings as an opportunity to renew their commitment to the struggle for social justice and to remind the nation that Lincoln had confirmed their right to full citizenship through his proclamation of freedom. The perceived promise of the document sustained them for several generations, but the legacy of slavery eventually led to disillusionment and abandonment of the idea that the Emancipation Proclamation would enable them to secure their rights.

Emancipation celebrations that focused on the issuing of the proclamation have long ago lost their attraction in the African American community. Today, when blacks do celebrate freedom, they do so through an appropriated Texas observance, "Juneteenth," which commemorates the date in 1865 in which enslaved people belatedly learned of their freedom in certain sections of that state. Concomitantly, reverence for Lincoln has diminished in proportion to the widening disinterest in his proclamation. One hardly recognizes the man whom freedpeople nearly worshiped.

Lincoln's evolving image in the African American community also reflects the logical consequence of a more sophisticated understanding of his complexity and an abandonment of sentimentality. Over the last several years of teaching, I have been impressed with the ability (and the willingness) of my students both to critique Lincoln's motivations for issuing the proclamation and to recognize the larger concerns with which he struggled in his conducting of the war. Moreover, African Americans have experienced a swelling pride and admiration for their Civil War–era antecedents. Awareness of the valor of black military men (their sacrifice both on and off the battlefield) and the agitation for freedom sustained by black leaders in pulpit and press have permitted African Americans to understand better the contributions of their own to the cause of the Union and emancipation.

Had Lincoln been one-dimensional, the task of the scholar would be easier. But it is the dichotomy between pragmatic politician and idealist that makes him so fascinating to us today. As W. E. B. Du Bois reminded us in his observance of Lincoln's birthday in the 1920s, flawless historical figures serve us poorly; in the end, we are left with "not the real man, but the tradition of the man—remote, immense, perfect, cold and dead!"[24] In assessing Lincoln's strengths and foibles, we achieve a better understanding of his greatness, and we begin to appreciate the extent of the journey undertaken in its attainment.

NOTES

1. See, for example, David Herbert Donald, *Lincoln Reconsidered: Essays on the Civil War Era* (New York: Knopf, 1956), and more recently his highly regarded *Lincoln* (New York: Simon and Schuster, 1995).

2. James McPherson, *Drawn with the Sword: Reflections on the American Civil War* (New York: Oxford University Press, 1996). See also Allen Guelzo, *Lincoln's Emancipation Proclamation: The End of Slavery in America* (New York: Simon and Schuster, 2004). Among those who have challenged the notion that Lincoln deserves the credit for emancipation and who argue for the consideration of the role of African Americans themselves is Barbara Jeanne Fields, "Who Freed the Slaves?" in *The Civil War: An Illustrated History,* ed. Geoffrey C. Ward, with Ric Burns and Ken Burns (New York: Knopf, 1990), 178–81; and Vincent Harding, *There Is a River: The Black Struggle for Freedom in America* (New York: Vintage Books, 1981), 231–37.

3. Lerone Bennett has suggested that Lincoln would have preferred that African Americans remain enslaved into the twentieth century. See *Forced into Glory: Abraham Lincoln's White Dream* (Chicago: Johnson Publishing, 2000).

4. I am reminded of an encounter with a young black woman a few years ago at the Civil War Institute in Gettysburg. She expressed her pleasure in finding me in attendance because her interest in Lincoln and the Civil War was not always understood by her peers and relatives.

5. See Edna Greene Medford, "Imagined Promises, Bitter Realities: African Americans and the Meaning of the Emancipation Proclamation," in *The Emancipation Proclamation: Three Views,* ed. Harold Holzer, Edna Greene Medford, and Frank J. Williams (Baton Rouge: Louisiana State University Press, 2006), 1–47.

6. Alexis de Tocqueville, *Democracy in America* (the Henry Reeve text, revised by Francis Bowen, further corrected and edited with introduction, editorial notes, and bibliographies by Phillips Bradley), 2 vols. (New York: Alfred A. Knopf, 1963), 1:359. Tocqueville had written that "the prejudice of race appears to be stronger in the states that abolished slavery than in those where it still exists; and nowhere is it so intolerant as in those states where servitude has never been known."

7. See Benjamin Quarles, *Lincoln and the Negro* (New York: Da Capo Press, 1991), 21–22.

8. Ibid., 22–23.

9. Ibid., 23–35.

10. In this instance, Lincoln argued military necessity, as he later would in issuing the Emancipation Proclamation. He suggested that as commander in chief, he had the authority to suspend the writ of habeas corpus in time of war. For a sympathetic discussion of the use of this power, see Mark Neely, *The Fate of Liberty: Abraham Lincoln and Civil Liberties* (New York: Oxford University Press, 1991).

11. "Reply to Emancipation Memorial Presented by Chicago Christians of All Denominations," in *The Collected Works of Abraham Lincoln*, ed. Roy P. Basler, 9 vols. (New Brunswick, N.J.: Rutgers University Press, 1953–55), 5:423.

12. Lincoln to James C. Conkling, August 26, 1863, in *Abraham Lincoln: His Speeches and Writings*, ed. Roy P. Basler (New York: Da Capo Press, 1990), 723.

13. "Speech at Peoria, Illinois, October 16, 1854," in *Think Anew, Act Anew: Abraham Lincoln on Slavery, Freedom and Union*, ed. Brooks D. Simpson (Wheeling, Ill.: Harland Davidson, 1998), 11.

14. Some African Americans did indeed support colonization (including certain prominent black leaders such as Martin Delany, James Holly, and Henry Highland Garnet), but the vast majority did not.

15. See Quarles, *Lincoln and the Negro*, 192.

16. "Address on Colonization to a Deputation of Negroes," August 14, 1862, in *Collected Works*, 5:371–72.

17. Ibid.

18. *Frederick Douglass: Selected Speeches and Writings*, ed. Philip S. Foner, abridged and adapted by Yuval Taylor (Chicago: Lawrence Hill Books, 1999), 551.

19. "Annual Message in Congress, December 3, 1861," in *Abraham Lincoln: His Speeches and Writings*, 619.

20. "Second Inaugural Address, March 4, 1865," in ibid., 793.

21. "Letter to Governor Michael Hahn," March 13, 1864, in ibid., 745.

22. "Last Public Address," April 11, 1865, in ibid., 800.

23. "Speech at Charleston, Illinois," September 18, 1858, in *Think Anew, Act Anew*, 45.

24. W. E. B. Du Bois, "Again, Lincoln," *Crisis*, September 1922.

Suspension of Habeas Corpus

Editors' note: Justice O'Connor recalls first learning about Abraham Lincoln from "a marvelous woman teacher with an understanding of history and Lincoln's place in it" while attending grade school in El Paso, Texas. From that point on, her interest in Lincoln developed to reading books on Lincoln as an adult.

In the early days of the Civil War, it looked as though the young American nation, "conceived in Liberty," might not "long endure." It faced so many threats. The Southern states had broken away. European powers were poised to intervene, to permanently divide the young nation into Union and Confederacy.

The war posed another sort of danger, as well—a danger less obvious, perhaps, than columns of soldiers marching through the countryside, but one far more insidious to a nation "conceived in Liberty." It was the danger that government at war might use its extraordinary powers to stamp out political opposition. And when President Lincoln suspended the writ of habeas corpus during the Civil War, there was a good chance of that happening.

Because it is an issue of considerable interest to lawyers and judges, my "lesson learned" is about Lincoln's suspension of habeas corpus. I will make three points. First, I will review a little bit of the history of habeas corpus: where it came from, what it means, and how it came to be viewed, by the beginning of the Civil War, as a principal guarantee of political liberty. Second, I will discuss what prompted President Lincoln to suspend the writ of habeas corpus in those first few days of the Civil War, when states were seceding left and right and our capital, Washington, was threatened with invasion. Finally, I will come to the main question: How did the Lincoln administration act once habeas corpus was suspended and it was free to take people into custody without arrest warrants issued by courts?

BACKGROUND ABOUT HABEAS CORPUS

Those who are *not* lawyers may recognize the term "habeas corpus" as a sort of criminal appeal. One may follow the ongoing debate about how to regulate habeas corpus proceedings brought by prisoners, particularly those on death row. In 2004, Congress passed a new law making it more difficult for prisoners to challenge their convictions or sentences by invoking the writ of habeas corpus. This new law has prompted quite a bit of activity in the courts, and it remains to be seen exactly what effects that law will have. But history shows that constant change is part and parcel of the remedy of habeas corpus.

We can trace the writ of habeas corpus as far back as the Norman Conquest of England. Back then, William the Conqueror sent royal judges to ride throughout the countryside of his new kingdom dispensing justice. These itinerant judges would, on occasion, order local sheriffs to "have the bodies" of accused criminals brought before their courts. That's where we get the Latin phrase "habeas corpus." It means, literally, "have the body." And we call it a "writ" because these traveling judges would put their orders into a "written" document.

So habeas corpus began as a way of dragging an unwilling suspect into court. But eventually people who were unlawfully imprisoned—say, by a corrupt mayor, or even the king—began asking royal judges to bring them out of jail and into court, where their jailers would have to justify why they were in custody. This explains why today, when a prisoner seeks a writ of habeas corpus, he technically names his prison warden as the defendant.

England grew to regard the writ of habeas corpus as a beacon of individual liberty against the gloom of tyrannical government. It was not a "Get Out of Jail Free" card, mind you, but it at least ensured that a prisoner could have his day in court. If you were to ask an Englishman to name the greatest legal documents in English history, right alongside the Magna Carta would be the Habeas Corpus Acts passed by Parliament in the 1600s, guaranteeing this remedy to all English subjects.

When English settlers moved to the New World, they brought with them more than hammers and saws to build new homes and plows and shovels to till new fields. They also brought with them the English common law to build their new legal system. That included habeas corpus. When tensions mounted between the colonies and the Crown, royal governors were known to lock up "troublemakers"—and local courts were known to issue writs of habeas corpus to release those troublemakers.

One of the guiding principles of the American Revolution, of course, was that governments should not be able to lock up citizens arbitrarily or simply because they raised their voices against the government. The Founding Fathers took this concern to heart at the Constitutional Convention. Like their ancestors, they saw the writ of habeas corpus as a bulwark against tyranny. So, to safeguard the writ, our new Constitution provided that "[t]he Privilege of the Writ of Habeas Corpus shall not be suspended, unless when in Cases of Rebellion or Invasion the public Safety may require it."

There was only one brief incident during the early days of the Republic when "public Safety" led to suspension of the writ. During the War of 1812, General Andrew Jackson imposed martial law in New Orleans. At one point, he locked up a newspaper editor who had been fiercely critical of the general. When a judge issued a writ of habeas corpus to free the editor, Jackson not only ignored the writ—he arrested the judge, too! Only a few days later, when a peace treaty had been signed and the British fleet sailed away from the coast, did Jackson release both editor and jurist. This proved to be an isolated incident. After that brief wartime interlude, courts went on issuing the writ as justice demanded.

As time went on, the writ of habeas corpus took on new dimensions. For a time, the writ became a lightning rod for people on both sides of the slavery issue. When runaway slaves were apprehended by slave catchers in Northern states, abolitionist lawyers helped them secure their freedom with writs of habeas corpus from sympathetic courts. Perhaps the most successful lawyer in this regard was Salmon P. Chase, secretary of the treasury under Lincoln and later chief justice of the United States. Chase extracted so many slaves from jail that he earned the moniker "Attorney General for Fugitive Slaves."[1]

While abolitionists interposed the writ as a shield to protect freed slaves, some proslavery forces tried to use it as a sword. Some Northern states let slave masters use the writ of habeas corpus to force local sheriffs to bring back runaway slaves.[2] But this fight over the soul of habeas corpus—a long-standing instrument of freedom—was interrupted by the Civil War.

THE CIVIL WAR: SUSPENSION OF THE WRIT

The year 1861 was a difficult one, to say the least. Barely a month after Lincoln's inauguration, Washington was abuzz with rumors that Confederate soldiers, gathering at Harper's Ferry in Virginia, might move against the capital. The Southern states had been seceding, one by one, and it looked as though Maryland—south of the Mason-Dixon Line and still a slave state—might be next. Lincoln himself had traveled incognito through Baltimore, at night, to avoid assassination plots on his way to his own inauguration.

In April, in the midst of all this confusion, a trainload full of Union soldiers passed through Baltimore en route to Washington. They were fresh recruits from Massachusetts, outfitted with polished boots and belt buckles, satin-trimmed coats and hats. They had been summoned to man the defensive fortifications around the capital.[3]

These soldiers were greeted not by brass bands and waving flags but by an angry mob of Southern sympathizers who were spoiling for a battle. The soldiers literally had to fight their way across the town of Baltimore to reach another station, where their train to Washington waited. Four of them did not make it out of town alive. Later that night, local authorities—whose sympathies clearly ran in a southerly direction—burned the bridges and cut the telegraph lines between Baltimore and Washington, claiming that Union soldiers might come back, looking for revenge after the riot.[4] But as one commentator has put it, "Bridge-burning looked like plain treason to the government in Washington, which was now defenseless and cut off from the rest of the North."[5]

Washington had a rebel army to its south and a secession-minded mob to its north. Congress was out of session. Lincoln felt the need to take things into his own hands. Invoking his power as commander in chief, he authorized local military commanders to suspend habeas corpus along the railroad line from Washington to Philadelphia. Essentially, this meant that the army could arrest civilians without getting a warrant from a court or without probable cause to believe a crime had been committed by the person arrested and without providing the speedy jury trial that the Constitution guarantees in times of peace.

Enter Mr. John Merryman, a member of the Maryland legislature. Merryman had been recruiting local men to march south and join the rebel army. When a Union general found out, he ordered Merryman's arrest and packed him off to Fort McHenry in Baltimore harbor (of "Star-Spangled Banner" fame) for the rest of the war. Merryman, in turn, applied for a writ of habeas corpus from his local federal circuit judge.

I mentioned earlier that royal judges in medieval England used to "ride circuit," holding court throughout the countryside. The Supreme Court worked in much the same way until late in the nineteenth century.[6] Justices of the Supreme Court sat together in Washington only part of the year. During their plentiful spare time, the justices would hop onto their horses and serve as federal circuit judges around the country. When Merryman filed his request with his local circuit judge, he went to none other than Roger Taney, chief justice of the U.S. Supreme Court.

The chief justice was no friend of the Republican administration, having written the *Dred Scott* decision only four years before. When he received Merryman's petition, Taney ordered the commander of Fort McHenry to bring Merryman to his court in Baltimore.[7] But instead of sending Merryman, the general sent back an aide bearing a polite message. The president had authorized the general, in this time of war, to suspend the writ of habeas corpus. Merryman would stay at Fort McHenry. This, as you can imagine, incensed the chief justice. He wrote a fiery opinion arguing that only Congress had power to suspend habeas corpus. The president could not. The president's job, he said, was merely to see that the laws be faithfully executed.[8]

Lincoln did not publicly respond to Taney's opinion until Congress met a month later, on July 4. Lincoln said that, had he not suspended habeas corpus immediately, Washington itself might now be in Southern hands. That, of course, would have prevented Congress from meeting, let alone from responding to the rebellion. Lincoln then took aim at Taney's claim that the president's job was to sit back and ensure that the laws be faithfully executed, even in the face of Merryman's recruiting soldiers for the Confederate cause. In the Confederacy, fully one-third of the country, the Constitution itself was being ignored. Should Lincoln's hands be tied by the writ of habeas corpus in such a national emergency? He asked: "[A]re all the laws, *but one*, to go unexecuted, and the government itself go to pieces, lest that one be violated?"[9]

Merryman stayed in jail. Now, Merryman was only one of many people arrested, without benefit of habeas corpus relief, in the early days of the war for providing military aid to the young Confederacy. Lincoln later said that he regretted not arresting even *more* traitors to the Northern cause—particularly the Robert E. Lees who had abandoned the Union army to lead its Southern enemy to victory after victory.[10]

Scholars still debate whether Lincoln had authority to invoke the constitutional provision suspending habeas corpus during the early days of the war. I will not wade into the muddy waters of that debate. I am more interested in talking about what Lincoln *did* after March 1863—when Congress gave Lincoln legislative authority to suspend the writ. From that point forward, Lincoln faced no constitutional obstacles. He could arrest whomever he chose, without courts interfering with writs of habeas corpus. What did Lincoln do at this point? Did he attempt to stifle political debate by imprisoning his opponents? In short, did he trample on the civil liberties that the writ of habeas corpus was meant to protect?

A recent historical study, *The Fate of Liberty*, says no. The author, Mark E. Neely, combed through the musty boxes of arrest records from the Civil War "to find out who was arrested when the writ of habeas corpus was suspended and why."[11] Neely concluded that, throughout the war, Lincoln was guided by a "steady desire to avoid political abuse under the *habeas-corpus* policy."[12]

According to the best estimates, about 38,000 civilians were arrested by the military during the Civil War. Who were they? Almost all fell within a few categories: "draft dodgers, suspected deserters, defrauders of the government, swindlers of recruits, ex-Confederate soldiers and smugglers."[13] And strikingly, most of these were Confederate citizens, caught behind Northern lines. The numbers show that very few civilians were taken from their homes and arrested. And of those few arrests, only a handful were colored by political considerations.[14]

Indeed, Lincoln issued his most sweeping proclamation suspending habeas corpus not to silence political dissent but to stop judicial interference in the draft. Early in the war, patriotic zeal was so strong that volunteers flooded into the army. But as the war dragged on, public enthusiasm ebbed. Eventually, the government was reduced to instituting a draft. Conscription was rather unpopular, to say the least. If you remember the burning of draft cards during the Vietnam War, imagine that unrest multiplied several times over in the New York City draft riots of 1863. The problem was especially bad in Pennsylvania. Coal miners attacked men thought to be "in sympathy with the draft."[15] State and federal courts added to the problem. They were churning out writs of habeas corpus, freeing soldiers as soon as they were drafted. Lincoln observed that "[t]he course pursued by certain judges is defeating the draft."[16]

Lincoln's response was to suspend the writ throughout the North in any case that involved military arrest of deserters or draft dodgers. And for good measure, he threw in prisoners of war, spies, and those giving assistance to the enemy—say, by smuggling goods to the Confederate government.[17] But his focus was always on military necessity. Lincoln never tried to suppress political dissent. He understood that a democracy only grows stronger by allowing people to voice their opposition to the government, even in the midst of war. He understood that the strength of the Union lay not only in force of arms but in the liberties that were guaranteed by the open, and sometimes heated, exchange of ideas. And as one historian has put it, "The opposition press in the North was vibrant, vigorous, and often vicious."[18]

This point is illustrated by the most sensational arrest of the Civil War: that of Clement Vallandigham, a former Democratic congressman from Ohio. Vallandigham was an outspoken Confederate sympathizer, a man who minced no words expressing his contempt for the Lincoln administration. He was one of the "Peace Democrats," or "Copperheads," who originally earned their name from "the poisonous snake that attacks without notice." The Copperheads co-opted the title, wearing the head of the goddess Liberty cut from copper pennies as lapel pins, to broadcast their opposition to the war.[19] It's a nice irony, I think, to remember whose head appears on the penny today! The Copperheads must be turning in their graves.

In May 1863, General Ambrose Burnside was in charge of the Department of the Ohio. Burnside, it turned out, is a man better remembered for his long whiskers—or "sideburns"—than for his political acuity. The general announced that anyone within his jurisdiction who was in the "habit of declaring sympathies for the enemy" would be arrested as a traitor.[20]

Vallandigham took Burnside's proclamation as a challenge. At a public rally opening his campaign for governor of Ohio, Vallandigham gave a vitriolic speech. He denounced the president as "King Lincoln," accused Burnside of being a heavy-handed tyrant, and called for a negotiated peace with the South.[21] Burnside read the speech, arrested Vallandigham, and shipped him off to a jail in Boston.

This, of course, was exactly what Vallandigham wanted. Overnight, he became a martyr for the Copperhead cause. The papers called him "Valiant Val."[22] Democrats triumphantly announced that Lincoln had finally shown his true colors: he was nothing more than a petty tyrant.

Lincoln, for his part, was not pleased by the general's actions. To be sure, he was not fond of Vallandigham. The former congressman had been constantly stirring up sentiments against the war, and Lincoln suspected that he was purposely fanning the flames of street violence in opposition to the draft.[23] But Lincoln realized that the arrest was valuable ammunition for his political opponents.

Burnside, ever the zealous soldier, had one more blunder to make. Turning his attention to Illinois, the general decided that the *Chicago Times* was getting too loud in criticizing the war effort. It was time to shut that paper down. So he sent out two companies of infantry, and they stopped the presses.

This was too much. Lincoln had to engage in what today might be called "damage control." Burnside had proclaimed that traitors would be either put on trial or sent "into the lines of their friends."[24] Lincoln decided to take the second option. Early one morning, Union troops escorted a bewildered Vallandigham to the Confederate lines in Tennessee and there set him free.[25] After some confusion, he made his way to Charleston, South Carolina. He exchanged some awkward pleasantries with his Confederate hosts and eventually caught a slow boat to Canada.

The next order of business was to get the *Chicago Times* back in circulation. Lincoln rescinded Burnside's order, called back the troops guarding the presses, and warned his overzealous general not to arrest any more civilians or shut down any more newspapers without express approval from Washington.[26]

Although Lincoln undid most of the damage, he still wanted to make a point. He explained to a group of New York Democrats that he would not allow civilians to be arrested merely for "damaging the political prospects of the administration or the personal interests of the commanding general."[27] Arrests would be made only to protect national security. Now, national security is always a difficult line to draw, especially during a civil war. But the line had to be drawn somewhere, if the Union was to be preserved. Lincoln asked: "Must I shoot a simple-minded soldier who deserts, while I must not touch a hair of a wily agitator who induces him to desert? . . . I think that, in such a case, to silence the agitator and save the boy is not only constitutional, but withal a great mercy."[28]

CONCLUSION

The Vallandigham episode is emblematic of Lincoln's approach to political liberties during the Civil War. The president was not out to trample on the First Amendment. He was not out to crush his political opposition. He suspended the writ of habeas corpus in response to perceived military threats to the Union. After he, and later Congress, removed that constitutional safeguard, the Lincoln administration did not use its power selfishly or arbitrarily. It arrested only those people who actively supported the Confederate war machine—people like Merryman, who recruited troops to march south. And when people walked the fine line between political dissent and treason, as Vallandigham did, Lincoln tried to err on the side of free speech.

Midway through the war, Lincoln predicted that habeas corpus would quickly be reinstituted after the war was over. He could not bring himself to believe Americans would allow the wartime suspension of habeas corpus to extend into peacetime, he said, "any more than I am able to believe that a man could contract so strong an appetite for emetics during temporary illness as to persist in feeding upon them during the remainder of his healthful life."[29] Lincoln died before he could see the writ of habeas corpus restored.

In one of his famous debates with Stephen Douglas, Lincoln spoke about how a society that tolerates slavery corrodes the very foundations of its own liberty. These words, I think, reveal Lincoln's awareness that he wasn't just battling for territory on a map; he was battling to preserve a nation "conceived in Liberty." Lincoln asked:

> What constitutes the bulwark of our own liberty and independence? It is not our frowning battlements, our bristling sea coasts, the guns of our war steamers, or the strength of our gallant and disciplined army. These are not our reliance against a resumption of tyranny in our fair land. All of them may be turned against our liberties, without making us stronger or weaker for the struggle. Our reliance is in the *love of liberty* which God has planted in our bosoms. Our defense is in the preservation of the spirit which prizes liberty as the heritage of all men, in all lands, everywhere. Destroy this spirit, and you have planted the seeds of despotism around your own doors. Familiarize yourselves with the chains of bondage, and you are preparing your own limbs to wear them. Accustomed to trample on the rights of those around you, you have lost the genius of your own independence, and become the fit subjects of the first cunning tyrant who rises.[30]

So today, let us heed the wisdom of a man who led our nation to a "new birth of freedom." Let us always be, first and foremost, lovers of liberty.

NOTES

1. Paul Finkelman, "Civil Liberties and Civil War: The Great Emancipator as Civil Libertarian," *Michigan Law Review* 91 (1993): 1353, 1354.

2. Mark E. Neely, *The Fate of Liberty: Abraham Lincoln and Civil Liberties* (New York: Oxford University Press, 1991), xv.

3. Ibid., 4–6; David Herbert Donald, *Lincoln* (New York: Simon and Schuster, 1995), 297–99.

4. Donald, *Lincoln,* 297.

5. Neely, *Fate of Liberty,* 5.

6. Circuit Court of Appeals Act (1891) after *In re Neagle,* 135 U.S. 1 (1890) (federal marshal Neagle shot David Terry to protect Justice Stephen Field, a Lincoln appointee from California).

7. *Ex parte Merryman,* 17 F. Cas. 144, 146 (C.C.D. Md. 1861) (No. 9,487) (Taney, C.J. in chambers).

8. Ibid., 149.

9. "Message to Congress in Special Session," July 4, 1861, in *Abraham Lincoln: His Speeches and Writings,* ed. Roy P. Basler (Cleveland: World Press, 1946), 601.

10. "Letter to Erastus Corning and Others," June 12, 1863, in ibid., 703.

11. Neely, *Fate of Liberty,* xvii.

12. Ibid., 92.

13. Ibid., 114, 136–37.

14. Ibid.

15. Bruce Catton, *The Army of the Potomac: Glory Road* (New York: Doubleday, 1952), 223.

16. Neely, *Fate of Liberty,* 69.

17. Ibid., 72.

18. Finkelman, "Civil Liberties and Civil War," 1376.

19. Donald, *Lincoln,* 417 (snakes); Catton, *Army of the Potomac,* 230 (pennies); James M. McPherson, *Battle Cry of Freedom: The Civil War Era* (New York: Oxford University Press, 1988), 494 n. 8 (both).

20. Donald, *Lincoln,* 419.

21. Ibid.

22. Neely, *Fate of Liberty,* 66.

23. "Letter to Matthew Birchard and Others," June 29, 1863, in *The Collected Works of Abraham Lincoln,* ed. Roy P. Basler, 9 vols. (New Brunswick, N.J.: Rutgers University Press, 1953–55), 6:304.

24. Catton, *Army of the Potomac,* 232.

25. Ibid.

26. Ibid.

27. "Letter to Erastus Corning and Others," 704.

28. Neely, *Fate of Liberty,* 68.

29. "Letter to Erastus Corning and Others," 705.

30. "Speech at Edwardsville, Illinois," September 11, 1858, in *Abraham Lincoln: His Speeches and Writings,* 473.

Lincoln and the Meaning of Equality:
How I Became a "Lost Cause" Apostate

During an episode of Ken Burns's magnificent 1990 PBS series on the Civil War, the late Shelby Foote recounted a story about a discussion he once had with an elderly lady in his Mississippi hometown. He told her that he thought that the Civil War produced two uniquely American geniuses: the remarkable Confederate cavalryman Nathan Bedford Forrest and Abraham Lincoln. The lady paused for a second and then replied, "Well, we didn't think much of Mr. Lincoln in our household."

I laughed when I heard Foote's anecdote because the elderly lady's story was mine as well. I too grew up in a "Lost Cause" household. Both my paternal and maternal forebears had fought for the Confederacy, and I grew up worshiping at the altar of Robert E. Lee and Thomas Jonathan "Stonewall" Jackson. One of my father's most cherished possessions was a first edition of John Esten Cooke's *Wearing of the Grey*, a panegyric to the leaders of Lee's Army of Northern Virginia.

The Lost Cause narrative of the Civil War holds that the cause of the war was not slavery but "states' rights" versus the oppressive power of the central government, which wished to tyrannize over the Southern states. The South only wished to exercise its constitutional right to secede but was thwarted by a power-hungry Lincoln. Like Foote's elderly Mississippi neighbor, I fervently believed these things.

As Edward A. Pollard wrote in the 1867 book that gave the Lost Cause interpretation its name, "all that is left in the South is the war of ideas." The Lost Cause narrative is neatly summarized in an 1893 speech by a former Confederate officer, Colonel Richard Henry Lee. "As a Confederate soldier and as a Virginian, I deny the charge [that the Confederates were rebels] and denounce it as a calumny. We were not rebels, we did not fight to perpetuate human slavery, but for our rights and privileges under a government established over us by our fathers and in defense of our homes."[1]

After graduating from college, I received a commission in the Marine Corps, serving as an infantry platoon leader in Vietnam during the period from 1968 to 1969. Several years later, I decided to leave active duty to pursue a Ph.D. in political philosophy at the University of Dallas. While I had come to appreciate elements of Lincoln's greatness, I still subscribed to the Lost Cause.

When I was younger, I had read *A Constitutional View of the Late War Between the States* by Alexander H. Stephens, the vice president of the Confederacy, and I decided to write my dissertation on the book.[2] Stephens had, after all, produced the most complete and logical constitutional defense of secession in the tradition of the Lost Cause school. But then something happened that forever altered my views on secession and the causes of the Civil War and placed me on the path to the house of Lincoln.

During the spring of my last year of courses, the politics department of the University of Dallas hosted a conference on Shakespeare's politics. One of the participants was Harry Jaffa, a professor at Claremont McKenna College. I had never met Professor Jaffa and had no idea who he was. I certainly did not know that he had written *Crisis of the House Divided*, a path-breaking study of the Lincoln-Douglas debates.[3]

We chanced to speak during a break in the proceedings, and he asked me about my progress toward the degree. I mentioned that I intended to write my dissertation on Stephens's *Constitutional View.* He listened without comment, but when I had finished, he asked me if I had ever read Stephens's "Cornerstone" speech, an address that he delivered as vice president of the Confederacy on March 21, 1861, in Savannah. I replied that I had not. Without any hint at the content of the address, he suggested that I look at it.

To say that this speech was eye-opening is like saying the sun is warm. According to Stephens, the Founders were absolutely wrong about the basis of republican government.

> The new [Confederate] constitution has put at rest, forever, all the agitating questions relating to our peculiar institution—African slavery as it exists amongst us—the proper status of the negro in our form of civilization. This was the immediate cause of the late rupture and present revolution. Jefferson in his forecast, had anticipated this, as the "rock upon which the old Union would split." He was right. What was conjecture with him, is now a realized fact. But whether he fully comprehended the great truth upon which that rock stood and stands, may be doubted. The prevailing ideas entertained by him and most of the leading statesmen at the time of the formation of the old [Federal] constitution, were that the enslavement of the African was in violation of the laws of nature; that it was wrong, in principle, socially, morally, and politically. It was an evil they knew not well how to deal with, but

the general opinion of the men of that day was that, somehow or other in the order of Providence, the institution would be evanescent and pass away. This idea, though not incorporated in the constitution, was the prevailing idea at that time. The constitution, it is true, secured every essential guarantee to the institution while it should last, and hence no argument can be justly urged against the constitutional guarantees thus secured, because of the common sentiment of the day. Those ideas, however, were fundamentally wrong. They rested upon the assumption of the equality of races. This was an error. It was a sandy foundation, and the government built upon it fell when the "storm came and the wind blew."[4]

Here Stephens does not waste his time discussing the constitutional right of secession or "states' rights." Instead, he asserts that the Southern states had seceded because of slavery and that they had formed a constitution the "cornerstone of which was the great truth that the negro is not equal to the white man; that slavery—subordination to the superior race—is his natural and normal condition."

The more I read, the more I became convinced that my understanding of the United States had been distorted by viewing the American Founding through the lens of the Lost Cause narrative. I resolved to go back to the beginning and look at things anew. Accordingly, I turned my attention to the Founding period and wrote my dissertation on Alexander Hamilton.

But I also concluded that if Stephens was wrong about the American Founding, then perhaps Lincoln had something to teach. I was right. Contrary to the claims of Stephens and other apologists of the Lost Cause, Lincoln did not destroy the Founders' constitutional order; he completed it.

Like most who esteem Lincoln, I admire his character. But in my view, it is the quality of his political thought and the clarity and constancy of his political principles that constitute his greatest contribution to the survival and prosperity of the American Republic. And the "cornerstone" of that political thought, and of the Republic upon which it is founded, is the principle of *equality* as articulated in the Declaration of Independence. Lincoln believed that Thomas Jefferson meant what he said when he wrote "all men are created equal" and that this meant simply that no person has the right to rule over another without the latter's consent. In other words, "equality" means "equal political liberty."

Jefferson himself expressed this meaning of the Declaration in a letter to Roger Weightman shortly before his death in 1826. By helping to open the eyes of mankind to "the rights of man," the Declaration of Independence was illuminating "the palpable truth, that the mass of mankind has not been born, with saddles on their backs, nor a favored few booted and spurred, ready to ride them legitimately, by the grace of god."[5]

Lincoln constantly invoked the Declaration of Independence as the well-spring of his theory of republican government. Indeed, for Lincoln the Declaration of Independence was prior to the Constitution not only temporally but philosophically. Lincoln saw the Constitution principally as a framework for sharing power within a republican government, which was the real thing he aimed to preserve, because only republican government was capable of protecting the liberty of the people. Lincoln saw the Declaration of Independence as the foundation of such a government and the Constitution as the means of implementing it.

Lincoln explained the relationship between the Declaration of Independence and the Constitution in a fragment that he probably composed in 1860, perhaps as the basis for some speeches he gave in New England. Here Lincoln observes that as important as the Constitution and Union may be, there is "something back of these, entwining itself more closely about the human heart. That something is the principle of 'Liberty to all'" as expressed in the Declaration. With or without the Declaration, Lincoln continues, the United States could have declared independence, but "without it, we could not, I think, have secured our free government and consequent prosperity."[6]

Lincoln refers to the Declaration's principle of equal liberty for all as a "word 'fitly spoken,' which has proved an 'apple of gold' to us. The Union and the Constitution, are the picture of silver, subsequently framed around it," not to conceal or destroy the apple "but to adorn, and preserve it. The picture was made for the apple—not the apple for the picture. So let us act, that neither picture [n]or apple, shall ever be blurred, or broken."[7] In other words, equality and republican liberty were the real things to be preserved by the Constitution.

Lincoln saw more clearly than his critics, then or now, that equality is inseparable from democracy. As he remarked in 1859: "All honor to Jefferson—to the man who, in the concrete pressure of a struggle for national independence by a single people, had the coolness, forecast, and capacity to introduce into a merely revolutionary document, an abstract truth, applicable to all men and all times, and so embalm it there, that to-day, and in all coming days, it shall be a rebuke and a stumbling-block to the very harbingers of re-appearing tyranny and oppression."[8]

Lincoln believed that it was the incorporation of the moral principle of equality into the Union that made the United States unique and constituted the foundation of American nationhood. In a speech delivered just after Independence Day 1858, Lincoln articulated the relationship between the moral principle of equality and nationhood. When we celebrate the Fourth of July, Lincoln told his listeners in Chicago, we celebrate the founders, "our fathers and grandfathers . . . [those] iron men."

> But after we have done this we have not yet reached the whole. There is something else connected with it. We have besides these men—descended by blood from our ancestors—among us perhaps half our people who are not descendants at all of these men, they are men who have come from Europe—German, Irish, French and Scandinavian—. . . finding themselves our equals in all things. If they look back through this history to trace their connection with those days by blood, they find they have none, they cannot carry themselves back into that glorious epoch and make themselves feel that they are part of us, but when they look through that old Declaration of Independence they find that those old men say that "We hold these truths to be self-evident, that all men are created equal," and then they feel that the moral sentiment taught in that day evidences their relation to those men, that it is the father of all moral principle in them, and that they have a right to claim it as though they were blood of the blood, and flesh of the flesh of the men who wrote that Declaration, and so they are.[9]

This commitment to the moral principle of equality made the United States a fundamentally decent regime, worthy of emulation. Thus, in his eulogy on Henry Clay, Lincoln argued that Clay's "predominant sentiment, from first to last, was a deep devotion to the cause of human liberty. . . . He loved his country because it was his own country, but mostly because it was a free country; and he burned with a zeal for its advancement, prosperity and glory, because he saw in such, the advancement, prosperity and glory, of human liberty, human right and human nature."[10] In his second annual message to Congress, he spoke of the United States as "the last best hope of earth."[11] For indeed, if republican government failed in North America, where else would it ever flourish again?

Lincoln argued that the shortcomings of this fundamentally decent regime could be attributed to the failure to live up to the fundamental principle articulated by the Declaration. The greatest affront to republican government was slavery. In his speech at Peoria on the Kansas-Nebraska Act, Lincoln declared that he hated slavery "because it deprives our republican example of its just influence in the world—enables the enemies of free institutions, with plausibility, to taunt us as hypocrites—causes the real friends of freedom to doubt our sincerity, and especially because it forces so many really good men amongst ourselves into an open war with the very fundamental principles of civil liberty—criticising the Declaration of Independence, and insisting that there is no right principle of action but self-interest."[12]

Needless to say, the argument that equality is the cornerstone of American republicanism has been the source of great controversy. What does "equality" mean, anyway? Did the Founders, especially Thomas Jefferson, the man who penned the passage cited by Lincoln, really believe in equality? Jefferson was, after all, a slaveholder. Or did Lincoln "pull a fast one," attributing to equality an importance never intended by the Founders? These are not unimportant questions. They have implications for us today, especially at a time when, despite the triumph of the United States in the Cold War, the American political system is often denounced as undemocratic, racist, and imperialist.

Lincoln's view of equality has been attacked from both the Left and the Right: on the one hand by radical egalitarians who claim that equality means nothing less than "equality of results," and on the other by conservative critics who claim that, by illegitimately emphasizing equality, Lincoln "derailed" the "authentic" American political tradition, compact-based majoritarianism.[13]

For the radical egalitarian, equality requires a complete leveling of society. An example of what this leveling sort of equality means is provided by historian Barbara Fields in the final episode of Ken Burns's PBS television series on the Civil War: "[The war] established a standard that will not mean anything until we have finished the work. . . . If some citizens live in houses and others live on the street, the Civil War is still going on. It is still to be fought, and . . . it can still be lost."

Contrast this with Lincoln's comments in his speech on the *Dred Scott* decision (1857): "I think the authors of [the Declaration of Independence] intended to include all men, but they did not intend to declare men equal in all respects. This did not mean to say that all were equal in color, size, intellect, moral developments, or social capacity. They defined with tolerable distinctness, in what respects they did consider all men created equal—equal in 'certain inalienable rights, among which are life, liberty, and the pursuit of happiness.'"[14]

Unlike the equality of the radical egalitarian, which would require massive coercion and is accordingly completely at odds with liberty, Lincoln's equality is inseparable from freedom. To be free is to be equal.

If radical egalitarians would argue that Lincoln's conception of equality does not go far enough, some conservative critics argue that it goes too far and indeed starts us down the slippery slope leading to radical egalitarianism. They argue that Lincoln illegitimately transformed the meaning of equality. Garry Wills, echoing his teacher Willmoore Kendall, writes in *Lincoln at Gettysburg* that Lincoln's Gettysburg Address was meant to "cleanse the Constitution—not, as William Lloyd Garrison had, by burning an instrument that countenanced slavery. He altered the document from within, by appeal from its letter to the spirit, subtly changing the recalcitrant stuff of that legal compromise, bringing it to its own indictment. By implicitly doing this, he performed one of the most daring acts of open-air sleight-of-hand ever witnessed by the unsuspecting. Everyone in that vast throng of thousands was having his or her intellectual pocket picked. The crowd departed with a new thing in its intellectual luggage, that new constitution Lincoln had substituted for the one they brought there with them. They walked off, from those curving graves on the hillside, under a changed sky, into a different America. Lincoln had revolutionized the Revolution, giving people a new past that would change their future indefinitely."[15]

The idea that the Founders meant by equality something different than the clear sense of the words "all men are created equal" has a long lineage, predating the Civil War. At best, according to Stephen Douglas, "all men are created equal" could mean nothing more than "all British subjects on this continent were equal to British subjects born and residing in Great Britain."[16] Douglas's view was merely a variation of an argument advanced by John C. Calhoun and given judicial sanction by Chief Justice Roger Taney in his *Dred Scott* decision.

According to Calhoun, the proposition that "'all men are created equal' as now expressed and now understood, is the most false and dangerous of all political errors. . . . We now begin to experience the danger of admitting so great an error to have a place in the declaration of independence. For a long time it lay dormant; but in the process of time it began to germinate, and produce its dangerous fruits. It had a strong hold on the mind of Mr. Jefferson, the author of that document, which caused him to take an utterly false view of the subordinate relation of the black to the white race in the South; and to hold, in consequence, that the former, although utterly unqualified to possess liberty, were as fully entitled to both liberty and equality as the latter; and that to deprive them of it was unjust and immoral."[17]

In a similar vein, Taney held that the black man, whether freeman or slave, had no rights that the white man was bound to respect. Taking his cue from Calhoun, Senator John Pettit of Indiana claimed that the document Lincoln called "the father of all moral sentiment among us" was "a self-evident lie."[18] And as noted above, Alexander H. Stephens contended that the Confederate constitution, the "cornerstone" of which was the "great truth" of slavery and inequality, would correct the fatal error advanced in the Declaration of Independence.

We have already observed that Lincoln saw that equality, properly understood, is inseparable from democracy. "Every nation," he said, "has a central ideal from which all its minor thoughts radiate."[19] For Lincoln, this central idea was equality. Democracy cannot entail a right to enslave another. Once the principle of inequality is accepted, where do we draw the line? If democracy can accommodate the enslavement of some by others on the basis of color, what principle prevents slavery based on other criteria?

> If A can prove, however conclusively, that he may, of right, enslave B—why may not B snatch the same argument and prove equally, that he may enslave A?—You say A is white, and B is black. It is color, then; the lighter, having the right to enslave the darker? Take care. By this rule, you are to be the slave to the first man you meet, with a fairer skin than your own.
>
> You do not mean color exactly?—You mean the whites are intellectually the superiors of the blacks, and, therefore have the right to enslave them? Take care again. By this rule, you are to be the slave to the first man you meet, with an intellect superior to your own.[20]

Without public sentiment in support of equality, free government would be lost. Lincoln understood the critical importance of public sentiment in a democracy. "Our government rests in public opinion. . . . Whoever can change public opinion, can change the government, practically just so much. . . . In this and like communities, public sentiment is everything. With public sentiment, nothing can fail; without it nothing can succeed. Consequently he who molds public sentiment, goes deeper than he who enacts statutes or pronounces decisions. He makes statutes and decisions possible or impossible to be executed."[21] Lincoln was concerned that public sentiment was being prepared to accept the rightness of slavery. It was being prepared by Stephen Douglas's doctrine of "popular sovereignty," which professed indifference to the moral aspect of slavery, leaving the question to the preferences of the community. It was being prepared by Chief Justice Taney, whose argument in *Dred Scott* that blacks had no rights that whites were bound to respect repudiated the "central idea" of the Declaration and thereby American republicanism.

Lincoln fought to save this "central idea" from its contemporary detractors. Contra Calhoun and Taney, Lincoln argued that the founders compromised on slavery out of necessity, not because they believed it to be right. "They found the institution existing among us, which they could not help; and they cast blame upon the British King for having permitted its introduction." Before the Constitution, they prohibited the introduction of slavery into the Northwest Territory. The words "slave" and "slavery" do not appear in the Constitution. "Thus, the thing is hid away, in the constitution, just as an afflicted man hides away a wen or cancer, which he dares not cut out at once, lest he bleed to death; with the promise, nevertheless, that the cutting may begin at the end of a given time. Less than this our fathers COULD not do; and MORE they WOULD not do. Necessity drove them so far, and farther they would not go."

But the Kansas-Nebraska Act, the *Dred Scott* decision, and Douglas's idea of popular sovereignty were preparing public sentiment to accept the transformation of the slavery question from one of "hostility to the PRINCIPLE, and toleration, ONLY BY NECESSITY" to slavery as a "sacred right."[22]

Current leftist critics of Lincoln contend that although he rhetorically opposed slavery, he did not truly believe that blacks and whites were equal. For instance, according to Lerone Bennett, Lincoln embodied the "racist" American tradition. With regard to abolishing slavery, they argue, he did not move fast enough or far enough.[23]

Allen Guelzo has demonstrated beyond a reasonable doubt that Lincoln planned to begin the process of emancipation from the outset of his presidency, but he was limited in how fast he could move by political reality and "public sentiment." The charges of those such as Bennett reflect an inability to understand the role of *prudence* in politics, especially democratic politics. Prudence, says Aristotle, is the virtue most characteristic of the statesman. Prudence is the ability to adapt an overarching principle to particular conditions. For Lincoln, the Declaration of Independence constituted the overarching principle of the American Republic. But existing conditions, especially the attitude of whites toward blacks during the middle part of the nineteenth century, constituted an obstacle to achieving the equality spoken of therein.[24]

Lincoln attributes a prudential approach to the Founders. When they wrote that "all men are created equal," they meant what they said. But, he concludes, "They did not mean to assert the obvious untruth, that all men were then actually enjoying that equality, nor yet, that they were about to confer it immediately upon them. In fact they had no power to confer such a boon. They meant simply to declare the right, so that the enforcement of it might follow as fast as circumstances should permit. They meant to set up a standard maxim for a free society, which should be familiar to all, and revered by all; constantly looked to, constantly labored for, and even though never perfectly attained, constantly approximated, and thereby constantly spreading and deepening its influence, and augmenting the happiness and value of life to all people of all colors everywhere."[25] Lincoln's approach was also prudential. Before he became president, his approach was primarily rhetorical, aimed at changing public sentiment regarding the institution of slavery. As president, he both spoke and acted, but his actions were of necessity constrained by his constitutional responsibilities and powers.

This accounts for Lincoln's emphasis on the priority of the Union. The preservation of the Union was, of course, his official duty. But he also understood that if the Union failed, nothing would stand in the way of slavery. This was the flaw in the abolitionist stance of "no union with slaveholders!" The cost of the abolitionists' sense of moral superiority would be the continuation of slavery in the South forever. Moreover, slave states and free states would be constantly at war, contending for the western territories.

Lincoln's preferred solution to the slavery issue was to limit its expansion, form public opinion against its morality, and, like the Founders, take steps leading to its gradual extinction, convincing the legislatures of the slave states to abolish the institution in return for federal compensation to slaveholders. Even after secession, Lincoln pursued this option but was rebuffed by the slave states that remained in the Union. Emancipation came more quickly, but at a very high cost to the Republic.

Abraham Lincoln should be viewed as a second Washington, a *re-founder* of the Republic, not the author of something wholly new. Wills and Kendall are wrong: Lincoln did not "derail" the American political tradition by emphasizing equality. He did not change the work of the Founders but helped fulfill it.

This point must be emphasized in response to those like Lerone Bennett who charge that the American tradition is "racist." Nothing could be further from the truth. Individual Americans can be and have been racists. There have been laws perpetuating the inequality of the races. Indeed, the Constitution itself at one time protected the institution of slavery. But these examples have always been in violation of the "central idea" of the American Republic.

Lincoln understood something that Bennett and other critics of the American political tradition either cannot or will not see. When the United States declared its independence in 1776, slavery was a worldwide phenomenon. But slavery was only part of a greater political reality. Before the American founding, all regimes were based on the principle of interest—the interest of the stronger. That principle was articulated by the Greek historian Thucydides: "Questions of justice arise only between equals. As for the rest, the strong do what they will. The weak suffer what they must."[26]

The United States was founded on different principles—justice and equality. No longer would it be the foundation of political government that some men were born "with saddles on their backs" to be ridden by others born "booted and spurred." In other words, no one had the right to rule over another without the latter's consent.

Slavery, of course, was a violation of this principle, but as Harry Jaffa has written: "It is not wonderful that a nation of slave-holders, upon achieving independence, failed to abolish slavery. What is wonderful, indeed miraculous, is that a nation of slave-holders founded a new nation on the proposition that 'all men are created equal,' making the abolition of slavery a moral and political necessity."[27]

It took the founding of the United States on the principle of equality to undermine the principle of inequality—that the strong by nature should rule the weak—upon which slavery was based. If critics of the American political tradition cannot appreciate the role of the American founding in ending the worldwide system of slavery that existed in 1776, perhaps they should listen to Frederick Douglass, former slave and abolitionist: "I would not, even in words, do violence to the great events, and thrilling association, that gloriously cluster around the birth of our national independence." He continued, "No people ever entered upon pathways of nations, with higher and grander ideas of justice, liberty and humanity than ourselves."[28]

Thanks to the Founders and Lincoln, American policy must be justified on the basis of something beyond the interest of the strong. Because of Lincoln's uncompromising commitment to equality as America's "central idea," the Union was not only saved but saved so "as to make, and to keep it, forever worthy of the saving."[29] And thanks to Harry Jaffa for illuminating for me and for so many others the source of Lincoln's greatness.

NOTES

1. Edward A. Pollard, *The Lost Cause: A New Southern History of the War of the Confederates* (1867; New York: E. B. Teal and Co., n.d.), 750; Lee quoted in David W. Blight, *Race and Reunion: The Civil War in American Memory* (Cambridge: Belknap Press of Harvard University Press, 2001), 190.

2. Alexander H. Stephens, *A Constitutional View of the Late War Between the States*, 2 vols. (Philadelphia: National Publishing Company, 1868).

3. Harry V. Jaffa, *Crisis of the House Divided: An Interpretation of the Issues in the Lincoln-Douglas Debates* (Chicago: University of Chicago Press, 1959).

4. Alexander H. Stephens, "Cornerstone Speech," Savannah, Georgia, March 21, 1861, *TeachingAmericanHistory.org*, http://www.teachingamericanhistory.org/library/index.asp?document=76.

5. Thomas Jefferson to Roger C. Weightman, June 24, 1826, *TeachingAmericanHistory.org*, http://www.teachingamericanhistory.org/library/index.asp?document=5.

6. *The Collected Works of Abraham Lincoln*, ed. Roy P. Basler, 9 vols. (New Brunswick, N.J.: Rutgers University Press, 1953–55), 4: 513 (hereafter *Collected Works*).

7. Ibid.; Proverbs 25:11: "A word fitly spoken is like apples of gold in pictures of silver" (KJV).

8. *Collected Works*, 3: 489.

9. Ibid., 2: 401–2.

10. Ibid., 2: 270.

11. Ibid., 5: 688.

12. Ibid., 2: 291.

13. See, e.g., the essays of Willmoore Kendall in *Willmoore Kendall Contra Mundum,* ed. Nellie Kendall (New Rochelle, N.Y.: Arlington House, 1971).

14. *Collected Works*, 2: 361.

15. Garry Wills, *Lincoln at Gettysburg: The Words That Changed America* (New York: Simon and Schuster, 1992), 38.

16. *Collected Works*, 2: 361.

17. John C. Calhoun, speech on the Oregon Bill, June 27, 1848, in *Union and Liberty: The Political Philosophy of John C. Calhoun,* ed. Ross Lence (Indianapolis: Liberty Fund, 1992), 565, 569–70.

18. *Collected Works*, 2: 500.

19. Ibid., 2: 386.

20. Ibid., 2: 223–24.

21. "First Joint Debate at Ottawa," August 21, 1858, in *The Lincoln-Douglas Debates,* ed. Robert W. Johannsen (New York: Oxford University Press, 1965), 65.

22. *Collected Works*, 2: 276.

23. Lerone Bennett, *Forced into Glory: Abraham Lincoln's White Dream* (Chicago: Johnson Publishing, 2000).

24. Allen Guelzo, *Lincoln's Emancipation Proclamation: The End of Slavery in America* (New York: Simon and Schuster, 2004).

25. *Collected Works*, 2: 361.

26. Robert B. Shassler, ed., *The Landmark Thucydides: A Comprehensive Guide to the Peloponnesian War* (New York: Free Press, 1996), 352.

27. Harry V. Jaffa, "The False Prophets of American Conservatism," February 12, 1998, *The Claremont Institute*, http://www.claremont.org/publications/pubid.670/pub_detail.asp.

28. Quoted in Glenn Ellmers, "P.C. in the Bayou," November 26, 1997, *The Claremont Institute*, http://www.claremont.org/publications/pubid.490/pub_detail.asp.

29. *Collected Works*, 2: 277.

WILLIAM D. PEDERSON

Crossing Borders to an International Lincoln

Unlike most contributors to this volume, my interest in Abraham Lincoln developed late and then rapidly moved in an international direction. To a large extent, this is due to my origins and training. I am a political scientist who was born and reared in Eugene, Oregon. My graduate training centered on comparative politics and political theory, but my teaching assignments have been primarily in American government and politics. It took a number of years before I became involved with America's sixteenth president as modern (post–World War II) political science deals mostly with the "institutionalized" presidency since Franklin Roosevelt's administration. The behavioral movement had little interest in earlier administrations, particularly those from a horse and buggy era.

After teaching for four years in Texas, Missouri, and South Dakota, I accepted a position at Louisiana State University in Shreveport in 1981. It was my first time in the Deep South, and it is where I remain today. Missionary work takes time.

Located near the Texas border in the extreme northwest corner of Louisiana, the traditionally isolated and relatively obscure city of Shreveport and its twin, Bossier City, are separated by the Red River. The main historical distinction of the area stems from the fact that it was the final Confederate command to surrender at the end of the Civil War. It was here Jefferson Davis was headed when he fled Richmond. Even today, it is the home of the Northwest Brigade of the Sons of Confederate Veterans, General Richard Taylor Camp, No. 1308, named in honor of the Confederate son of former president Zachary Taylor, who owned a plantation in south Louisiana. What Shreveport and I shared on my arrival was that we were both Lincolnless. The purpose of this chapter is to tell the story of how that would change over the next quarter century and conclude with the lessons that I have drawn from this experience.

My first step in a Lincoln direction came quickly and indirectly. At the end of my first year of teaching in Shreveport, I was asked to prepare a new humanities course, Heroes in History, for the honors program in the fall.

None of the historians was interested in a new preparation that would be a one-shot proposition, so the task fell on the proverbial new kid on the block. To lighten my lecture preparations, I invited my colleagues in the College of Liberal Arts to deliver presentations on the hero of their choice. A philosophy professor came dressed as Socrates, a criminologist spoke on Robert E. Lee, and the department's most popular historian, who offered courses on revolutionary France and the American Civil War, spoke on Napoleon Bonaparte. I later learned that he had never visited the Lincoln Memorial but openly wept at Jefferson Davis's grave. There were no volunteers to lecture on Abraham Lincoln.

More significant than the guest speakers was the student response. At the end of the course, one nontraditional student, a middle-aged woman from Shreveport, indicated an interest in endowing a program that would send students to Washington, D.C., for an experiential component of their education and also bring outside speakers to Shreveport in a distinguished lecture series. She had participated in a travel program during her high school days and remained an advocate of experiential learning. Because of my summer stints during graduate school at the State Department in Washington and at the National Institutes of Health in Bethesda, Maryland, I was appointed the director of the newly endowed American Studies program. Our first Washington mini-semester began in May 1983, and the lecture series was launched during the fall. Among the first well-known speakers brought to campus over the following years were James MacGregor Burns, Arthur Schlesinger, and William E. Leutchenburg. For the most part, the speakers tended to be presidential scholars, in part due to my teaching and research on the American presidency.[1]

While acting as a part-time academic impresario and teaching three courses each semester, I also continued my research on the American presidency and political leadership. My first book was an effort to integrate my teaching and research by bringing together polls on the rankings of political leaders with case studies. This material was set in an international context so that students could determine for themselves whether there was a difference between a Napoleon and a Lincoln.[2] The new book also reflected my interest in the psychology of collective behavior to understand the motivation of leaders and followers.[3] Or to put it more bluntly, as Barbara Tuchman formulated the question, why are there so many stupid political leaders in history compared to most human endeavors?[4]

A foreshadowing of what I would later encounter both with my Lincoln work and in developing a presidential conference series in the South came in 1989 after I delivered a paper on ranking presidents at a presidential conference at a small midwestern college. At the end of my presentation, I was told by some of the historians whose specialty was on the less-than-great American presidents that the ranking of presidents was "ahistorical." Worse yet, my categorization of Woodrow Wilson as having an inflexible streak made no sense.

Despite this early rebuke, I continued with my "ahistorical" research. Later that year, I was contacted by the International Lincoln Association (ILA) to deliver its annual keynote address. ILA members had learned of my book on presidential rankings, so they felt that I might be an appropriate speaker. That meeting marked my first encounter with Lincoln enthusiasts. The organization had been founded in 1986 by a group of retired lawyers and political scientists in California. Although I didn't know it at the time, this incident began my venture down the Lincoln road. The nature of that road became clear after meeting a professor of literature from Communist China at the ILA meeting. He had gone through the forced reeducation process during Mao's so-called Cultural Revolution. He had already known about Lincoln's values before that time, and they only grew in importance to him.

It was also at this same time that the distinguished lecture series on my campus faced a juncture. Big-name speakers were becoming increasingly expensive. As an alternative, despite considerable nay-saying by those who argued that outside academics would not come to Shreveport, a triennial presidential conference was planned for 1992. Yet the critics had a point. As a midsize city, the Shreveport-Bossier metropolitan area was the last major population area in the nation to acquire a National Public Radio station. Moreover, because of the enduring hostility that Huey P. Long had felt toward Shreveport, which had resisted his programs, it would be another decade before I-49 connected Shreveport with New Orleans. The counterargument against our size and isolation for attracting outside academics here was that this was precisely why the area needed such a program, to offset our traditional isolation.

As a result, planning for the first conference went forward from 1989 to 1992. With modest funding from the Division of Continuing Education and Public Service at LSU in Shreveport, the ILA, and eventually the Abraham Lincoln Association, a two-day conference, "The Life, Times and Legacy of Abraham Lincoln," was held on our campus during the fall of 1992. It grew into the Deep South's largest conference ever held on America's sixteenth president. During the planning process, one of the historians on the program had told me that a Lincoln conference was impossible without the participation of Frank Williams. At the time, that was only a name I had seen on paper. That soon changed.

The rationale for holding the first conference on Lincoln stemmed from his ranking in virtually all the polls of scholars. The order of future conferences would reflect presidents' position in the polls, at least until the greatest presidents had been exhausted. An underlying theme of the series was to explore the impact that Lincoln had on subsequent presidents and the possible impact that prior presidents might have had on him. The success of the Lincoln conference led to a string of publications, as well as to the expansion of the conference from a two-day to a three-day event.[5] Keeping with my own experience before the series began, the conferences were designed to be multidisciplinary. Typically, they attract fifty to sixty scholars on the program itself, and half are historians. Ironically, by holding a conference on Lincoln at our university, I instantly became "the Lincoln guy" on campus and in the community.

Major spin-offs from the conference began with the Summer Teachers Institute on Lincoln for secondary school teachers, which was held during the summer of 1993.[6] Funded by the Louisiana Endowment for the Humanities (LEH), it became the first such endeavor in the nation. By that time, Frank Williams and I had become friends. We acted as codirectors of the institute. Part of the success of that institute was owed to Frank's wife, Virginia, and Myra Miller, his mother-in-law. Both were once public school teachers themselves. In fact, Myra had graduated from a local Shreveport high school. The institute also recruited volunteers from the Lincoln conference, so that the twenty-five teachers invited that year were exposed to a variety of Lincoln scholars. The impact of the institute on the participants is perhaps best reflected in the fact that one of the teachers launched a Louisiana Lincoln group. It publishes a newsletter, *The Lincolnator*.

A requirement of the LEH grant was to have a follow-up session with the secondary teachers the following year. That requirement became the basis for the annual Frank and Virginia Williams Abraham Lincoln Lecture. Frank delivered the first lecture in 1994. Several of the contributors to this volume have served as subsequent lecturers in the series. It is the only Lincoln lecture series in Louisiana, thus institutionalizing America's sixteenth president at LSU in Shreveport.

As one might expect, these lectures attracted protesters from the Sons of Confederate Veterans. One year they handed out "Wanted for War Crimes" flyers with Lincoln's image on them. On Lincoln's birthday in 1999, I received a letter from one of the members of the local chapter of the Sons of Confederate Veterans, which reads in part:

> It seems that you blind fools of the North will never cease trying to make a silk purse out of a sow's ear. Book after book has been written exposing Dishonest Abe for what he was—a bloody tyrant. . . .
>
> You bubble-headed ultra liberal college professors insist on perpetuating the Lincoln Myth and trying to make a god of that backwards

Hitler. No wonder our kids don't know anything. The uneducated cannot educate!

Whenever ya'll bring your damyankee [*sic*] propagandists down here to spread their lies about that Illinois white trash, our boys from the Sons of Confederate Veterans will always be there to return fire. We will not suffer idiots to pollute our land.[7]

Perhaps more surprising is how few protesters the lecture now draws. The overwhelming majority of Shreveporters have been very open to the Lincoln lecture series.

The Lincoln lecture series has spawned several other Summer Teachers Institutes also funded by the LEH on broader topics, including White House first couples, the American presidency, and the U.S. Constitution. The American Studies program also funds three local teachers to attend the Summer Teachers Institute at Colonial Williamsburg.

A few years ago, the American Studies program launched a second annual lecture series on James Madison. In fact, the first non-great chief executive to be covered by the triennial presidential conference series was held on Madison in 2006. The rationale was that federalism and Lincoln's leadership style are the two greatest gifts of American government to world democracy. Appropriately, Frank Williams delivered the first lecture in the series.

By the late 1990s, a number of events came together that further developed my interest in Abraham Lincoln's legacy abroad. In the fall of 1998, unexpectedly a political science major enrolled in my introductory class. As it turned out, she was from Lincoln, Argentina. By the next summer, I made my first trip to Latin America to deliver a speech for the ILA at Lincoln College in Lincoln, Argentina. If Lincoln had created a town in his own image, it might resemble this modest-size town, one of only two outside the United States named in his honor. The success of that trip led to the formation of an ILA chapter there and of many subsequent links between Shreveport and Lincoln, Argentina.

In December 2002, I had a second opportunity to visit Latin America, this time Havana, Cuba, and the surrounding area. Probably no area per square mile in the world outside the United States has more tributes to America's sixteenth president. In part, this is due to the influence of its independence leader, José Martí, who admired the Great Emancipator. It continued before and during the reign of Fulgencio Batista and Fidel Castro. There are Lincoln stamps, statues, and schools named in his honor, as well as a hotel in downtown Havana. Not only do liberals and conservatives identify with him, but so do dictators, whether capitalist or Communist.

A few years earlier, the influence of Frank Williams the collector finally caught up with me. Up to that time, I purposely had tried to avoid collecting anything. Because I lacked space for even books, if I collected anything it would have to be small. From elementary school, I had kept a two-volume stamp collection, though that was from a short-lived hobby that lasted only from the third to the sixth grade. Nonetheless, during those years I had taught myself more geography and the names and faces of leaders from abroad than my peers, and even my teachers. Though I could not recall any stamps from abroad with Lincoln's image on them, I decided that resuming that hobby might make for a simple solution to being around a major collector. The assumption was that this could be easily accomplished with a single volume of stamps, since surely there could not be too many foreign stamps with Lincoln on them. Twenty-some volumes later, I now have virtually every stamp (and numerous duplicates) bearing Lincoln's image. These stamps (first-day covers, souvenir sheets, and the like) eventually formed the beginnings of large framed wall displays for what would become the International Lincoln Center.

In 2001, the American Studies program (the Washington, D.C., program and conference and lecture series) was transformed into the International Lincoln Center by the LSU Board of Supervisors.[8] It is now housed in an office and a vacated classroom set up to display Lincoln items from abroad. As the best-known political figure outside the United States, virtually every area of the world has a stamp, street, statue, school, or some other tribute in his honor.[9] I have had the opportunity to present several papers on Lincoln in India, the largest democracy in the world and the nation now with the largest number of English speakers. Lincoln was admired by both Mahatma Gandhi and Jawaharlal Nehru, India's founding prime minister, and is featured in the country's secondary school textbooks. Moreover, in my role as the director of the Association of Third World Studies, I have had the additional opportunity to visit several other countries in Latin America. If you have ever happily eaten Lincoln pizza at the Lincoln Road Restaurant located on Lincoln Avenue in the capital of the Dominican Republic, it might mean that you are a Lincolnator.

More important, while in Santo Domingo, I learned that its Lincoln Avenue was not named during the reign of Rafael Trujillo, the notorious dictator who came to power in 1930 and was eventually assassinated in May 1961. This was personally important to me. When I was in junior high school in Eugene, Oregon, I had learned that Trujillo had kidnapped Jesus Galindez, a young critic of his who had just completed his doctorate at Columbia University, flew him back from New York to the Dominican Republic on a small plane piloted by Gerald Murphy, and then had Galindez murdered. The same fate befell Murphy after he began to tell others in Santo Domingo what had happened.[10] Because Murphy's family was from Eugene, our local congressman, Charles O. Porter, took up the case against Trujillo. I had gone to school with Murphy's younger twin sisters. Unfortunately, the locals in Eugene turned against Porter, defeating him in the next election for paying too much attention to international rather than local matters. Nonetheless, the former congressman had the satisfaction of witnessing Trujillo's bloody fall in May 1961, and I had the satisfaction of finding, forty years later, that the naming of Lincoln Street was made only after Trujillo's assassination.[11] To gain favor with the United States, Trujillo had once named a street after its first president but never its sixteenth. Lincoln was too democratic.

After spending the last quarter century of my professional life in the Deep South, my interests have evolved from a general concern with the American presidency to our greatest presidents and finally to Lincoln's legacy abroad. I have learned several Lincoln lessons during these years.

First, just as my interests have expanded, many Southerners now recognize that their antebellum roots in the original political development of the United States and its Constitution are of more importance than just the "Lost Cause."

Second, many Southerners seem more open to Lincoln research than some scholars who have become specialists, defending only their professional turf.

Third, both liberals and conservatives generally admire Lincoln, but so do democrats and even dictators. There are more schools named for America's sixteenth president in Cuba than in any other nation outside the United States.

Fourth, the study of Lincoln's legacy abroad remains the most neglected area in Lincoln studies today. It seems to be changing.[12]

Though some of these lessons are depressing, overall it is hard to remain pessimistic for long. For example, Qatar Airways launched a new ad campaign in 2007 featuring Lincoln, not sitting on a throne in Washington, D.C., but enjoying himself lounging in one of Qatar's passenger recliner chairs. As impressive as the large and humorous ads are themselves, they were brought to my attention by a young instructor of literature in India.[13] Ironically, the legacy of America's sixteenth president might rest better in the hands of younger generations abroad, if our own at home fail to learn the lesson.

NOTES

1. William D. Pederson, "Amnesty and Presidential Behavior," *Presidential Studies Quarterly* 7, no. 4 (Fall 1977): 175–83.

2. William D. Pederson and Ann McLaurin, eds., *The Rating Game in American Politics: An Interdisciplinary Approach* (New York: Irvington Publishers, 1987).

3. William D. Pederson, "Inmate Movements and Prison Uprisings: A Comparative Study," *Social Science Quarterly* 59, no. 3 (December 1978): 509–24; and "Inmate

Revolts in the Soviet Union," in *Modern Encyclopedia of Russian and Soviet History*, ed. Joseph L. Wieczynski (Gulf Breeze, Fla.: Academic International Press, 1979), vol. 14, 184–88.

4. Barbara Tuchman, "An Inquiry into the Persistence of Unwisdom in Government," in Pederson and McLaurin, *Rating Game*, 197–212.

5. Frank J. Williams, William D. Pederson, and Vincent J. Marsala, eds., *Abraham Lincoln: Sources and Style of Leadership* (Westport, Conn.: Greenwood Press, 1994); Frank J. Williams and William D. Pederson, eds., *Abraham Lincoln Contemporary: An American Legacy* (Campbell, Calif: Savas Woodbury Publishers, 1996); and Frank J. Williams and William D. Pederson, eds., "Special Issue on Abraham Lincoln," *Quarterly Journal of Ideology* 17, nos. 1–2 (June 1994); as well as William D. Pederson and Frank J. Williams, "Deep South Conference Produces Living Lincoln Legacy," *Lincoln Newsletter* 14, no. 1 (Spring 1995): 6–8.

6. William D. Pederson and Frank J. Williams, "Abraham Lincoln and Lead-ership: A Summer Institute for Secondary Teachers," *Lincoln Newsletter* 12, no. 4 (Winter 1993) 3, 6–7.

7. Letter to author, February 12, 1999. Another member of the same organization, John D. Long, publishes pamphlets; see his *The Confederate Book of Arguments: 100 Questions Your Teacher Did Not Want You to Ask in School* (2004) and *Justice at* [...] th self-published in Shreveport. He [...] onwide.

[...] nternational Lincoln Center in the [...] 2): 63–70.

[...] oes Beyond U.S. Borders," *Washing-* [...] n, *The Legacy of Lincoln* (New York: [...]

[...] ictatorship to Democracy in the Do-*dies* 23, no. 1 (Spring 2006): 13–16.

[...] 'orter," *Washington Post*, January 6,

12. The first international conference, "Lincoln and Democracy," was held in Taiwan in 1989; see Y-Tang D. Lew, ed., *The Universal Lincoln* (Taipei: Chinese Culture University Press, 1995). Several symposia have been held on Lincoln's legacy abroad: in Santo Domingo, Dominican Republic, in 2005; in Barcelona, Spain, and Udaipur, India, in 2006; and in Lima, Peru, and Washington, D.C., in 2007.

13. *The Times of India*, June 12, 2007, and *The Hindu*, June 20, 2007.

Tell Me What You Want to Believe, and
I'll Tell You What You Will Believe

L ike most individuals, I was first exposed to Abraham Lincoln while a
   student in grade school. It was the 1940s, and World War II seemed to
dominate everything from school activities to playtime with patriotism as an
underlying theme. My earliest recollection of Lincoln is typical, I suspect, of
most children who grew up during that period. Above the blackboard were
two large framed portraits, one of George Washington, the other of Abraham
Lincoln. That Washington was the father of our country and Lincoln was its
savior was too abstract for young minds to understand. Rather, I was taught
that Washington never told a lie (the cherry tree caper) and Lincoln was
honest to a fault (walking several miles to return two cents to a poor woman
he had inadvertently overcharged when clerking at his store in New Salem).
These simple examples that every schoolchild could understand—always
tell the truth and be honest in all dealings with other people—sometimes
proved hard to follow as I grew older.

The real Lincoln did not attract my interest until many years later when I
was a graduate student at the University of Pennsylvania. It all began with a
used copy of selected writings by Lincoln. Lincoln students will appreciate
my fascination with his skillful use of words and his ability to explain the
most complex problems in simple terms. By the time I graduated and started
working at the National Institutes of Health in Bethesda, Maryland, I was a
"Lincoln buff" on my way to becoming a "Lincoln scholar."

To anyone interested in the Civil War, Washington is an ideal place to live.
Within a half-day drive, one can find the sites of most of the major battles
of the Army of the Potomac and its vaunted enemy, the Army of Northern
Virginia. But little did I know that Washington is "ground zero" for Lincoln's
assassination. Beginning with Ford's Theatre in downtown Washington, one
can follow the escape of Lincoln's assassin over the same roads and past many
of the houses and farms where he hid out or lingered in his dash to escape his
pursuers. It was while retracing the footsteps of John Wilkes Booth and his co-
hort, Davy Herold, that I became hooked, so to speak, on the assassination.

My story begins in July 1977, when I attended a Civil War show in Gettys-burg. During an afternoon lull, I struck up a conversation with an old friend, Dave Zullo. Dave had recently retired from the Air Force and decided to try his hand as a bookseller. Books were what Dave loved most, and he eventually built his effort into a respectable business, including publishing important reference works under the name "Olde Soldier Books, Inc."

As we talked about the show—what items impressed us and what trea-sures we did or didn't find—Dave asked me what I knew about the "missing pages" from Booth's diary. "Not much," I answered. What I learned came a few years later. When Booth was killed at the Garrett farm on April 26, 1865, one of the items taken from his body was a little memorandum book he used as a diary during his twelve-day escape into Virginia. The book was turned over to Secretary of War Edwin M. Stanton by Booth's captors. The "diary" was never introduced at the trial of the eight defendants accused of Lincoln's murder. When it did appear two years later during the 1867 trial of conspirator John Surratt, people noticed that several pages were missing. Some claimed the "missing pages" held the key to a greater conspiracy in-volving prominent members of the North's political, military, and business communities, including Lincoln's own secretary of war.

In 1937, amateur Civil War historian Otto Eisenschiml published a revi-sionist account of Lincoln's assassination in a book entitled *Why Was Lincoln Murdered?* Eisenschiml, without directly accusing Stanton of complicity in the assassination, filled the pages of his book with innuendo implicating Stanton. This left the reader with the impression that Stanton was behind Lincoln's assassination, just what Eisenschiml intended. His theory became a favorite with conspiracy buffs and the media; the idea of a government cover-up proved a profitable sell. Refuted by many competent historians, the theory nevertheless refused to die and, like Lazarus of old, kept rising from the grave. Lazarus, or rather Stanton, walked across the assassination landscape with blood dripping from his fingers, thanks to Eisenschiml. It was an undeserved libel on a great American patriot who helped save the Union in its hour of greatest peril.

In 1975, the assassination community was stunned to learn that the missing pages had surfaced in the possession of a Stanton descendant. An individual who identified himself as "Mr. X" acted as a "go-between" for the descendant and certain individuals interested in the "missing pages." Mr. X eventually identified himself as Joseph Lynch, a dealer in rare books and Americana living in Massachusetts. According to Lynch, he had been contacted by a member of the Stanton family to appraise the material in the "descendant's" possession. At some point, Lynch acquired copies of the missing pages.

A movie company, Sunn Classic Pictures, learned of the missing pages and contacted Lynch in an effort to obtain the rights to the pages for a movie. After Sunn Classic acquired the rights to a transcription of the alleged missing pages, a movie and a book, both titled *The Lincoln Conspiracy*, were released in 1977. The book, written by David Balsiger and Charles E. Sellier Jr., and movie, directed by James L. Conway (screenplay by David Balsiger and Jonathan Cobbler), relied heavily on the information in the missing pages. Both the book and the movie were sensational, to say the least. Once again, Edwin Stanton became the dark angel of death, plotting with high-ranking government officials and powerful businessmen to remove Lincoln from office. With Lincoln out of the way, his assassins were free to plunder the South and reap fortunes from Southern cotton and land deals.

Enter James O. Hall, the dean of Lincoln assassination researchers. During the period between the alleged discovery of the missing pages and the release of the book and movie, Hall attempted to track down the missing pages and their owner. He worked closely with Richard E. Sloan, past president of the Lincoln Group of New York and the publisher and editor of an informative newsletter that specialized in Lincoln's assassination, *The Lincoln Log*.

Sloan doggedly pursued the rumors and made contact with Lynch, eventually gaining his trust.[1] Lynch told Sloan that he discovered the missing pages in 1974 in the possession of one of Stanton's great-granddaughters, who also insisted on anonymity. As the story unfolded over a period of several months, Sloan kept his subscribers to the *Lincoln Log* informed with the latest news, as it became available to him.[2]

Hall, in the meantime, had contacted the known Stanton descendants and came up dry. None knew of missing pages, nor had they ever heard any family stories or suggestions that such pages ever existed.[3] On informing Lynch of Hall's inability to locate a Stanton heir with knowledge of the missing pages, Hall and Sloan were told that the mysterious heir was descended from an *illegitimate* son of Stanton's whose identity was kept secret from family members. It was the illegitimate son who had come into possession of the missing pages after his father's death. The two Lincoln sleuths had hit a wall. They needed to see the pages, or at least a typescript of them, before they could pass judgment on their authenticity.

Sunn Classic Pictures included excerpts from these missing pages in the film's press kit. Sloan published them in the March-April 1977 issue of his newsletter, along with a brief history of the diary.[4] The transcript revealed a wide conspiracy involving "Senator John Conness of California, Northern financier Jay Cooke, Confederate Secretary of State Judah Benjamin, New York political boss Thurlow Weed, U.S. Senator Zachariah Chandler, Confederate Secret Service commissioner Jacob Thompson, U.S. Secret Service

Chief Lafayette Baker, Col. Everton J. Conger [member of Baker's agency who led the posse that killed Booth], and several others."[5]

Toward the end of the entries, Booth wrote: "By the Almighty God, I swear that I shall lay the body of this tyrant [Lincoln] dead upon the altar of Mars [Mars was Lincoln's nickname for Stanton]. And if by this act, I am slain, they too shall be cast into Hell for I have given information to a friend who will have the nation know who the traitors are."[6]

After carefully examining the typescript, Hall formally told Sloan, "I would not stake my life on the 'missing pages' being forgeries, but . . . no responsible researcher can say that they are authentic until they are released for scientific study. Booth could have made the whole thing up to damage the hated Radicals and Baker."[7] Privately, Hall confided to him that he believed the missing pages a clever hoax.[8]

In the same issue of the *Lincoln Log* in which Sloan published the excerpts, a notice appeared announcing a guided tour along John Wilkes Booth's legendary trail. The daylong trip was scheduled for the fall. The tour, the newsletter announced, would be conducted by the most knowledgeable expert on the subject, James O. Hall.[9] As a result of Dave's story about the missing pages, I was becoming intrigued with the controversy, even though Lincoln's assassination was still in the background of my interests. I picked up the phone and called Joan Chaconas, my good friend from the Lincoln Group of the District of Columbia who arranged the tours for the Surratt Society. Joan reserved a seat for me.

Arriving at the Surratt House in Clinton, Maryland, at 6:15 A.M., I was greeted by Joan, standing in the middle of the parking lot with a clipboard checking off the "Boothies" as they arrived. Parked across the lot was a bright yellow school bus. It was too early for schoolkids to be visiting the Surratt House, I thought to myself. What was a school bus doing at the Surratt House at this early hour? I soon found the answer. The bus was for us, complete with hard seats, no shocks or air conditioning (only a few windows would open), and no public address system or rest room.

Joan, acting like a drill sergeant, barked out orders telling us to board. She had reserved a seat for me up front across the aisle from her. I recently had a ruptured disk surgically removed from my lower back, and Joan thoughtfully made sure I didn't wind up sitting over one of the wheels.

As the bus made its way out of the parking lot and onto Surratt Road, I couldn't help feeling I was in for a very bad day. Joan must have noticed the look on my face. Waving her hand in the air, she said, "Not to worry. You are gonna love it. Trust me."

She was right. Beginning at Ford's Theatre, we headed east past the Capitol into southeast Washington, where we drove over the Navy Yard Bridge toward southern Maryland. Our first stop was at the Surratt House (where we had started two hours earlier), then on to Dr. Mudd's house, followed by St. Mary's Church and the Bryantown Tavern. Booth had stayed at the tavern on at least two occasions, and it was there that Mudd introduced him to Thomas Harbin, a Confederate agent who would later make arrangements for horses and a guide to help Booth in his escape in Virginia.

Before long, the dread of a long trip had completely evaporated. Everyone was enthused and loving Hall's narration. The bantering back and forth added to our enjoyment. John Brennan, a legend among Booth "trippers," delighted us with his demonstration of "dousing for bodies" at St. Mary's Cemetery (where Dr. Mudd and several of his Confederate cohorts are buried).

The trip through southern Maryland was like stepping back into the past. The same roads that Booth used were still there (only paved). Many of the mailboxes along the route carried the same names of the people who lived there in the 1860s. And several of the places where Booth stopped or where his Confederate friends lived were still standing, and we were invited inside to see and feel the history that was surrounding us.

Midway into the tour, the bus pulled into a McDonald's restaurant in LaPlata, Maryland, for lunch. I decided to follow Hall and use the time to ask him several questions that were puzzling me. Toward the end of our meal, I happened to casually mention the missing pages from Booth's diary. I told him I had a friend who had a friend who knew the fellow who had the original pages. Hall's ears perked up immediately. He wanted to know the details, but Joan ended our conversation by herding everyone back on the bus. It was time to go, she said, and Booth was only a few miles ahead of us. If we hurried, we just might catch him. As I boarded the bus, Hall said he wanted to talk with me further when the tour ended.

Six hours later, the bus pulled into the Surratt House parking lot. Tired but happy, the crowd gave Joan and Hall a rousing cheer. When the last of the cars left, Hall pulled me aside. We sat down on the front steps of the old house, and he asked me what I knew about the pages and this fellow who was supposed to have them. I couldn't tell him a whole lot because I didn't know a whole lot, but I told him about my conversation with Dave Zullo back in July at the Gettysburg Civil War show. The story went something like this: Dave had a friend with whom he had served in the Air Force; they had retired at the same time. His friend then went into the home renovation business somewhere in New Jersey. Seems his friend had purchased an old Victorian house he was renovating for resale—Dave wasn't sure where the house was located. Anyway, his friend had uncovered beneath a staircase a closet that had been plastered over and covered with wallpaper. The house had once belonged to some famous person who had been a close friend of Lincoln's.

Dave couldn't remember who the "famous person" was, but his friend told him he had found several items associated with Lincoln's assassination in the hidden closet. Among the items were some pages from Booth's diary. The only solid information Dave had was the name of his friend and his renovation company located in New Jersey. Hall wrote down the information and slipped the paper in his shirt pocket. We chatted a few minutes longer before parting and heading home.

The next day my phone rang. It was Hall. He said my story, fuzzy as it was, checked out on the particulars. He had located Dave's friend and had spoken with him. He had confirmed the story of the hidden closet and the items found inside it. There were three large books, a few papers, a fancy box, a woman's bonnet, and some other items he couldn't remember. The story got better. The house had been owned at one time by Thomas Eckert, the man in charge of the War Department telegraph office and later assistant secretary of war under Stanton. Eckert was Lincoln's first choice to accompany him and his wife to the theater the night Lincoln was killed, but Stanton told Eckert he couldn't spare him; he needed Eckert to work in the telegraph office. Eckert's absence that fateful night has fueled speculation that Stanton deliberately prevented Eckert from accompanying the president to the theater so that Booth would have a better chance of entering the box and shooting Lincoln.

Dave's friend told Hall that he had sold the items to a Civil War collector who lived near Newton, New Jersey. He had the man's name and address. Hall then contacted the collector. Yes, he still had the items he originally bought from Dave's friend. Hall asked if he might visit the collector and see the items. The collector said he would be happy to show them to Hall, who left the impression he was interested in purchasing some of the items. Hall then asked if I could go with him the next day to New Jersey. He wanted the two of us to visit the collector and examine the "secret papers" from Eckert's closet. Sure, I said. I was pleased he invited me along for the ride. It sounded rather exciting.

At eight o'clock the next morning, Hall pulled into my driveway. I had been up for over an hour, anxious to get on the road. The anticipation of what we might find had taken hold of me. I slid into the passenger side of the car, and Hall handed me a map. "You're the navigator," he said. We were traveling about as far up in New Jersey as one can go before crossing over into Pennsylvania. The trip was long, but time passed quickly as the two of us talked assassination. I would ask a question; Hall would answer. By the time we pulled into the motel later that evening, I felt as though I had just finished a graduate course on Lincoln's murder.

We had a nine o'clock appointment the next morning with the collector. I was up at six, ready to go, but Hall showed no sign of anticipation. In fact, he seemed almost indifferent. He had been through so many wild goose chases that he had become used to their amounting to nothing. It was that rare instance, however, when you just might get lucky and find something of great importance that kept Hall running down rumors.

A few minutes after nine, we pulled up to the collector's house. The anticipation was building. The more we talked with him, the greater it became. After several minutes of small talk, Hall asked about the house with the closet. Was it really a "hidden closet" in Thomas Eckert's house? Yes, it was true; Thomas Eckert had once owned the old house. Under the staircase was a closet that had been covered up many years earlier. Inside the closet were several items of great historical importance. There were papers, some in code or cipher. The collector was sure the coded papers had to do with the assassination. He told us that an alleged authority had already examined the papers and told him they contained critical evidence that pointed to Stanton's involvement in Lincoln's murder. The collector told us the documents were worth a great deal of money.

The more he talked, the more I wanted to get started. Hall had cautioned me before we arrived that we would probably have to spend some time just sitting and chatting. It was natural for the collector to size us up, to determine how knowledgeable we were, how serious we were. The collector had never met us, but he knew of Hall by reputation. Finally, after what seemed an agonizingly long time, the collector asked us if we would like to see some of his things. "Finally," I mumbled. I looked over at Hall sitting comfortably on the sofa. "That would be nice," he said, smiling. "Good," the collector said. "I think it would be best if we went into the dining room where we can sit around the table."

He motioned for us to take a seat at one end of a large rectangular table. At the other end were several items carefully arranged. The collector picked up the first item: a small book, beautifully bound in maroon leather with gold lettering. It was a special presentation copy of *Lincoln in the Telegraph Office* by David Homer Bates.[10] Bates was one of the telegraphers that worked in the War Department telegraph office. Lincoln was a constant visitor to the office, sitting with his feet propped on one of the desks while reading through a stack of daily telegrams, regaling the telegraphers with funny stories if the news wasn't too bad. Inside the front cover of the book, on the flyleaf, was an inscription to General Thomas T. Eckert, signed and dated by Bates.

The special presentation copy was one piece of evidence that supported the collector's story. But there was more—a woman's bonnet said to be assassination conspirator Mary Surratt's, removed on the scaffold before the hood was placed over her head and the noose around her neck. There was a beautiful rosewood box with a lid made of beveled French glass. On the front of the box was a small silver plate with Eckert's name engraved on it. Inside the box were short lengths of twisted cable carefully lined up from left to right, each succeeding piece larger than the preceding one. Each section of cable had a thin band of gold metal slipped over it like the band on a cigar. Each band was inscribed with a date. The sections, the collector said, were cut from successive telegraph cables laid across the ocean bottom from North America to Europe. The box was a special presentation piece given to Eckert in recognition of his service to commercial telegraphy. Eckert had organized and run the military telegraph during the Civil War. After the war, he supervised several telegraph companies owned by Jay Gould, eventually becoming president of Western Union.

The items were clearly authentic and belonged, at one time, to Eckert. He was close to Stanton and was in the right place at the right time. I was beginning to believe there just might be missing pages among the treasures stacked at one end of the table. The collector suddenly left the room, and when he returned he was carrying two large ledger books. They were bound in brown cloth and stamped with gold letters bearing the dates 1864 and 1865. He set the ledgers down on the table between Hall and myself and placed one hand on top of the books. He said the pages were very fragile, being made of some sort of tissue-like paper. Some of the pages were in code, and they were the important pages because they contained the incriminating evidence telling of Booth's greater conspiracy. That's why they were in code, he said. I thought to myself, Why write anything down? Why chance the possibility that an enemy might be able to break the code and expose the traitorous plot?

We were welcome to go through the books, the collector said, but we were not to write anything down. Whatever we took away from our meeting would be in our heads, not anywhere else.

Hall took the book dated 1865 and pushed the other, marked 1864, toward me. We carefully opened the books and began reading the elegant script that ran across each page in neatly formed rows. Clerks during the war were hired for their penmanship more than anything else. The thin pages, Hall later explained to me, were known as "flimsies"—copies made by pressing tissue paper backed by a damp cloth against the original page written in ink. When carefully done, these "press" copies transferred some of the ink from the original to the tissue paper, where it gave a positive copy of the original. The "flimsies" were bound in large volumes and served as file copies of the originals.

The collector sat impatiently waiting for some sign from Hall that he had finally found the Holy Grail he had been looking for all these years, but there was no expression of "Eureka!" or anything else from Hall. The best he managed was an occasional "Hmmm," or a nod of the head with a low murmured "Ahhh."

My book was filled with telegrams detailing the mundane business of running a war from inside an office building: shipping supplies, requests for statistical reports, instructions concerning bounty payments for enlistment, orders to report, and so on. The collector reminded us that the important pages were written in cipher—they were the key. Could Hall read them? He had been able to read some of the simple cipher, enough to understand the topic of the message. After looking over several coded pages, Hall said that most of the cipher seemed to deal with confiscated rebel land that was being auctioned. Bids were to be kept sealed. Secrecy was of the utmost importance to prevent fraud. There were several telegrams dealing with the conspirators and the assassination. Their names appeared in several places: Payne, Herold, Arnold, O'Laughlen, and Mrs. Surratt. There were telegrams to Chapel Point in southern Maryland ordering the troops to seize, search, arrest, commandeer, send at once under guard, patrol the river, and so on, and telegrams to the Navy Yard to prepare the monitors *Montauk* and *Saugus* to receive prisoners.

Hall finessed his remarks. The material was very interesting. It shed light on the daily and even hourly activities of searching for Lincoln's killers, transporting those arrested, gathering evidence, and preparing to carry out the sentences of the tribunal. But no missing pages, no smoking gun, nothing that would suggest a desperate Stanton covering his tracks, a government cover-up. The books, Hall explained, were bound copies of War Department telegrams. Similar volumes for the earlier years were in the National Archives. These two volumes somehow escaped. Hall speculated that Eckert kept the two books when he left his job at the end of the war because they contained detailed information concerning the operation of the military telegraph, information that would prove valuable in establishing a commercial telegraph company in the postwar period: names and locations of telegraphers, maintenance men, all of the nuts and bolts needed to run an efficient telegraph. Such information, Hall said, would be vital to setting up postwar companies. Eckert was a smart businessman. The books were certainly interesting and valuable for what they were, but nothing more.

The collector would have none of Hall's explanations. He had it on good authority that inside the ciphered messages was buried the key to a greater government conspiracy.

Hall then surprised me by asking if the books were for sale. The collector hesitated for a minute as if sizing up Hall. He had to get $10,000 for them, he said. They were too important. Hall stood up and thanked the collector for his hospitality. We shook hands and left.

I was disappointed, of course, at not finding the missing pages that would unlock the mysteries and answer all the questions about why Lincoln was murdered. Hall pointed out there were no pages that held incriminating information about a grand conspiracy. So why, I asked Hall, did he go to all the trouble to drive several hundred miles to examine the collector's materials? He explained that someday someone will claim to have secret papers from Thomas Eckert exposing a government conspiracy, and when it happens, we will be in a position to expose it for what it is. Hall has a file cabinet filled with hoaxes and confabulations. He pointed out that wanting to believe can be a very strong emotion. When faced with a choice between fact and fiction, fiction is often the winner. And conspiracy is a powerful force. "Americans," he said, "love conspiracy."

The trip was quite an education for me. Hall had introduced me to the inner sanctum of the Lincoln assassination. I was hooked. Over the next twenty-five years, we became good friends, and he has always been a generous resource. I will forever remember that sobering first experience and something he said on the drive back home. We were cruising along the New Jersey turnpike, resting from our conversation, when suddenly he said, "Tell me what you want to believe, and I'll tell you what you will believe." The truth of that statement has come back to me time and again over the years. They are, perhaps, the greatest lesson I learned from James O. Hall.

NOTES

1. Richard E. Sloan, "The Case of the Missing Pages," *Journal of the Lincoln Assassination* 9, no. 3 (December 1995): 38–44. This periodical is a privately printed newsletter edited by Frederick Hatch and published by Autograph Press, P.O. Box 2616, Waldorf, Md.

2. Sloan reported the story in the *Lincoln Log* beginning with the November–December 1976 issue (vol. 1, no. 11) and continuing through October–November 1977 (vol. 2, no. 6).

3. James O. Hall, interview with author, May 1977.

4. Richard Sloan, "The Missing Pages," *Lincoln Log* 2, no. 3 (March–April 1977).

5. Ibid., 1.

6. Ibid., 4.

7. Richard Sloan, ed., "Comments on Conspiracy Film," *Lincoln Log* 2, no. 4 (May–June 1977), 9.

8. Hall interview.

9. Sloan, "Missing Pages," 14.

10. David Homer Bates, *Lincoln in the Telegraph Office* (New York: Appleton-Century Company), 1907.

Sixteen Feet Tall: Abraham Lincoln and History

My first association with Abraham Lincoln was in the fall of 1950 when as a four-year-old kindergarten student I walked with my older sister past orange groves and a field of amaryllis plants to my first day at Lincoln Elementary School in Anaheim, California. Actually, it was called simply Lincoln School, and it still exists, though it looks nothing like it did five-plus decades ago. I attended it for six years, leaving briefly in the fifth grade to attend Clara Barton School—another name with a strong Civil War connection—because of overcrowding in the fast-growing Anaheim of the 1950s (Disneyland opened in 1955). I returned to Lincoln School to graduate from the sixth grade into (of all places) John C. Fremont Junior High School. Perhaps my interest in the Civil War was fated from the beginning.

What I remember most about Lincoln School was its old brick facade. It was constructed of pale golden-yellow bricks, rough in texture, that contrasted with the darker red bricks around the heavy doors and the tall double-sash windows that stretched up to the high ceilings in the classrooms—ceilings so high that there was a perceptible echo to the teacher's instruction. In the middle of that brick facade was a protruding gable with an enormous archway framing a recessed alcove—at least, it seemed enormous to me at the time. I realize now, thinking back, that it could not have been as large as it seems in my memory, for Lincoln School was but a single story high, so the arch in question could not have been more than twelve to fourteen feet high. Inside the alcove, which was always cool even in the summer, was a bronze statue of the sixteenth president for whom the school had been named. He was standing—not seated as he is at the Lincoln Memorial—on a pedestal that was perhaps two feet high. I can't remember now if he held anything in his hands, but I think he was hatless, for I recall how his hair was sculpted into wayward tufts. It may have been a life-size statue, but on that pedestal, inside that soaring arch, his lank form loomed above me with awe-inspiring gravitas. To me, Lincoln was sixteen feet tall.

I report this early memory as a possible metaphor for those of us who study Abraham Lincoln. The historical figure who has come down to us through generations of awed students and who has been honed to a near deity by Carl Sandburg and other admirers looms at least as large in the public histori- cal consciousness as that bronze figure did over the diminutive elementary students who gazed up at it more than a half century ago. Let me hasten to say that this is not necessarily a bad thing. Lincoln deserves our awe. In almost every poll, year after year, professional historians rate Lincoln as the greatest of American presidents, with Washington and the two Roosevelts trailing.[1] I think their judgment—our judgment, since I number myself among them—is accurate. But on the other hand, we must be careful not to assume that Lincoln was, in fact, sixteen feet tall, for to do that actually diminishes his accomplishments since it suggests that his greatness came naturally to him, without effort.

Lincoln's all-but-ignored first-term vice president, who bore the won- derful nineteenth-century name of Hannibal Hamlin, later insisted that "eulogists make the mistake of constructing a Lincoln who was as great the day he left Springfield as when he made his earthly exit four years later." Hamlin, too, admired Lincoln. But Hamlin believed that historically there were two Lincolns: "The one who came from Illinois, inexperienced in wield- ing great power," and the one who emerged over the next four years as "the conqueror of a gigantic civil war, the emancipator of slaves, master of the political situation, and savior of the nation." He became those things—he grew to be sixteen feet tall—but it was part of a metamorphosis that began almost the day he arrived in Washington and that continued until the day he died. Hamlin believed that "no man ever grew in the executive chair in his lifetime as Lincoln did."[2]

Lincoln's greatness was a process, not a gift. He was arguably less prepared for the presidency than any man who ever ascended to that position. He had served only two years in the national government, as a one-term Whig con- gressman in the 1840s. He was less well educated and less well traveled than any other president before or since. He spoke no language other than English, and he spoke that with a reedy backwoods patois that frequently led more precise elocutionists to underestimate him. We explain away these presumed disadvantages by noting that Lincoln compensated for his lack of experience with great political instinct, a sense of humor, the ability to work effectively with almost anyone, and a deep devotion to the principles of democratic gov- ernment. Without a doubt. But he also possessed a determination to learn, to adjust, to change, and to improve, and that, in the end, is what allowed him to become the bronze hero that still awes elementary schoolchildren.

Of course, growth can occur only through experience. One learns at least as much from mistakes as from success, and Lincoln's admirers need to acknowledge that he made a number of mistakes and miscalculations, especially early in his presidency. It is curious that conventional explanations of Abraham Lincoln emphasize his astonishing trajectory from humble roots to national greatness without acknowledging that this trajectory continued into and during his presidency. Lincoln was not a great president from the day he took office. He groped hesitantly toward a policy for the offshore forts in South Carolina and Florida, and after the first shots were fired at Fort Sumter (which Lincoln and others invariably spelled "Sumpter"), he approached the problem of how to fight the war with equal diffidence and uncertainty. He struggled morally and politically with the Gordian knot of slavery, and after emancipation he struggled to define the precise character of black freedom in a postwar America. In all these areas, he knew what he wanted to accomplish, but he had no clear idea of how to do it. As a result, Lincoln's early decision-making was both ad hoc and experimental. He relied heavily on his advisers, especially William Henry Seward, and when those advisors offered conflicting opinions, as they frequently did, Lincoln generally asked each of them to state their case before the group. If consensus did not emerge, he often asked them to commit their views in writing—something he forced himself to do as well. Even then, he disliked having to choose, preferring to blend the views of his advisers whenever possible. When, only hours after the first shot at Fort Sumter, he asked the members of his cabinet how many soldiers he should call into service under the Militia Act, their suggestions ranged from 50,000 to 100,000. Lincoln split the difference and called up 75,000. Especially during the early months of the war that followed, Lincoln was as much an adjudicator as a leader—more Franklin Roosevelt than Andrew Jackson.

None of this diminishes Lincoln's greatness. Indeed, it enhances it, for it demonstrates how Lincoln struggled, adjusted, shifted his ground when necessary, and learned to be an effective—indeed, a brilliant—president and commander in chief. Of course, a candid acknowledgment of the trajectory of Lincoln's growth from 1861 to 1865 makes his death in April 1865 that much more tragic. Though some have suggested that Lincoln's martyrdom, coming literally at the moment of his greatest triumph, played a large role in his public reputation, it is equally likely that had he lived, he would have continued to grow in stature, soaring past sixteen feet to take on truly Homeric proportions.

Some twenty years after meeting Lincoln eyeball-to-kneecap as a four-year-old, I found myself engaging in serious contemplation of Lincoln as commander in chief. In the early 1970s, I taught at the U.S. Naval War College in Newport, Rhode Island. It was, to say the least, an unusual teaching environment for me. I was a navy ensign fresh out of Officer Candidate School and cast by a variety of circumstances as a "professor of strategy" charged with teaching students who were immeasurably senior to me. The Naval War College had been founded by Stephen B. Luce a century earlier to prepare senior navy officers for flag-rank responsibilities by requiring them to think strategically rather than tactically—to think, in other words, like an admiral rather than as a ship commander. The course I taught, along with other talented and more experienced scholars, was called Strategy and Policy; it began with a careful reading of Thucydides' *History of the Peloponnesian War* and then examined historical case studies of decision-makers from Napoleon to Bismarck to Churchill. One case focused on the American Civil War.

The book that my war college students read for the Civil War case study was T. Harry Williams's *Lincoln and His Generals*, first published in 1952. (This is not to be confused with a multivolume work with a similar title: *Lincoln Finds a General* by Kenneth P. Williams.) T. Harry Williams argued that Lincoln was "a great natural strategist, a better one than any of his generals." He admitted that Lincoln had a steep learning curve as a military strategist, especially in the early months of the war, but Williams insisted that Lincoln not only was an excellent judge of men but also had an instinctive, common-sense grasp of military strategy and that it was Lincoln more than anyone else who was the chief architect of Union victory.[3] For many of the students in those seminar groups, Lincoln's management of his generals was the "school solution"—a kind of how-to manual for heads of state in wartime.

The American conception of the civil-military relationship is quite specific. We believe that while the decision to go to war is one properly made by the civil government, we also believe that once war begins, it is the generals who should organize it and manage it, handing authority back over to the civil government once the war is over. According to this view, if a president or some other representative of the civil government attempts to impose a particular strategy on the generals, we look upon that as "meddling" or "micromanaging." One of the lessons we tried to teach our war college students was that such a view is simplistic, for theoretically, at least, wars are fought to achieve political objectives, and success in war therefore requires consultation and cooperation between civil and military authority. Still, the traditional template of a sharp divide between president and his field generals was—and is—hard to shake.

Lincoln himself has been accused of micromanaging his generals, though not as often as his counterpart, Jefferson Davis. Davis was a West Point graduate and a hero of the Mexican War and thought of himself as the literal as well as the constitutional commander in chief. For his part, however, Lincoln knew that he was no military expert and characteristically mocked his own short stint as a militiaman in the Black Hawk War. He would have been happy to turn military strategy over to the professionals, but the capriciousness of those generals compelled him, over time, to grip the reins of government more firmly than he had initially intended. Initially, Lincoln hoped that seventy-four-year-old General Winfield Scott could manage the war, but despite his successes in earlier wars, it soon became evident that this new conflict was beyond him. After Scott stepped aside, Lincoln placed his hope in George B. McClellan, who at age thirty-four was four decades younger than his predecessor. Lincoln was initially inclined to give McClellan as much authority and time as he needed, but as time passed and nothing happened, he began to prod him, then to push him, and finally he took to pleading with him. "I beg to assure you," he wrote Little Mac in April 1862, "that I have never written you or spoke to you in greater kindness of feeling than now, nor with a fuller purpose to sustain you, so far as in my most anxious judgment, I consistently can. *But you must act.*"[4] Even this could not move McClellan into action, and in the end, of course, Lincoln had to let him go.

All this time, Lincoln maintained a serious and continuous study of military principles to which he applied a commonsense logic based on his understanding of the particular strengths of the Union as contrasted to the Confederate states. The North, Lincoln knew, had more men and more resources. A strategy based on the simultaneous and relentless application of this manpower and matériel superiority would eventually lead to victory as long as public opinion continued to sustain the war effort. Alas, he could not get his generals to see it this way. They sought to win brilliant victories by virtue of their tactical planning and ingenious maneuvers. All too often, those tactics and maneuvers led to disappointment—even disaster. Over time, Lincoln's own confidence in his strategic views grew, and eventually he became the activist commander in chief who crafted the final victory. Here, too, it was a process of growth, not merely the application of native genius, that made Lincoln great. Moreover, Lincoln's restraint, patience, tolerance, and commitment to a republican form of government allowed him to become an activist wartime president without threatening the fundamental relationship between the head of state and the army.

My war college students invariably developed a great admiration for Lincoln as commander in chief. If anything, they thought he ought to have dumped McClellan sooner and been even more proactive in forcing his strategic vision on his generals. They agreed that while generals were duty-bound to offer their professional views and opinions, they also believed that when the civil head of government gives an order, it becomes a soldier's duty to obey that order with his full commitment and enthusiasm. If he can't do that, he should resign. Such a view is comforting simply because it is so clear: salute smartly and obey, or resign and keep quiet. Moreover, this view protects the concept of civilian control of the military, one of the great bulwarks of our democracy. But few complicated issues can be reduced to such a simple formula. In 2006, a number of retired U.S. Army and Marine Corps generals went public in protest of what they saw as harmful behavior and poor decision-making by the American secretary of defense during the war in Iraq. Critics asked why these generals had remained on active duty if they disagreed so strongly with the strategy imposed on them or, alternatively, why, after staying on active service until retirement, they decided to speak up at all. Very likely, these men felt constrained by the conventional protocols of the civil-military relationship while on active duty. Unwilling to resign in the midst of an ongoing campaign, in effect abandoning their soldiers on the battlefield, they kept a public silence and did their jobs the best they could. But equally unwilling to remain silent forever, they spoke out once their jobs were over.

This recent episode shows that the issue of civil-military relations in America is not simply a matter of applying a strict set of rules. Lincoln's great strength as a commander in chief is that he understood that nuance was important, even essential, in defining the civil-military relationship. He was patient with McClellan (too patient, some would say); he boosted Ambrose Burnside's fragile confidence; he tolerated Joseph Hooker's bloviated posturing; and he gave both William T. Sherman and Ulysses S. Grant the kind of loose rein that allowed them to complete their triumphant campaigns. In the end, therefore, it was not merely Lincoln's willingness to adapt himself to the existing protocols of the civil-military relationship but also the sensitivity he demonstrated in the care and feeding of his various generals that allowed the United States to survive a bloody four-year civil war without damaging the constitutional relationship.

What I hope my senior-grade officer-students at the war college learned from their study of Abraham Lincoln as a wartime commander in chief is that while patriotism, determination, and a clear articulation of the war's objective are all valuable characteristics in a president, they are not enough. Lincoln's ability to listen, adapt, compromise, and subordinate his own preferences to the greater public good were also elements of his greatness, and they were critical to eventual Union victory.

Soon after leaving the war college in 1975, I began a thirty-year teaching career at the U.S. Naval Academy where I taught both American naval history and the history of the Civil War and Reconstruction. The naval history course was required of all midshipmen and was great fun; it is hard to imagine a more salubrious educational environment than teaching naval history to midshipmen. The Civil War course was an upper-level elective, and it, too, was great fun. The students were bright and dedicated and came from every state in the Union. I usually had a good cross section of "Rebs" and "Yanks" along with a number of "orphans" from such places as North Dakota or Hawaii, some of whom scratched their heads in perplexity at the intensity of the class arguments over the causes of the war, Sherman's behavior in Georgia and South Carolina, or the relative greatness of Lee and Grant.

Naturally, this course included a discussion of Lincoln as commander in chief, but it also covered Lincoln and slavery. Indeed, in many ways, that became the heart of the course. Like Lincoln himself, I sought to make a clear distinction for my students between the existence of slavery in the Deep South states and the issue of its extension into the western territories. Nevertheless, many students were surprised to learn that Lincoln had been willing to guarantee the future of slavery in the South before the war, that he had promised to enforce the Fugitive Slave Law, and that even once the war began, his Emancipation Proclamation technically freed no slaves since it applied only to those areas where Lincoln's armies could not enforce it. Lincoln was also slow to accept the idea of black soldiers, disciplining both John Fremont and David Hunter and dismissing his first secretary of war, Simon Cameron, for getting ahead of themselves on that issue. So what, then, was Lincoln's view of slavery? Was he really the Great Emancipator?

It is a question that is still asked, and like many historical questions, it requires some explanation rather than a simple yes or no. It was not possible for me simply to tell the midshipmen the answer even if I knew what it was, since like all good students they wanted to see the evidence. As every teacher knows, it is better to allow students to discover the important answers for themselves than simply to tell them, because that way they "own" the information. So to engage this issue, we explored the broader question of Lincoln and slavery, and once again, a key to understanding that issue is appreciating the trajectory of Lincoln's growth and his ability to adjust.

Lincoln hated slavery. Of that we can be fairly certain. "If slavery is not wrong, nothing is wrong," he declared in 1864, adding, "I can not remember when I did not so think, and feel."[5] Politician though he was, he did not quail at the final conclusion of his logic. When during a debate in 1858, Stephen A. Douglas charged that a vote for Lincoln was a vote for "nigger equality," the smart political move would have been for Lincoln to deny it. Even in Illinois, there were few white voters who could tolerate the notion of racial equality in 1858. Instead, however, Lincoln replied that "[i]n the right to eat the bread, without leave of anybody else, which his own hand earns, he is my equal and the equal of Judge Douglas, and the equal of every living man."[6] It was a bold assertion, well ahead of public opinion at the time, and one with great political risk.

Lincoln was a politician, and he knew that adopting the abolitionists' position and simply calling slavery a sin not only was fatuous but courted political suicide. Instead of cursing the darkness, Lincoln lit a single candle. His hope and belief was that if the nation could stop the spread of slavery into the West, the continued growth of the black population by natural increase, combined with the refusal to expand the amount of productive land that the slaves could work, would eventually create a labor surplus where there were more slaves than there was work for them to do. The law of supply and demand would depress the price of slaves, and soon it would cost more to maintain slaves as property than an owner could gain from their labor. When that occurred, slavery would perish by its own dead weight. In making this assumption, Lincoln almost certainly underestimated the determination of a slave-holding society to maintain race dominance, even if it was economically unremunerative. Still, this vision was the source of Lincoln's determination to prevent slavery from going into the Mexican Cession and later into Kansas Territory. It was the core of his objection to the *Dred Scott* decision. It was what led him back into the political arena in 1854 and to the presidency in 1860. It was also why he expressed a willingness to guarantee the protection of slavery where it existed in 1861 while remaining adamant that it should not be allowed to expand.

It is hard to know how swiftly Lincoln expected the restriction of slavery would lead to eventual emancipation. There is some suggestion that he believed it might take as long as a hundred years. But war is a great accelerator; in terms of social change, war is history's fast-forward button. Lincoln realized only a few months into the war that it would be possible to accomplish several generations of change in a very short period. To be sure, his preliminary emancipation proclamation did not free any slaves at the moment it was announced in September 1862. Nor, for that matter, did the final proclamation on New Year's Day of 1863. But Lincoln's contemporaries knew—as he did—that once that proclamation was out, it meant that so long as the Union won the war, slavery was doomed.

Lincoln *was* the Great Emancipator, and he was that precisely because he did *not* do what William Lloyd Garrison and the other abolitionists did: angrily curse the darkness. Instead, he approached the problem with his usual pragmatism and political good sense wrapped around a central core of moral conviction. A proclamation earlier than the fall of 1862 or one that fatuously declared that all slaves, in all the states, were at once free would not only have antagonized the slave-holding border states but would have had no more practical effect than the fabled papal bull against Halley's comet.

But if Lincoln was so clearly antislavery, what role did he envision for the former slaves once they were free men? This is a harder question to answer, for not only was he killed before he could address that question meaningfully, but he kept his cards very close to his vest on the issue, reluctant as he was to antagonize any of the various elements of his fragile wartime coalition until the war was won. A few of his modern-day critics charge that Lincoln, in addition to being a reluctant emancipator, was also a racist who could not conceive of blacks as equal citizens in a multiracial United States.[7] Lincoln, I think, would have acknowledged that; he knew he was imperfect, and one of his characteristics—a very rare one among presidents, or anyone else for that matter—was his willingness to be self-critical. Like every other member of his generation, Lincoln had certain preconceptions about differences in the particular skills and abilities of the two races. Conscious of his preconceptions and fearing that free blacks would be unable to escape the prejudices of his own race, Lincoln toyed for years with the notion of sending freed slaves to Africa, even though the vast majority of them had lived in America all their lives. "My first impulse would be to free all the slaves and send them to Liberia," he declared in 1858. Indeed, Lincoln gave up on the idea of re-colonization only when it became evident that it was logistically impossible. But unlike most members of his generation, Lincoln saw that if the two races were going to live together, black men and women must be "entitled to all the natural rights enumerated in the Declaration of Independence."[8] That, too, was a very advanced position for his time.

How, then, would this attitude have translated into the complex and sorrowful era known to us as Reconstruction? Would Lincoln have allowed—even demanded—black suffrage? Would he have ensured free public education for the freed slaves? Would he have supported the distribution of land to them so they could be economically independent of their former masters? When I asked my students these questions, I acknowledged that we could never know the answers with any certainty, but we could intuit the answers based on what we know about his previous behavior and his character. Noting that a few of my students wore the popular bracelets that rhetorically asked, "What Would Jesus Do?" (WWJD), I sometimes wrote on the blackboard "WWLD."

What would Lincoln do? Or more accurately, what would Lincoln have done? Based in part on the poetic peroration of his second inaugural address in which he asked all Americans to bind up the nation's wounds "with malice toward none; with charity for all," many students of the war have concluded that if Lincoln had lived, he would have been more sympathetic with the South than the Radicals who seized power in 1867. The common wisdom is that Lincoln's death was a greater tragedy for the South than it was for the North because he would not have imposed on the (white) South the harsh requirements of the Radicals, thereby avoiding a hundred years of bitterness. The problem with this assumption is that in order to accommodate the white South, Lincoln would have had to allow white Southerners to define the postwar circumstances of the freed blacks. While Lincoln did not seek punishment for "traitors," neither, I suspect, was he willing to abandon the nation's responsibility to the freed slaves.

My own view was—and is—that for all his hesitancy about black soldiers or his apparent diffidence about black citizenship, Lincoln was, in fact, something of a secret Radical. Thaddeus Stevens and the other Radicals who saw him as a roadblock to the social revolution they sought seriously mistook their man. As in his approach to the issue of emancipation, Lincoln was a master of the possible. He would take the country as far in the direction of black civil rights as the majority of public opinion would allow him to go—and he was an excellent judge of how far that was. Hard-line Radicals thought that public opinion should have nothing to do with it—that it was a simple matter of right and wrong. They wanted Lincoln to issue a sweeping pronouncement that all blacks would be made citizens at once, granted the right to vote, to serve on juries, and to hold public office. Some argued that they were entitled to the ownership of at least some of the land belonging to their former masters. After all, they had worked it for generations without compensation. Lincoln knew that such proclamations would provoke passionate resistance in the South, as they did in the years after 1867. But while he would not go as far or as fast as the Radicals desired, theirs was the direction he would have taken.

In regard to black voting rights, Lincoln was "clear and decided" about his postwar policy as early as January 1864. He was convinced that black veterans had "heroically vindicated their manhood on the battle-field" and "demonstrated in blood their right to the ballot." He did not issue any proclamations—it was too early for that—but to the first Reconstruction governor of Louisiana, he wrote to suggest privately "whether some of the colored people may not be let in." Even then, he was quick to add that "this is only a suggestion, not to the public, but to you alone."[9] Just as emancipation for blacks held in the rebellious states was a foot in the door for complete emancipation, suffrage for some blacks—in this case for black veterans—would eventually lead to universal black suffrage. In the years after Appomattox, Lincoln would almost certainly have sought to extend this limited franchise, moving toward black civil rights as fast and as fully as public opinion would allow.

Conventional textbook wisdom is that Lincoln wanted to let the South up easy—that his form of Reconstruction would have been less vindictive and more supportive of the white population in the South than the Reconstruction program espoused by the Radicals. But Lincoln's difference with the Radicals was more one of process and timing than content. The great tragedy of his death, then, is not that he would have allowed white Southerners to have their way but that he would have imposed civil rights judiciously and realistically and thereby advanced the re-United States more swiftly toward a humane America.

All too often, historians discover that peeling back the layers of time reveals that their once-revered heroes were mere mortals after all. This has not been true in my research into the life of Abraham Lincoln. The more I study him, the more I admire the personal characteristics that allowed him to become our greatest president. My respect and admiration—my sense of awe—is greater now than when I first gazed up at the sixteen-foot-tall bronze figure at Lincoln School.

The statue is no longer there. A recent inquiry to school administrators about it brought no satisfaction. A few of them remembered the statue, but no one knew what had happened to it when they modernized (tore down) the old facade. It is another manifestation of progress in a society obsessed with progress. Still, it is sad to me that students at Lincoln School will not encounter that grave and imposing figure at the outset of their education. After all, it might have led one or more of them to a lifelong study of America's greatest president.

NOTES

1. The most recent such survey ranked the top five presidents this way: (1) Lincoln, (2) Franklin Roosevelt, (3) George Washington, (4) Theodore Roosevelt, (5) Harry Truman. For context, see Arthur M. Schlesinger Jr., "Rating the Presidents: Washington to Clinton," *Political Science Quarterly* 11, no. 2 (Summer 1997): 179–90.

2. Charles E. Hamlin, *The Life and Times of Hannibal Hamlin* (Cambridge, Mass.: Riverside Press, 1899), 393.

3. T. Harry Williams, *Lincoln and His Generals* (New York: Dorset Press, 1952), vii.

4. Lincoln to McClellan, April 9, 1862, in *The Collected Works of Abraham Lincoln,* ed. Roy P. Basler, 9 vols. (New Brunswick, N.J.: Rutgers University Press, 1953–55), 5:185 (emphasis in original). This passage is quoted by Williams in *Lincoln and His Generals* on p. 84.

5. Lincoln to A. G. Hodges, April 4, 1864, in *Collected Works*, 7:281.

6. Speech at Ottawa, Illinois, August 21, 1858, in ibid., 3:16.

7. Lerone Bennett, *Forced into Glory: Abraham Lincoln's White Dream* (Chicago: Johnson Publishing, 2000).

8. Speech at Ottawa, Illinois.

9. Lincoln to James Wadsworth, January 1864[?], and Lincoln to Michael Hahn, March 13, 1864, both in *Collected Works*, 7:101, 243.

Historian, Editor, and the Assassination Legacy

My longstanding interest in Abraham Lincoln and the Civil War came from my parents. My mother always told me of a family tradition that I can't actually verify, that during the Lincoln-Douglas debates my great-great grandfather stayed in a hotel room where he heard Senator Douglas next door practicing for one of his debates. My father majored in history in college and was for part of his career a junior high school social studies teacher. I inherited a love of history from my dad, and we often went on vacations to historical sites. My uncle Earle served in the army during World War II, where he met and married my aunt Myra, who was an army nurse. After the war, they settled in Alexandria, Virginia, and my uncle went to work as a bookkeeper for the *Army Times*. Since my father had a week off in April and his summers were free, we usually went twice a year to visit.

While I'm sure that we studied Lincoln in grammar school, and I have memories of cutting out silhouettes of both Lincoln and Washington, among my earliest recollections of Lincoln are from those visits to Washington. In the early 1950s, there were no security worries in the nation's capital, and one could easily park along the mall and walk to the tourist sites. We never tired of visiting the Lincoln Memorial, the White House, and Ford's Theatre. I particularly recall that Ford's Theatre was simply a shell—it had not yet been restored—and the door to Lincoln's theater box, with a hole bored into it (which had allowed one to look into the box at the people seated there), was placed on the floor. Someone had traced footsteps in front of the door, supposedly imitating Booth's escape route, and we were thrilled to put our own feet where the assassin had fled. I was a lot older before I realized that the tracings probably had no connection to Booth, but it was a great deal of fun nonetheless.

While I always continued to have an interest in Abraham Lincoln, that interest really deepened when I encountered Professor Kenneth A. Bernard at Boston University (BU). The BU history department was an exciting place to be in the late 1950s and early 1960s. My first course with Professor Bernard was the standard U.S. history survey. Above and beyond several assigned books, every week we were to read at least a hundred additional pages from three additional books. We then had to summarize our reading on 3x5 cards, which we turned in every Monday. In his Civil War course, Professor Bernard assigned an additional two hundred pages a week on which we had to take extensive notes. I had never worked so hard in my life academically, nor had I ever learned so much.

Some students shied away from Professor Bernard because of the heavy workload and the impression that this sometimes gave, which was that he was not very approachable. When you got to know Ken Bernard well, however, he was a very warm man who possessed a wonderful, dry sense of humor. I'll never forget the time I went to his office to consult with him on some issue and he said to me, "In class you always have a twinkle in your eye, which tells me you are thinking about something, but I'm not sure it's always history." I had to concede that he was right.

When I was a senior, he invited me to sign up for his Lincoln seminar, the topic being Lincoln's assassination. I was the only undergraduate; the other five students were working on master's degrees or doctorates. The first paper I submitted came back with so many red marks that one of my classmates, who became a dear friend, said that it looked like it had been hacked to pieces with a sharp sword. I took the positive criticism to heart and through Professor Bernard's skillful guidance produced a 125-page paper (150 if you count the annotated bibliography) that earned me an A and became the basis for my dissertation and first book, *Beware the People Weeping*.[1]

I remained at Boston University to pursue both my MA and Ph.D., eagerly looking forward to the prospect of continuing to study with Professor Bernard. I was an ROTC student and had been commissioned a second lieutenant in 1963, and so my studies were interrupted by active army duty from 1965 to 1967. I served a year overseas, and Lincoln even accompanied me to Korea—or, more accurately, I found Lincoln in Korea. I was stationed on the island of Kangwha along the Demilitarized Zone where the Han and Imjin rivers run into the Yellow Sea. We were within sight of North Korea and lived in a reconditioned Quonset hut. Someone had painted a bulls-eye in front of the orderly room where the first artillery shells would land if renewed conflict occurred. Needless to say, we didn't have much in the way of a library. On a trip to the PX in Seoul, I was delighted to discover a copy of Carl Sandburg's abridged biography of Lincoln, which I still possess. I read and reread Sandburg during the cold winter nights as the wind howled and the temperature hovered at thirty below zero. Since I always seemed to be reading the same book, Captain Bob Hahn, my commanding officer, and Chief Warrant Officer Leonard Van Camp, who were very close friends, used to kid me that they understood why it was taking so long to finish my degree, since I was such a slow reader.[2]

In 1967, I left the army and returned to my studies, then finished my doctorate in 1971. Many graduate students, once they obtain their degrees, find themselves taking positions in other parts of the country and therefore probably have less frequent direct contact with their mentors as the years go by. But since I landed a job in Massachusetts—at Bridgewater State College, one of nine state colleges in the Massachusetts public higher education system—I continued to have a close friendship with Professor Bernard up until the time of his death. I joined the Lincoln Group of Boston and saw him frequently at meetings and also visited him at his Cape Code home. When I married my wife, Lois Joyce, in 1969, we invited Ken and Dorothy Bernard to the wedding. We both chuckled when the Bernards replied that the Lincoln Group was meeting on that Saturday, so they would miss the ceremony, but that they would be able to make the reception. Somehow, though, we understood, and we still cherish the copy of his book *Lincoln and the Music of the Civil War* that they presented us with as a wedding gift.[3]

I actually owe my long career at Bridgewater State to Abraham Lincoln. In the spring of 1971, as I was about to graduate, Professor Bernard prevailed on me to present a paper based on my dissertation to the Lincoln Group of Boston. Judge Carl Wahlstrom, a former group president, had donated his extensive collection to Endicott College in Beverly, Massachusetts, and the Lincoln Group often held one of its meetings on the campus.

Afterward, as we walked back to the car, I saw Dr. Jordan Fiore leaning against a fence that led to the parking lot. I didn't really know Jordan personally, but I knew who he was and that he chaired the Bridgewater History Department. Jordan rather casually motioned to me and said, "I understand you might be looking for a teaching job." Trying to be equally calm, although my heart was racing a mile a minute, I replied that I was seeking employment. The reason I was so excited was that I still didn't know what I would be doing in the fall. Since Lois was working as a social worker, we weren't going to starve, but history positions were not easy to obtain in the early seventies.

I was in the army reserves, and I indicated to Jordan when he asked me to come for an interview that I was leaving on Thursday for two weeks of annual training. Being in the reserves wasn't always in vogue in that period of the Vietnam War, but since Jordan had been a major in World War II, I guess that was already a plus. We agreed that I would come to Bridgewater on Tuesday. I had interviews with Jordan and a couple of deans, ate lunch with some department members in a very noisy student cafeteria, and finally met with Dr. Adrian Rondileau, the president of the college. At the end of the interview, Dr. Rondileau said, "Welcome aboard," which I took to be a positive sign. I was told to call the next day, and I was informed that I had been hired.

I subsequently discovered that I had almost missed this opportunity. Dr. Fiore had actually gotten into his car and begun to pull out of the parking lot, but he had been accompanied to the meeting by Jean Stonehouse, another history department faculty member. Jean, who has remained my colleague and friend for all of the years I have taught, mentioned that the paper had been pretty good and reminded Jordan that they were looking to hire someone. He turned the car around and waited by the fence. I often wonder what I might be doing now had those split-second events not occurred.

Of course, my younger colleagues can hardly believe this story. When we hire today, there is all kinds of paperwork to fill out. We must also advertise widely and make sure that we adhere to affirmative action procedures. The department can usually expect seventy-five to a hundred applications for any position, and if the process begins in September, we are lucky if by February or March we are ready to invite three or four candidates for on-campus interviews. There is little wonder that they are incredulous that I could have been unemployed on Saturday and hired on Wednesday.

It was also fortunate for me that the hiring process was not overly rational in 1971. Today, we would be looking for someone in a very specific academic specialty and would not want to overlap with our current offerings. However, not only were Jordan and Jean interested in Lincoln and the Civil War but another colleague and longtime friend, Arthur Oien, was already teaching the Civil War course. Today I would never have been hired, given those circumstances.

Therefore, early in my career I was limited to teaching basic survey courses in American history and western civilization as well as U.S. foreign relations, which was one of my minor academic specialties. Before long I did begin to nibble around the edges of Lincoln studies, teaching a seminar that Jordan had developed and also a course on American assassinations. Ultimately, when Arthur Oien retired, I picked up the Civil War, which I have taught ever since and which, of course, contains a liberal dose of Abraham Lincoln. We have developed a very good working Lincoln collection over the years at the college's Maxwell Library, from items largely given by Lincoln Group of Boston members. This has allowed generations of Bridgewater students to conduct research on the sixteenth president.

Bridgewater State College started as a normal school in 1840. Indeed, it is one of the oldest teacher training institutions in the United States and takes great pride in its heritage. While I always thought of myself as a teacher first and despite a heavy teaching load, I was able to pursue a scholarly career of research and publication. I will never forget the thrill when I submitted the paper I had delivered to the Lincoln Group and received notification from Dr. R. Gerald McMurtry, the editor of the *Lincoln Herald*, that my article was accepted for publication. McMurtry was a well-known and respected Lincoln scholar, and part of my excitement was the fact that he had found it worthy. The article, which began a lifelong association with the *Lincoln Herald*, was published in two parts in 1976.[4]

I was eventually asked by Dr. Gary Planck, the *Herald's* review editor, to do reviews and went on to serve on the advisory and editorial boards. When Joseph Suppiger left as editor in chief, I assumed the editor's position with the fall 1991 issue and am currently the longest-serving editor in that publication's lengthy history.

One of the real joys and wonders of editing the *Herald* has been the opportunity to work with both well-established scholars and those new to the field. While some journals can accommodate the work of only rather senior scholars, the *Herald* has room for both senior and beginning authors. For example, we have published articles by such noted scholars as Frank Klement and Hans Trefousse, historians who are well known and respected in the Civil War field. I still admit to feeling rather strange when approached by historians of this stature and asked, "Do you think this article would be okay for the *Herald*?" It is refreshing that such great scholars are so genuinely humble.[5]

On the other hand, newer scholars such as Allen Spiegel and Mark Reinhart come to mind. While both are very talented, some of their initial work appeared as articles in the *Herald's* pages. I'm sure that both would have gone on to publish books without their *Herald* experience, but I like to think that the encouragement they received from this Lincoln publication gave them the confidence to seek a broader venue.[6]

Editing the *Herald* has also been an interesting exercise in itself. Large journals have a huge staff with numerous associate editors and copy editors and all the resources they require. We run the *Herald* with a very small staff and budget with the major editors scattered geographically throughout the country. Before I conclude my duties, I hope to write an article about how to edit a journal from the corner of your desk, which is usually where the upcoming manuscripts are located. Somehow we manage to do the job moderately well, and one of the pleasures has been to work with people of the caliber of Gary Planck, Steve Rogstad, Ed Steers, and Frank Williams.

My interest in Lincoln has also opened opportunities to me that I would never have dreamed of while I was growing up in Quincy, Massachusetts. In 1982, I gave my first major presentation to the Abraham Lincoln Association in Springfield, Illinois. Since the symposium was held in the Old State Capitol building, the speakers literally stood where Lincoln had given his "House Divided" speech. Some presenters stayed with the Herndon family; Lew

Herndon was related to Lincoln's law partner, and they possessed William Herndon's dictionary, in which he had made annotations. I went with one of their neighbors to New Salem, where on a cold winter day we went through almost every building that was reminiscent of what life would have been like for Lincoln. Over the years, I have spoken at the Library of Congress and Ford's Theatre, and in 2001 I delivered the Watchhorn Lecture in Redlands, California. I have always advised my own students to seek careers where they can find personal satisfaction, and it has been gratifying to have received recognition of my work from Bridgewater State College in the form of the lifetime Achievement Award for Research (2003) and the V. James DiNardo Award for Excellence in Teaching (2005).

Having had the opportunity to appear in a number of television programs, I have also learned just how powerful the image of Lincoln still remains in the public mind. If I write a new article or even a book, I can guarantee that as I walk across campus, no one will stop me and comment on my latest publication. However, if I appear in a television program, even one of the numerous reruns of *The Lincoln Assassination* on the History Channel, both students and faculty will stop me to say that they saw me on TV. Even the young man at the takeout restaurant where we often order pizza will immediately call me to the head of a long line (much to the consternation of some other patrons) because he wants to talk to me about the assassination. Admittedly, part of this is the sheer power of the media, but it is also the topic of Lincoln's assassination that has drawn them to the show in the first place.

This interest in Lincoln is manifested in additional ways. I am curious about a wide variety of subjects and can enjoy chatting with colleagues in physics, anthropology, or mathematics about their academic interests and specialties. However, very few of those areas engage the general public in a fundamental way, in the manner that Lincoln does, and not simply because an area of physics might be difficult for the non-scientist to grasp. In a manner that is unique, most people—whether scientists or medical doctors or ministers or lawyers—want to discuss Lincoln once they discover he is my area of expertise. Nearly all Americans grew up with Lincoln and think they know him. His impact is amazing.

While my deepest involvement with Lincoln studies has been the assassination, I have also learned many lessons from studying the life of Lincoln. Given his humble beginnings and accomplishments, I always viewed Lincoln as a prime example of the American success story. While my father was a teacher, my mother grew up in a large family and never graduated from high school, since she had to go to work to help her parents. My grandfather was a Canadian immigrant who worked at various low-paying jobs and needed the help of his children to survive. While I am not naive enough to think that everyone can duplicate the American success story, nonetheless Lincoln stood as a symbol that proved it was possible to better one's position in life.

The two colleges I have been most involved with during my academic career have reinforced this lesson for me. Bridgewater's motto is "Not to be ministered unto, but to minister." The idea of service is strongly ingrained in Bridgewater's history. Lincoln Memorial University, which publishes the *Herald*, was founded by General Oliver Otis Howard, who had told Lincoln that if they both survived the war, he wanted to do something for the loyal but poor citizens of eastern Tennessee. In 1897, Howard founded Lincoln Memorial University as a tribute to this ideal. Similarly, Bridgewater State has served since 1840 as a gateway to education for many students who were the first in their family to attend college, demonstrating that in the United States, education has always been one way to fulfill Lincoln's ideal that every person should have the right to rise to the level of his or her talents.

I have also learned from Lincoln's humility and patience. Teaching is a profession that by its nature requires some ego in order to successfully stand before a class of forty-five sometimes less-than-eager undergraduates. You have to work hard to motivate students, and while you may be an expert in a particular area, if you are honest, there is a great deal that you don't know. Lincoln was also a person of enormous patience. When scholarly battles have raged in the Lincoln field, it has been good for the combatants to pause and remember that the man we study was slow to anger and endured a great deal of criticism in silence. Patience is also an excellent trait for any teacher, since if you can't reach a student, it is all too easy to blame the student for lacking intelligence or initiative. Sometimes you may need to consider varying your own teaching techniques.

Another lesson that Lincoln teaches is persistence in the face of adversity. Lincoln was quoted to the effect that he was a slow walker, but he never walked back.[7] In an age when life seems so fast-paced and people make snap judgments that they sometimes regret, there is a great deal to be said for methodically approaching a problem. One example is the Emancipation Proclamation. The president was often criticized for being slow in dealing with emancipation, but once he decided on the proclamation he did not waver, noting that he would be condemned by history if he reneged on his promise.

Being a student of the assassination, I have also learned many lessons from the legacy of his death. One lesson that the assassination teaches is to be wary of sensational conspiracy stories. Among these charges are that the president was betrayed by members of his own administration and that Booth survived Garrett's barn. While historians need to carefully weigh the validity of sources in any area, this necessity is heightened in the assassination field, which so naturally attracts bizarre tales. A healthy skepticism is clearly in order.

Inevitably, though, while utilizing the proper caution, the student of both Lincoln's life and death must come to grips with mythology. Given his reputation as the Great Emancipator and savior of the Union and his death at the height of his triumph, Abraham Lincoln was probably destined to be viewed as a larger-than-life figure. Lincoln became a saint rather than a mere mortal. Interestingly, Lincoln was the creator of some of his own myths and was not above using them for political purposes. The idea of being born in a log cabin and rising to greatness has always proven to be a good vote-getter in the United States.

As is sometimes the case, however, myth and reality don't always coincide. The real Lincoln, who was seen as a rustic rail-splitter, tried to escape from his rural roots as quickly as he could. Lincoln was also not simply a joke-cracking man of the people but a man of great intellect, despite his limited education, who would pen two of the greatest addresses in the English language, the Gettysburg Address and his second inaugural address.

Just because the real Lincoln was somewhat different from the mythological Lincoln, though, it does not necessarily mean that we should abandon myth completely. Myth reveals the way Americans wish Lincoln had been, even if it does not always reveal the way he was.[8] It speaks well of Americans that the characteristics they attribute to one of the central figures in our history are the decent qualities of all civilized men: patience, tolerance, humor, sympathy, kindliness, and wisdom. Perhaps in the end, that is the long-lasting example that Lincoln provides and why each succeeding generation since his assassination has been drawn to him.

NOTES

1. Thomas R. Turner, *Beware the People Weeping: Public Opinion and the Assassination of Abraham Lincoln* (Baton Rouge: Louisiana State University Press, 1982).

2. Carl Sandburg, *The Prairie Years and the War Years*, 3 vols. (1954; New York: Dell, 1963).

3. Kenneth A. Bernard, *Lincoln and the Music of the Civil War* (Caldwell, Idaho: Caxton Publishers, 1966).

4. Thomas R. Turner, "Public Opinion and the Assassination of Abraham Lincoln," pts. 1 and 2, *Lincoln Herald* 78 (Spring 1976): 17–24; 78 (Summer 1976): 66–76.

5. For examples, see Hans L. Trefousse, "Abraham Lincoln and Germany," *Lincoln Herald* 93 (Fall 1991): 83–86, and "Abraham Lincoln and Thaddeus Stevens," *Lincoln Herald* 98 (Fall 1996): 79–85; and Frank L. Klement, "President Lincoln, the Civil War, and the Bill of Rights," *Lincoln Herald* 94 (Spring 1992): 10–23.

6. Allen D. Spiegel and Francis Kovaler, "Chicken Bones, Defense Lawyer A. Lincoln and a Malpractice Case," *Lincoln Herald* 99 (Winter 1997): 156–67; Allen D.

Spiegel, *A. Lincoln Esquire: A Shrewd Sophisticated Lawyer in His Time* (Macon, Ga.: Mercer University Press, 2002); Mark Reinhart, "The Lincoln Image on the Screen," *Lincoln Herald* 96 (Summer 1994): 56–62, and *Abraham Lincoln on Screen: A Filmography of Dramas and Documentaries Including Television, 1903–1998* (Jefferson, N.C.: MacFarland, 1999).

7. Allen C. Guelzo, *Abraham Lincoln: Redeemer President* (1999; Grand Rapids, Mich.: W. B. Eerdmans, 2003), 361.

8. Stephen B. Oates, *Abraham Lincoln: The Man behind the Myths* (New York: Harper and Row, 1984); David Herbert Donald, *Lincoln Reconsidered: Essays on the Civil War Era* (New York: Knopf, 1956).

FRANK J. WILLIAMS

The Compleat Lincolnator:
Enthusiast, Collector, and Scholar

A braham Lincoln permeates American culture—just as he has perme-
ated my own life.

Ronald Reagan once opined that to understand America requires an
understanding of its greatest president, Lincoln. As a second-generation
American—the grandson of Italian immigrant parents—I wanted to fit in, to
contribute to the promise of America, and my quest to understand Lincoln
began subconsciously. As this essay will recount, my life with Lincoln started
serendipitously while I was still a schoolboy.

First, I became interested in collecting books about Lincoln. Learning
about this man, who not only influenced my career but also helped shape my
life, gradually became my avocation. Over time, I became a serious student of
America's sixteenth president. I'm not sure that "I've Led Three Lives" worthy
of the television show from days past, but I've led at least two. One was as a
lawyer-judge, the other as a student of Lincoln. These dual tracks actually
complement each other. Using opportunities afforded to me by both, I have
endeavored to introduce others to Lincoln's significant legacy.

ELEMENTARY BEGINNINGS

I was first introduced to Lincoln through bedtime stories read by my mother,
who wanted me to learn about the heroes of her adopted land. Those memories of Lincoln were reinforced when I reached the sixth grade at Meshanticut
Park School in Cranston, Rhode Island. Mrs. Taylor, my teacher, assigned
seats alphabetically and sat me in the back row in the classroom beneath a
full-length portrait of Lincoln. As I think back, Mrs. Taylor qualifies as my
first mentor in American history, but in his own right, Lincoln was my distal
mentor, a heroic figure to a boy who figuratively and literally looked up to
him in that classroom. Years later, in the process of collecting Lincoln prints,
I learned that the Lincoln portrait that inspired, perhaps haunted, me wasn't
really a portrait of him. It turned out to be a composite portrait imposing
Lincoln's head onto the body of John C. Calhoun, Lincoln's polar opposite,

in nineteenth-century American political thought! The "Marx of the Master Class," as Calhoun is called, didn't leave a lasting impression on me, but the Great Emancipator's influence was ignited and continues yet.

Keeping it secret from my parents, I began diverting my lunch money—a quarter each day—to purchase my first books about Lincoln. They were used books, but I treasured them. I still recall the authors and titles of my first two acquisitions: Dale Carnegie's *Lincoln the Unknown* and Carl Sandburg's abridged version of his six-volume Lincoln biography, *The Prairie Years and The War Years*. Professional historians have little regard for either, but I remain impressed that Lincoln inspired two such diverse men—a salesman and a poet—to write about him. I have often suspected that my lifelong philosophy that Lincoln should not be the exclusive preserve of specialists somehow is rooted in that youthful epiphany.

By the time I was thirteen and attending Hugh B. Bain Junior High School, I aspired to become a lawyer. My career choice was influenced by Lincoln and his success in the field of law. When I entered Cranston High School in 1955, my Lincoln collection contained about two hundred books. When I graduated, it was twice that many. I also had begun collecting Lincoln artifacts. My first bust of Lincoln, acquired when I was thirteen, was an Alva reproduction of Leonard Wells Volk's beardless Lincoln. It always occupied a place of honor on my law office desk and is now displayed in my chambers in the Rhode Island Supreme Court.[1]

As an undergraduate majoring in government and history at Boston University, I audited Kenneth A. Bernard's symposium on Lincoln and the Civil War. This experience led me, at age nineteen, to join the Lincoln Group of Boston, in which Professor Bernard, author of such books as *Lincoln and the Music of the Civil War*, was so active. A friend and I even spent our spring break junior year camping out at Lincoln and Civil War sites, including Gettysburg.

Just as Lincoln absented himself from active politics between the end of his term in Congress and the enactment of the Kansas-Nebraska Act, I held my Lincoln collecting in abeyance while I served as a U.S. Army officer in Germany and Vietnam between 1962 and 1967. It was during this hiatus that I married my Southern-born wife, Virginia Elizabeth Miller. Lincoln may not have held elective office between 1849 and 1854, but he retained his keen interest in politics. In the same sense, while I was outside the United States and did minimal collecting, my interest in Lincoln remained undiminished.

THE LAWYER-COLLECTOR

On my return from military service abroad in 1967, two things occurred simultaneously: I resumed my Lincoln collecting in earnest, and I began law school at Boston University. As my law practice commenced, I found myself making presentations of my own to the Lincoln Group of Boston. The topic of my first talk to this group was Lincoln's visit to Rhode Island after his Cooper Union speech in February 1860. For that presentation I used slides, which remains a trademark of my public presentations. Of course, many of the slides were made from the paintings, prints, and other artifacts contained in my growing collection. I have always enlisted Virginia's extraordinary teacher skills to help organize and prepare these slides for my presentations. When the visuals go right, it's because of her talents. When they don't, it's because I've pressed the wrong button!

Within a few years of beginning my law practice, I was elected president of the Lincoln Group of Boston just as America celebrated its bicentennial. I served in that position for a dozen years, until 1988. Subsequently, I was elected president of the Abraham Lincoln Association in Springfield, Illinois—the first president from outside the state—and then founding chairman of the Lincoln Forum. In each of these leadership positions, I tried, as I still do, to promote the legacy of America's sixteenth president by working to expand not only organizational membership but also activities that reach out to others similarly motivated.

During those years of promoting Lincoln's legacy while I was a lawyer-collector, I sometimes heard comments that it was "impossible to hold a conference on Lincoln without Frank Williams." I occasionally pondered what was meant by that. One academician who did not yet know me concluded that I must be "an extremely old lawyer" given how many Lincoln conferences I had attended. I do not deny that I am an active Lincoln conference participant (or, by now, an old lawyer!). Among these events, two deserve special mention, since they epitomize my goal of reaching out to others who are interested in Lincoln.

The first was an international conference on Abraham Lincoln, virtually the first such conference to be held abroad, at least to my knowledge. It took place in Taipei, Taiwan, on November 12–15, 1989, in conjunction with Lincoln's 180th birthday observance. The proceedings of that conference appear in *The Universal Lincoln*, a volume appropriately titled for such a landmark event. I was particularly pleased that my conference paper, "Individuality and Universality," became my first paper on Lincoln to be published.[2]

The satisfaction that I derived from that experience was repeated when I endorsed and participated in the first Lincoln conference to be held in a Deep South state. Hosted by Louisiana State University in Shreveport in the fall of 1992, it generated additional venues in which the Lincoln legacy could be showcased. From it came my opportunity to serve as codirector of the first Lincoln Summer Teachers Institute in the nation, held at LSU in

Shreveport in 1993. It inspired the publication of three volumes in addition to several articles.[3] In addition, the conference led to the establishment of the International Lincoln Center at LSU in Shreveport. It yielded also the triennial presidential conference series, with its signature use of Lincoln as the touchstone for judging other presidents, an approach I fully support.[4]

THE JUDGE AS COLLECTOR AND SCHOLAR

My transition from practicing attorney to presiding judge coincided with my transition from a Lincoln enthusiast to more scholarly efforts. In late 1995, I became an associate justice on the Superior Court of the State of Rhode Island. I served in that capacity until 2001, when I became the chief justice of the state's supreme court.

By the time my first formal articles appeared in print in the early 1990s, I had already written for many years the annual surveys on Lincoln activities around the country. I took on the assignment in 1977 and continue it on a quarterly and annual basis for Lincoln publications.[5] In 2000, I was appointed by the Senate to the U.S. Abraham Lincoln Bicentennial Commission. At present, I serve on the executive committee of that commission. My first book of essays, *Judging Lincoln*, was published in 2002.[6]

When I look back to those first Lincoln book purchases made with saved lunch money, it's hard to believe that they were the precursors to today's Frank and Virginia Williams Collection of Lincolniana. The collection now includes some 12,000 books and pamphlets about the Civil War and on Lincoln himself; 20,000 items related to the Civil War, like sculptures, paintings, prints, numismatics, philately, campaign tokens, photographs, and manuscripts; and 40,000 newspaper clippings. I am proud to say that it is the most comprehensive collection of its type remaining in private hands. And I'm even prouder to report that it remains available as a resource to any scholar who desires to use it for research purposes. Many, many have done so.

LINCOLN LESSONS

I have synthesized what I have learned from my lifetime of collecting, researching, and speaking and writing about Lincoln into four primary lessons that I believe he teaches us.

First, the ideal of American opportunity. As I now look back over my life with Lincoln, it seems to me that I was initially attracted to him because he symbolized the successful life a poor boy, like I was, could attain through hard work. I wanted to emulate him. As a youth, I became an Eagle Scout, and the Scouts use Lincoln as an example of morality. If the Great Commoner could become a "self-made man," I had hope for becoming the same. I suppose that my appreciation of military life and its code of conduct in some way reinforced my desire to work hard and abide by the rules of fair play. In many ways, I appropriated the Lincoln standard of behavior as my personal moral compass.

Second, listen to others, even when you initially disagree with them. Lincoln surrounded himself with people and, as he put it, took "public opinion baths" during his presidency. He was open to what others thought. This takes patience, and Lincoln's reservoir of patience was uncommonly deep. Our judicial system is criticized frequently for taking too long to resolve issues, but that very characteristic is among its greatest virtues, for it allows time for passions to cool while issues are fully explored. As a product of New England, I have come to appreciate the region's town hall meeting tradition, which provides a public forum in which individuals can express their views. It is a vital part of the great democratic tradition that Lincoln embodied. One of the principles applied to the Frank and Virginia Williams Collection is that it should not be a museum but a working collection open to those seeking to learn more about Lincoln. Our perspective is that ours is truly a "people's collection."

Third, the Lincoln example helps to keep life in perspective. Judges and lawyers have to separate facts from the *obiter dicta* of life to which we all are subject, especially in the modern media age. I think of the wisdom of great Supreme Court justice Oliver Wendell Holmes Jr., who argued that "the life of the law has not been logic: it has been experience."[7] Unfortunately, I have known the occasional critical individual who became lost in either the law or "the facts." Such a person becomes, for me, a sad example of Victor Hugo's Inspector Javert in *Les Misérables*, an individual who inflicts great damage on himself and others in his grand, ill-advised, personal crusade for a mythical kind of justice.

Fourth, Lincoln is the classic example of someone who did not become a one-dimensional person but who evolved and grew. The energetic local lawyer became a prominent attorney; the state legislator developed into America's greatest president. If only to a small degree, I hope that my transition from collecting Lincolniana and speaking about Lincoln has been commensurate with my transition from lawyer to judge. I know I have heeded Lincoln's advice to would-be lawyers: "work, work, work."[8]

NOTES

1. Volk's beardless Lincoln eventually morphed into my monograph with Harold Holzer, *Lincoln's Deathbed in Art and Memory: The "Rubber Room" Phenomenon* (Gettysburg, Pa: Thomas Publications, 1988).

2. Frank J. Williams, "Individuality and Universality," in *The Universal Lincoln*, ed. Yu-Tang D. Lew (Taipei: Lincoln Society of Taipei and Chinese Culture University Press, 1995), 266–75.

3. Frank J. Williams, William D. Pederson, and Vincent J. Marsala, eds., *Abraham Lincoln: Sources and Style of Leadership* (Westport, Conn.: Greenwood Press, 1994); Frank J. Williams and William D. Pederson, eds., *Abraham Lincoln Contemporary: An American Legacy* (Campbell, Calif.: Savas Woodbury Publishers, 1996); and Frank J. Williams and William D. Pederson, eds., "Special Issue on Abraham Lincoln," *Quarterly Journal of Ideology* 17, nos. 1–2 (June 1994).

4. For example, see Mark J. Rozell, William D. Pederson, and Frank J. Williams, eds., *George Washington and the Origins of the American Presidency* (Westport, Conn.: Praeger, 2000); William D. Pederson and Frank J. Williams, eds., *Franklin D. Roosevelt and Abraham Lincoln: Competing Perspectives on Two Great Presidencies* (Armonk, N.Y.: M. E. Sharpe, 2003); Stephen K. Shaw, William D. Pederson, and Frank J. Williams, eds., *Franklin D. Roosevelt and the Transformation of the Supreme Court* (Armonk, N.Y.: M. E. Sharpe, 2004); and William D. Pederson and Frank J. Williams, eds., "Special Issue on Thomas Jefferson," *Journal of Contemporary Thought* (Summer and Winter 2004).

5. From 1977 to 1980 and 1982 to 1989 in *Hobbies Magazine*; then in an expanded version in the *Annual Papers of the Abraham Lincoln Association* and its successor, the *Journal of the Abraham Lincoln Association*, from 1982 to 1995; and from 1998 to the present in the *Lincoln Herald* journal as well as an annual Lincolniana survey for the quarterly *Lincoln Lore*, published by the Lincoln Museum in Fort Wayne, Indiana, from 1996 to the present.

6. Frank J. Williams, *Judging Lincoln* (Carbondale: Southern Illinois University Press, 2002), and then with Harold Holzer and Edna Greene Medford, *The Emancipation Proclamation: Three Views* (Baton Rouge: Louisiana State University Press, 2006).

7. Oliver Wendell Holmes and Sheldon M. Novick, *The Common Law* (Toronto: General Publishing, 1991), 1.

8. *The Collected Works of Abraham Lincoln*, ed. Roy P. Basler, 9 vols. (New Brunswick, N.J.: Rutgers University Press, 1953–55), 4:121.

SELECTED BIBLIOGRAPHY OF WORKS
BY CONTRIBUTORS

CONTRIBUTORS

PHOTO CREDITS

INDEX

Baker, Jean H. *Affairs of Party: The Political Culture of Northern Democrats in Mid-19th Century*. Ithaca, N.Y.: Cornell University Press, 1983.

———. *Ambivalent Americans: The Know-Nothing Party in Maryland*. Baltimore: Johns Hopkins University Press, 1977.

———. *James Buchanan*. New York: Henry Holt, 2004.

———. *Mary Todd Lincoln: A Biography*. New York: W. W. Norton, 1987.

———. *Sisters: The Lives of America's Suffragists*. New York: Hill and Wang, 2005.

———. *The Stevensons: A Biography of an American Family*. New York: W. W. Norton, 1996.

———. *Votes for Women: The Struggle for Suffrage Revisited*. New York: Oxford University Press, 2002.

Cuomo, Mario M. *Why Lincoln Matters: Today More Than Ever*. Orlando, Fla.: Harcourt, 2004.

Cuomo, Mario M., and Harold Holzer, eds. *Lincoln on Democracy*. 2nd ed. New York: Fordham University Press, 2004.

Daynes, Byron W., William D. Pederson, and Michael P. Riccards, eds. *The New Deal and Public Policy*. New York: St. Martin's Press, 1998.

Donald, David Herbert, and Harold Holzer, eds., *Lincoln in the "Times": The Life of Abraham Lincoln, as Originally Reported in "The New York Times."* New York: St. Martin's Press, 2005.

Fishman, Ethan, William D. Pederson, and Mark J. Rozell, eds. *George Washington: Foundation of Presidential Leadership and Character*. Westport, Conn.: Praeger, 2001.

Fornieri, Joseph, and Sara Vaughn Gabbard, eds. *Lincoln's America: 1809–1865*. Carbondale: Southern Illinois University Press, forthcoming.

Goodwin, Doris Kearns. *The Fitzgeralds and the Kennedys: An American Saga*. New York: Simon and Schuster, 1987.

———. *Lyndon Johnson and the American Dream*. New York: Harper and Row, 1976.

———. *No Ordinary Time: Franklin and Eleanor Roosevelt; The Home Front in World War II*. New York: Simon and Schuster, 1994.

———. *Team of Rivals: The Political Genius of Abraham Lincoln*. New York: Simon and Schuster, 2005.

———. *Wait Till Next Year: A Memoir*. New York: Simon and Schuster, 1997.

Holzer, Harold, comp. and ed. *Abraham Lincoln the Writer: A Treasury of His Greatest Speeches and Letters*. Honesdale, Pa.: Boyds Mills Press, 2000.

———. *Dear Mr. President: Letters to the President*. Carbondale: Southern Illinois University Press, 2006.

———. *Lincoln at Cooper Union: The Speech That Made Abraham Lincoln*. New York: Simon and Schuster, 2005.

———, ed. *The Lincoln-Douglas Debates*. New York: HarperCollins, 1993.

———, ed. *The Lincoln Mailbag: America Writes to the President, 1861–1865*. Carbondale: Southern Illinois University Press, 1998.

———. *Lincoln: Seen and Heard*. Lawrence: University Press of Kansas, 2000.

———, ed. *State of the Union: New York and the Civil War*. New York: Fordham University Press, 2002.

Holzer, Harold, Gabor S. Boritt, and Mark E. Neely Jr. *The Lincoln Image: Abraham Lincoln and the Popular Print*. New York: Scribner's, 1984.

Holzer, Harold, and Sara Vaughn Gabbard, eds., *Lincoln and Freedom: Slavery, Emancipation, and the Thirteenth Amendment*. Carbondale: Southern Illinois University Press, 2007.

Holzer, Harold, Edna Greene Medford, and Frank J. Williams. *The Emancipation Proclamation: Three Views*. Baton Rouge: Louisiana State University Press, 2006.

Holzer, Harold, and Mark E. Neely Jr. *Mine Eyes Have Seen the Glory: The Civil War in Art*. New York: Orion Books, 1993.

Howard, Thomas C., and William D. Pederson, eds. *Franklin D. Roosevelt and the Formation of the Modern World*. Armonk, N.Y.: M. E. Sharpe, 2003.

Jaffa, Harry V. *The Conditions of Freedom: Essays in Political Philosophy*. Baltimore: Johns Hopkins University Press, 1975.

———. *Crisis of the House Divided: An Interpretation of the Issues in the Lincoln-Douglas Debates*. Chicago: University of Chicago Press, 1959.

———. *A New Birth of Freedom: Abraham Lincoln and the Coming of the Civil War*. Lanham, Md.: Rowman and Littlefield, 2000.

Marszalek, John F. *Commander of All Lincoln's Armies: A Life of General Henry W. Halleck*. Cambridge, Mass.: Belknap Press of Harvard University Press, 2004.

———. *The Petticoat Affair: Manners, Sex, and Mutiny in Andrew Jackson's White House*. New York: Free Press, 1997.

———. *Sherman: A Soldier's Passion for Order*. New York: Simon and Schuster, 1992.

———. *Sherman's March to the Sea*. College Station, Tex.: McWhiney Foundation Press, 2005.

———. *Sherman's Other War: The General and the Civil War Press*. Tennessee: Memphis State University Press, 1981.

McPherson, James M. *Abraham Lincoln and the Second American Revolution*. New York: Oxford University Press, 1991.

———. *Battle Cry Freedom: The Civil War Era*. New York: Oxford University Press, 1988.

———. *Crossroads of Freedom: Antietam*. New York: Oxford University Press, 2002.

———. *Drawn with the Sword: Reflections on the American Civil War*. New York: Oxford University Press, 1996.

———. *For Cause and Comrades: Why Men Fought in the Civil War*. New York: Oxford University Press, 1997.

———. *Ordeal by Fire: The Civil War and Reconstruction*. 2nd ed. New York: McGraw Hill, 1992.

———. *Struggle for Equality: Abolitionists and the Negro in the Civil War and Reconstruction.* New Jersey: Princeton University Press, 1967.

———. *This Mighty Scourge: Perspectives on the Civil War.* New York: Oxford University Press, 2007.

Neely, Mark, Jr., and Harold Holzer. *The Lincoln Family Album.* 1990. Reprint, Carbondale: Southern Illinois University Press, 2006.

———. *The Union Image: Popular Prints of the Civil War North.* Chapel Hill: University of North Carolina Press, 2000.

Neely, Mark, Jr., Harold Holzer, and Gabor S. Boritt. *The Confederate Image: Prints of the Lost Cause.* Chapel Hill: University of North Carolina Press, 1987.

Pederson, William D., ed. *The "Barberian" Presidency: Theoretical and Empirical Readings.* New York: Peter Lang, 1989.

———. *The FDR Years.* New York: Facts on File, 2006.

Pederson, William D., and Ann McLaurin, eds. *The Rating Game in American Politics: An Interdisciplinary Approach.* New York: Irvington Publishers, 1987.

Pederson, William D., and Norman W. Provizer, eds. *Leader of the Pack: Polls and Case Studies of Great Supreme Court Justices.* New York: Peter Lang, 2003.

———, Norman W. Provizer, and Frank J. Williams, eds. *Classic Cases in American Constitutional Law.* St. Paul: West Group, 2001.

Pederson, William D., and Frank J. Williams, eds. *Creative Breakthroughs in Leadership: James Madison, Abraham Lincoln, and Mahatma Gandhi.* New Delhi: Pencraft International, 2007.

———. *Franklin D. Roosevelt and Abraham Lincoln: Competing Perspectives on Two Great Presidencies.* Armonk, N.Y.: M. E. Sharpe, 2003.

———. *The Great Presidential Triumvirate at Home and Abroad: Washington, Jefferson, and Lincoln.* New York: Nova Science Publishers, 2006.

———. "Thomas Jefferson." Special issue, *Journal of Contemporary Thought* 19–20 (2004).

Rozell, Mark J., and William D. Pederson, eds. *FDR and the Modern Presidency: Leadership and Legacy.* Westport, Conn.: Praeger, 1997.

Rozell, Mark J., William D. Pederson, and Frank J. Williams, eds. *George Washington and the Origins of the American Presidency.* Westport, Conn.: Praeger, 2000.

Shaw, Stephen K., William D. Pederson, and Frank J. Williams, eds. *Franklin D. Roosevelt and the Transformation of the Supreme Court.* Armonk, N.Y.: M. E. Sharpe, 2004.

Simon, John Y., and Harold Holzer, eds. *The Lincoln Forum: Rediscovering Abraham Lincoln.* New York: Fordham University Press, 2002.

Simon, John Y., Harold Holzer, and William D. Pederson, eds. *The Lincoln Forum: Abraham Lincoln, Gettysburg and the Civil War.* Mason City, Iowa: Savas, 1999.

Steers, Edward, Jr. *Blood on the Moon: The Assassination of Abraham Lincoln.* Lexington: University Press of Kentucky, 2001.

———. *His Name Is Still Mudd: The Case Against Doctor Samuel Alexander Mudd.* Gettysburg, Pa.: Thomas Publications, 1997.

———. *Lincoln Legends: Myths, Hoaxes, and Confabulations Associated with our Greatest President.* Lexington: University Press of Kentucky, 2007.

———. *The Quotable Lincoln.* Gettysburg, Pa.: Thomas Publications, 1993.

———. *The Trial: The Assassination of President Lincoln and the Trial of the Conspirators.* Lexington: University Press of Kentucky, 2003.

Symonds, Craig L. *Charleston Blockade: The Journals of John B. Marchand, U.S. Navy 1861–1862.* Newport, R.I.: Naval War College Press, 1976.

———. *Confederate Admiral: The Life and Wars of Franklin Buchanan.* Annapolis, Md.: Naval Institute Press, 1999.

———. *Decision at Sea: Five Naval Battles That Shaped American History.* New York: Oxford University Press, 2005.

———. *Joseph E. Johnston: A Civil War Biography.* New York: W. W. Norton, 1994.

———. *Stonewall of the West: Patrick Cleburne and the Civil War.* Lawrence: University of Kansas Press, 1998.

Turner, Thomas Reed. *The Assassination of Abraham Lincoln.* Melbourne, Fla.: Krieger Publishing, 1999.

———. *Beware the People Weeping: Public Opinion and the Assassination of Abraham Lincoln.* Baton Rouge: Louisiana State University Press, 1991.

———. *101 Things You Didn't Know about the Civil War: Places, Battles, Generals—Essential Facts about the War That Divided America.* Cincinnati, Ohio: Adams Media, 2007.

Williams, Frank J. *Judging Lincoln.* Carbondale: Southern Illinois University Press, 2002.

———, and William D. Pederson, eds. *Abraham Lincoln Contemporary: An American Legacy.* Campbell, Calif.: Savas Woodbury Publishers, 1996.

———, William D. Pederson, and Vincent J. Marsala, eds. *Abraham Lincoln: Sources and Style of Leadership.* Westport, Conn.: Greenwood Press, 1994.

Wolf, Thomas P., William D. Pederson, and Byron W. Daynes, eds. *Franklin D. Roosevelt, the New Deal and Its Aftermath.* Armonk, N.Y.: M. E. Sharpe, 2001.

Young, Nancy B., William D. Pederson, and Byron W. Daynes, eds. *Franklin D. Roosevelt and the Shaping of American Political Culture.* Armonk, N.Y.: M. E. Sharpe, 2001.

Jean H. Baker is the Elizabeth Todd Professor of History at Goucher College.

Mario M. Cuomo is the former three-term governor of the state of New York. He is now of counsel at the law firm Willkie, Farr and Gallagher, LLP.

Joan Flinspach is the past president of the Lincoln Museum in Fort Wayne, Indiana.

Sara Vaughn Gabbard is the editor of *Lincoln Lore,* the bulletin published by the Lincoln Museum in Fort Wayne, Indiana, which was recognized in 2005, 2006, and 2007 by the *Chicago Tribune* as one of the nation's fifty best magazines.

Doris Kearns Goodwin is a nationally recognized historian and political commentator. She is the recipient of a 1995 Pulitzer Prize, the 2006 Lincoln Prize, and the inaugural New-York Historical Society Book Prize.

Harold Holzer is co-chairman of the U.S. Lincoln Bicentennial Commission and senior vice president for external affairs at the Metropolitan Museum of Art. He is the recipient of the 2005 Lincoln Prize.

Harry V. Jaffa is the Henry Salvatori Research Professor of Political Philosophy, Emeritus, at Claremont McKenna College and Claremont Graduate University. He is at present a Distinguished Fellow at the Claremont Institute for the study of statesmanship and political philosophy.

John F. Marszalek is the Giles Distinguished Professor Emeritus of History and retired Mentor of Distinguished Scholars at Mississippi State University, and managing editor of *The Papers of Ulysses S. Grant.*

James M. McPherson is the George Henry Davis '86 Professor of American History Emeritus at Princeton University and a recipient of the 1989 Pulitzer Prize, the 1998 Lincoln Prize, and the 2007 Pritzker Military Library Literature Award.

Edna Greene Medford is a professor of history at Howard University and a nationally recognized lecturer on African Americans in nineteenth-century America.

Sandra Day O'Connor is an associate justice of the Supreme Court of the United States (Ret.).

Mackubin Thomas Owens is associate dean of academic strategy for electives and directed research and professor of national security affairs at the U.S. Naval College and also editor of *Orbis.*

William D. Pederson is a professor of political science, the American Studies chair, and director of the International Lincoln Center at Louisiana State University in Shreveport.

Edward Steers Jr. is an independent writer who lives in Berkeley Springs, West Virginia. He is a 2002 recipient of the Achievement Award from the Lincoln Group of New York.

Craig L. Symonds is professor emeritus at the U.S. Naval Academy and the author of eleven books on the Civil War and U.S. naval history.

Thomas Reed Turner is a professor of history at Bridgewater State College and the editor in chief of the *Lincoln Herald*.

Frank J. Williams is the chief justice of the Rhode Island Supreme Court, the founding chairman of the Lincoln Forum, a member of the U.S. Lincoln Bicentennial Commission, and a major Lincoln collector.

PHOTO CREDITS

Photo of Jean H. Baker by Ellen Warner

Photo of Mario M. Cuomo by Don Pollard Photography

Photo of Joan Flinspach by Samuel Hoffman,
The Journal Gazette, Fort Wayne, Indiana

Photo of Sara Vaughn Gabbard by Jim Gabbard

Photo of Doris Kearns Goodwin by Richard N. Goodwin

Photo of Harold Holzer by Don Pollard Photography

Photo of Harry V. Jaffa by Claremont Institute

Photo of John F. Marszalek by Russ Houston, Mississippi State University

Photo of James M. McPherson by David K. Crow

Photo of Edna Greene Medford by Thomas A. Medford Jr.

Photo of Sandra Day O'Connor by Dane Penland, Smithsonian Institution

Photo of Mackubin Thomas Owens by Mackubin T. Owens III

Photo of William D. Pederson by Louisiana State
University Office of Media/Public Relations

Photo of Edward Steers Jr. by Kiernan McAuliffe

Photo of Craig L. Symonds by Jeff Symonds

Photo of Thomas Reed Turner by Bridgewater State College

Photo of Frank J. Williams by Matthew A. Poyant

abolitionism and abolitionists, 58–59,
    118–19, 148
abolition of slavery, 82, 84, 95
Abraham Lincoln (Charnwood), 66
Abraham Lincoln Association, 50, 155–
    56, 162
Acton, Lord, 57
African Americans: Civil War–era an-
    tecedents, 98–99; and colonization,
    95–96; Fourteenth and Fifteenth
    Amendments and, 84–85; at Gan-
    non College, 68–69; political rights
    of, 97–98, 149; as soldiers of Civil War,
    95, 146; Johnson C. Whittaker court
    martial, 67
Allen, Wendy, 51
American Colonization Society, 96–97
American conservatism, 57–58, 60
American Presidents Series (C-SPAN),
    91
American Revolution, and *habeas cor-
    pus*, 1–2
ancien régime, 59
Aristotle, 61, 118
Arnold, Isaac, 14

Bailey v. Cromwell, 94
Baltimore riot, 103–4
Barzun, Jacques, 49
Bates, David Homer, 136
Bates, Edward, 33–35, 37–39
Batista, Fulgencio, 126
Bedell, Grace, 44
bed sharing, in 19th century, 35
Beecher, Catharine, 8
Beesly, Edward, 84
Bennett, Lerone, Jr., 26, 99n. 3, 118
Bennett, Tony, 51
Berlin, Isaiah, 85
Bernard, Kenneth A., 151–53, 161

Beveridge, Albert J., 55
Bill of Rights, 86
Bishop, Michael, 50
Booth, John Wilkes: and assassination of
    Lincoln, 87, 130; diary of, 131–33, 138;
    memory of, 52, 56–57; missing pages
    of diary of, 138; tour of trail taken by,
    133–34
Boritt, Gabor, 45, 48–49, 51
Bradwell, Myra, 15–16
Bradwell v. Illinois, 15–16
Brady, Mathew, 42
Brennan, John, 134
Bridgewater State College, 154–55, 157
British Reform Act of 1832, 80
Buckley, William, 57
Burns, Ken, 110
Burnside, Ambrose, 106–7, 145

Calhoun, John C., 57, 86, 116
Cameron, Simon, 146
Cannibals All (Fitzhugh), 58
Carnegie, Andrew, libraries of, 29
Castro, Fidel, 126
Chaconas, Joan, 133
Charles Scribners's Sons, 49
Charnwood, Lord Geoffrey Rathbone
    Benson, 66
Chase, Salmon P., 33–39, 103
Chicago Times, 107
circuit judges, during Civil War, 104
civil-military relationship, 143, 145
civil rights movement, 68–70
civil society, 61–63
Civil War: African American soldiers of,
    95, 146; circuit judges, 104; as democ-
    racy on trial, 79–81, 84; in diary of
    Emma Holmes, 72; foreign-born sol-
    diers of, 79; Mary Todd Lincoln and,
    12–13; Lincoln on legacy of, 82–83;

Civil War (*continued*)
Lincoln's awareness of significance of, 75–76; Lincoln's search for generals, 26; Lincoln's strategy for victory, 144; Lost Cause narrative of, 110; military draft, 106; John Stuart Mill on, 81; re-enactors of, 57; secession and threat of, 76; as struggle for all human beings, 88; study of, 93; suspension of *habeas corpus*, 103–7; symposia on, 152, 161
Civil War amendments, 25, 82, 84–85, 87, 97
Clay, Henry, 114
Clinton, William J., 50
Cobb, Josephine, 46, 53–54n. 7
Collected Works of Abraham Lincoln, 18–19
colonization solution, 95–97, 100n. 14
Committee of Five, 95–96
compact (social contract), 56, 61–63
Confederates in the Attic (Horwitz), 57
Confiscation Acts, 95
conscription, 106
conservative movement, 57–58, 60
conspiracy theories, 131–33, 139, 157–58
Cooke, John Esten, 110
Copperheads, 106–7
"Cornerstone" speech (Stephens), 111–12
Crisis of the House Divided (Jaffa), 55, 111
Crooks, William, 12

Darkness at Noon (Koestler), 60
Darwinism, 57–58
Davis, David, 13, 35, 37
Davis, Jefferson, 143
Declaration of Independence: central idea of, 117; idea of nature as basis of, 58; Lincoln and principles of, 19, 27, 77; meaning of "equality" in, 113–17; moral law and, 62–63; political theory implicit in, 60–61; relationship of, to Constitution, 113; slavery references in, 30; universality and timelessness of, 77–78
Delany, Martin, 96
democracy: American experiment in, 78–81, 84; inseparability of equality, 113, 116–17; Lincoln's definition and

legacy, 2; Lincoln's presidency and, 20; public sentiment in, 117–18; Alexis de Tocqueville on, 80
Democracy Project, 18
Democratic Party, 88
divine right of kings, 61
Dix, Dorothea, 86
domestic feminism, 12
Douglas, Stephen A., 62, 116–18. *See also* Lincoln-Douglas debates
Douglass, Frederick, 96, 120
Dred Scott decision, 94, 104
Du Bois, W. E. B., 99
Durbin, Richard, 50

Eckert, Thomas, 135–38
education, in 19th-century America, 8, 30, 34–35
Edwards, Elizabeth Todd, 9
Edwards, Ninian, 9
Eisenchiml, Otto, 131
elective franchise, 97
Elements of Military Art and Science (Halleck), 71
Emancipation Proclamation: celebrations of, 98; effect of, during Civil War, 146; as encouragement for self-liberation efforts by African Americans, 97; as groundwork for abolition of slavery, 82; in "I Have a Dream" speech, 68, 75; Leland-Boker edition, 25; Lincoln's prudential approach to, 118, 157; as political tool and inspiration, 72
England, impact of American Civil War on, 84
English common law, and *habeas corpus*, 102
equality: in dominion, 61–63; as equal political liberty, 112–13; Lincoln's definition of and commitment to, 87, 94, 98; meaning of, in Declaration of Independence, 113–17; principle of, in nation's founding, 119–20; self-evident proposition of, 59–61; Alexander Stephens on, 111–12
Europe, and American Civil War, 80–81, 84
evolutionary theory, 58

Farber, Joseph C., 49
Fate of Liberty, The (Neely), 105
federalism, 126
Felicite, Louise, 28
Fields, Barbara, 115
Fifteenth Amendment to the Constitution, 84–85, 87
Fink, Sam, 51
Fiore, Jordan, 153–54
Fish, Daniel, 25
Fitzhugh, George, 58
flimsies, 137
Flinspach, Joan, 1, 30
folklore, 66
Foote, Shelby, 110
Ford's Theatre, 151
Ford's Theatre Museum, 42
Fornieri, Joseph, 31
Forrest, Nathan Bedford, 110
Fort Sumter, 142
Founders: central idea of, 59; and *habeas corpus*, 102; Lincoln on compromise of, over slavery, 30, 117; Lincoln on connection of all citizens to, 113–14; Lincoln on intentions of, 77; Lincoln on prudential approach of, 118; and principle of equality, 119–20; Alexander Stephens on, 111–12
Fourteenth Amendment to the Constitution, 84–85, 87
Frank and Virginia Williams Abraham Lincoln Lecture, 125
Frank and Virginia Williams Collection of Lincolniana, 164
Frech, David, 52
freedom, and equality, 115
freedom of the press, 85–86
Freeport, Illinois, 51
Fremont, John, 146
French, Daniel Chester, 42, 47
Friends of the Lincoln Museum, 24
Fugitive Slave Law, 146

Galindez, Jesus, 127
Gandhi, Mahatma, 127
Gannon College (Erie, Pennsylvania), 67–69
Gardner, Alexander, 42
Garfield, James, 87

Garrera, Joseph, 50
Garrison, William Lloyd, 148
Gelfund, Lawrence, 24
Geneva conventions, 2
Georgia Female College (Wesleyan College), 8
Gettysburg Address, 83, 115–16, 158
government, responsibility of, 19
Grant, Ulysses S., 71, 145
Griffith, Albert H., 25
Guelzo, Allan, 118

habeas corpus: American Revolution and, 1–2; background of, 101–3; suspension of, and national security, 107–8; suspension of, as military necessity, 100n. 10; suspension of, during Civil War, 103–7; use of, for and against runaway slaves, 103
Haiti, 96–97
Hall, James O., 132–38
Halleck, Henry W., 71–72
Hamlin, Hannibal, 44, 141
Harbin, Thomas, 134
Havana, Cuba, 126
Haycraft, Samuel, 24
Hayes, Rutherford B., 67
Hegel, 58
Helm, Emilie, 13
Helm, John, 24
Helm, Katherine, 7
Herndon, Lew, 156
Herndon, William, 5
Herold, Davy, 130
Hesler, Alexander, 42
Hohenstein, Anton, 44–45
Holmes, Emma, diary of, 72
Holmes, Oliver Wendell, Jr., 164
Holy Alliance, and American conservatism, 58
Holzer, Harold, 1, 21
Holzer-Boritt-Neely partnership, 45, 49–50, 54n. 10
Hooker, Joseph, 145
Horwitz, Tony, 57
Howard, Oliver Otis, 157
Hunter, David, 146
Huntington Library, 88

"I Have a Dream" speech (King), 68
Ile à Vache, Haiti, 96
individual rights, 56, 63
International Lincoln Association (ILA), 124, 126
International Lincoln Center, 2, 127, 162
International Partnership Program, 21

Jackson, Andrew, 86, 103
Jaffa, Harry V., 2, 111
Jefferson, Thomas, 77–78, 112–13, 116
Judd, Norman, 38
judicial system, in 19th-century America, 15, 104
Julian, George, 87
Juneteenth, 98

Kansas-Nebraska Act, 94
Kennedy, Jacqueline, 75
Kennedy, John F., 66, 75, 92
King, Martin Luther, Jr., 68, 75
Kirk, Russell, 57
Klement, Frank, 155
Koestler, Arthur, 60

laws, and equal protection, 62
Lee, Elizabeth Blair, 33
Lee, Richard Henry, 110
Lee, Samuel Phillips, 33
Liberia, diplomatic relations with, 96–97
liberty, 84–87, 112–13
Library of Congress, 42
Life magazine, photograph of President Nixon, 44–45
Lincoln, Argentina, 126
Lincoln, Illinois, christening of, 28
Lincoln, Abraham: admiration for, 127–28; and assumptions of authority, 61; compared to cabinet colleagues, 34–39; conference on legacy of, 124–25; contributions of, greatest, 112; critical assessments of, 92–93; decision making by, 26, 75; elevated sense of ambition, 39; eloquence of, 37–38; evolution and growth of, 67–68, 141–42, 164; as example of American success story, 156–57, 163–64; as focus of unity, 69–70; as the Great Emancipator,

147–48; as historical figure, 140–41; humanity of, 72–73; international legacy of, 2, 126, 128, 129n. 12; leadership of, 2, 20, 34, 126; and lifelong learning, 26; management of generals by, 143–45; as master of the possible, 149; mythology of, 158; parables of, 85; patience and persistence of, 157; political struggle of, 63; as politician, 146–47; principles of, 27; racial divide in memories of, 91–92; ranking of, 91, 141, 150n. 1; on shortcomings of United States, 114; views of, by Mary Todd's family, 9
Lincoln, Abraham, images of: bust by Leonard Wells Volks, 25, 161, 164n. 1; on election poster, 43–44; enduring power of, 53; exhibitions, 49; hands, 25; iconography of, 45, 52; interest in, by the public, 50; life mask, 25; paintings, 51; photographs of, 42, 44–45, 48; portraits, 160–61; on postage stamps, 127; sculptures, 51–52; symbolism in, 41
Lincoln, Abraham, speeches by: in Baltimore (April 1864), 85; in Chicago (1858), 113–14; Henry Clay eulogy, 114; to Congress, first annual message, 82; to Congress, second annual message, 82–83, 114; to Congress special session (July 4, 1861), 78–79; on Dred Scott decision, 115; at Edwardsville, Illinois (1858), 108; final public address, 97; Gettysburg Address, 83, 115–16, 158; inaugural address, first, 27; inaugural address, second, 26, 30, 83, 97, 148, 158; metaphors in, 36; in Peoria, 36, 55, 77, 95–96, 114; in Philadelphia, on Washington's Birthday, 77; in Trenton, to New Jersey legislature, 76
Lincoln, Abraham, works by: Collected Works of Abraham Lincoln, 18–19; themes in, 19–20. See also Lincoln, Abraham, speeches by
Lincoln, Eddie, death of, 13
Lincoln, Mary Todd: and Abraham's political career, 7, 11–12; and Civil War, 12–13; compared to Eleanor Roosevelt,

32; courtship of Abraham and, 9–10; early life of, 7; education and intellect of, 8; historical evaluations of, 5–6, 10, 12; images of, 4–5; independence of, 9; insanity file on, 17; insanity trial of, 14–15; interest in politics, 10–11; story of, as woman's tale, 16; tragedies in life of, 13; as unfit subject for academic historians, 6; as widow, 13–14

Lincoln, Robert T., 13–16, 67–68

Lincoln, Tad, 14, 52

Lincoln, Willie, death of, 13

"Lincoln and Democracy" (conference), 129n. 12

Lincoln and Freedom (Holzer and Gabbard), 30–31

Lincoln and His Generals (Williams), 143

Lincoln: A Picture Story of His Life (Lorant), 42

Lincolnator, The (newsletter), 125

Lincoln collections: Frank and Virginia Williams Collection of Lincolniana, 161–64; Lincoln Museum, Fort Wayne, Indiana, 24–25; Maxwell Library, Bridgewater State College, 154

Lincoln Conspiracy, The (Balsiger et al.), 132

Lincoln-Douglas debates, 55, 94, 98, 108, 146

Lincoln-Douglas debates reenactment (C-SPAN), 91

Lincoln Enigma, The (Boritt), 51

Lincoln Financial Group Foundation, 24

Lincoln Forum, 50, 162

Lincoln fraternity, 17n. 12

Lincoln Group of Boston, 153–54, 161–62

Lincoln Group of New York, 50

Lincoln Herald (journal), 155

Lincoln Image, The (Holzer, Boritt, Neely), 49

"Lincoln in Modern Art" (Holzer), 51

Lincoln in the Telegraph Office (Bates), 136

Lincoln lecture series, LSU, 125–26

Lincoln Log, The (newsletter), 132–33

Lincoln Lore (periodical), 26, 30, 46

Lincoln Memorial (Washington, D.C.), 42, 51, 59, 66

Lincoln Memorial University, 157

Lincoln Museum (Fort Wayne, Indiana), 24–27, 29, 47–48

Lincoln National Life Insurance, 24

Lincoln on Democracy (Cuomo and Holzer), 21–22

Lincoln Presidential Library and Museum (Springfield, Illinois), 51

Lincoln's America (Gabbard and Fornieri), 31

Lincoln School (Anaheim, California), 140

Lincoln seminar, Boston University, 152

Lincoln Summer Teachers Institute, LSU, 125, 162

London Working Men's Association, 80

Long, John D., 129n. 7

Lorant, Stefan, 42, 46–48

Lost Cause narrative of Civil War, 110

Louisiana Endowment for the Humanities (LEH), 125

Louisiana State University (LSU), 122–27, 162–63

Luce, Stephen B., 142–43

Lynch, Joseph, 131–32

Macon, Nathaniel, 86–87

Madison, James, 56

Madison lecture series, LSU, 126

Mahan, Dennis Hart, 71

majority rule, 62–63

March on Washington, 68

Martí, José, 126

Mauldin, Bill, 66

McClarey, John, 51

McClellan, George B., 71, 144–45

McMurtry, R. Gerald, 25, 44–46, 155

Merryman, John, 104–5, 108

Meserve, Frederick Hill, 42

military draft, during Civil War, 106

Militia Act, 142

Mill, John Stuart, 81

Miller, Myra, 125

Mississippi State University, 69

moral law, 62

Mudd, Samuel Alexander, 134

Murphy, Gerald, 127–28

National Republican Chart, 43–44
National Review, 57
nature, standard of, 58
Naval War College, 142–44
Neely, Mark E., Jr., 25, 45, 48–49, 105
negative liberty, 85–87
Nehru, Jawaharlal, 127
New Birth of Freedom, A (Jaffa), 57
New York City draft riots, 106
Nichols, Roy, 55
19th-century America: bed sharing, 35; contradictions and inconsistencies in, 93; courtship in, 9–10; education of women, 8; juries, 14; male friendships, 35; marital disability, 15; widows, 13
19th-century European thought, and American conservatism, 58
19th-century political history: Gabbard's study of, 31; gender in study of, 5; women in, 6
Nixon, Richard, 44–45
Norman Conquest of England, 102
Northwest Ordinance, 78

Oberlin College, 8
"O Captain! My Captain!" (Whitman), 65, 73
Oglehurst, Lincoln, Illinois, 28
Oglesby family, 28
Oien, Arthur, 154
Ostendorf, Lloyd, 47–48
Owens, Mackubin Thomas, 1–2

parlor politics, 4
Payne, Daniel A., 96
Peace Democrats, 106
Pennsylvania coal miners, and military draft, 106
Pensamiento Español (periodical), 81
Pettie, John, 116
Picasso, Pablo, 51
Pierce, Franklin, 86
Plato, 57–58
Platt, Charles D., 50
Poland, 18–19
political community, 62
political parties, reversal in positions of, 88

Poor Man's Guardian (newspaper), 80
popular government, 78–79
popular sovereignty doctrine, 62, 117
Porter, Charles O., 128
positive liberty, 85–87
presidents, rankings of, 91, 141, 150n. 1
public opinion baths, 26, 164

Qatar Airways, 128
Quarles, Benjamin, 96

racism in America: Alexis de Tocqueville on, 93, 99n. 6; Robert T. Lincoln and, 67–68; as violation of central idea of the American Republic, 119
Randall, Ruth Painter, 7, 46
Rating Game in American Politics, The (Pederson and McLaurin), 123–24
Reagan, Nancy, 11
Reconstruction, 69–70, 148–50
Reform Bill (1867), 84
Reinhart, Mark, 155
Republic (Plato), 57–58
Republican National Convention (1860), 36–37
Republican Party, 87–88
Rondileau, Adrian, 153–54
Roosevelt, Eleanor, 32
Ross, Ishbel, 7
rule of law, 61

Sandburg, Carl, 152–53
Savannah, Georgia, 71
Scalia, Antonin, 62
Scott, Winfield, 144
secession, 55–58, 76–78, 87, 111–12
secessionists, appeasement of, 92, 94
self-evident truths, 59–60
self-government, 63
Seward, Fanny, 33
Seward, William Henry, 33–39, 142
Shelby, John, 94
Sherman, Ellen, 67
Sherman, William T., 66–67, 70–71, 145
Shreveport-Bossier City, Louisiana, 122. *See also* Louisiana State University (LSU)
Shrewsbury, Earl of, 81

slaveholders, 86–87, 94

slavery: abolition of, 82, 84, 95; arguments against, in Lincoln-Douglas debates, 94; in Civil War course at U.S. Naval Academy, 146–48; and criteria for enslavement, 116–17; Declaration of Independence and, 30; Holy Alliance and defense of, 59; interest of the stronger as basis of, 119; Lincoln on, in speeches, 36, 77, 114; Lincoln's fight against, 81–82; as moral wrong, 60, 62; positive good theory of, 57–59; proponents of, 56–57, 86–87; tragedies of, 26; U.S. Constitution and, 30, 81–82

slaves: effect of Lincoln's appeasement policy on, 94; role of, in liberation, 93; runaway, and writ of *habeas corpus*, 103

slave states, Lincoln's appeasement of, 94

Sloan, Richard E., 132–33

social contract, 56, 61–63

Solidarity Union, 18

Sons of Confederate Veterans, 122, 125–26

Southern Partisan (periodical), 57

Speed, Joshua, 10, 35

Spiegel, Allen, 155

Sprague, Kate Chase, 33

Sprague, William, 33

Stanton, Edwin M., 33–35, 71, 75, 131–32

Stashin, Leo, 43, 46

state of nature, 61

state sovereignty, 86–87

states' rights, 56

Stephens, Alexander H., 110, 116

Stevens, Thaddeus, 149

Stonehouse, Jean, 154

suffrage, 98, 149

Sunn Classic Pictures, 132

Surratt, John, 131

Surratt, Mary, 136

Surratt Society, 133

Swett, Leonard, 14

Taney, Roger, 104–5, 116–17

television portrayals of Lincoln, 41, 156

Thirteenth Amendment to the Constitution, 25, 82, 87, 97

Thompson, Richard, 25

Thucydides, 119

Times (London), on Civil War, 81

Tocqueville, Alexis de, 80, 93, 99n. 6

Todd, Robert, 7

Tolpo, Lily, 51

Tolstoy, Leo, 75

town hall meeting tradition, 164

Tracy, Albert, 35

Trefousse, Hans, 155

Tripp, C. A., 10

Truesdell, Winfred Porter, 48

Trujillo, Rafael, 127–28

Truth, Sojourner, 96

unanimous consent, 62

Union of Soviet Socialist Republics (USSR), secessions from, 55–56

U.S. Constitution: Fourteenth and Fifteenth amendments, 84–85, 87; and Lincoln's fight against slavery, 81–82; relationship of Declaration of Independence to, 113; slavery and, 30, 81–82; and Alexander Stephens's defense of secession, 111–12; Thirteenth Amendment, 25, 82, 87, 97

U.S. Historical Society, 52

U.S. Lincoln Bicentennial Commission, 50, 163

U.S. military, 106, 143–45

U.S. Naval Academy, 145–46

Vallandigham, Clement, 106–7

Vindication of the Rights of Women, A (Wollstonecraft), 8

Volk, Leonard Wells, 25, 161, 164n. 1

voting rights, 98, 149

Wahlstrom, Carl, 153

Walesa, Lech, 21–22

War Department telegrams, 138

Warren, Louis A., 24–25, 46

Washington, D.C., 104, 130

Washington, George, 76

Watson, Robert, 94

Wearing of the Grey (Cooke), 110